VOICES FROM THE SWEETWATER SEAS:
A GREAT LAKES ANTHOLOGY

By William F. Keefe

Christmas '97

Jim - Thanks for the wonderful care -

Wally Keefe -

VOICES FROM THE SWEETWATER SEAS: A GREAT LAKES ANTHOLOGY

By William F. Keefe

Action Research Institute
New Buffalo, Michigan

Distributor:
Action Research Institute
P.O. Box 40
New Buffalo, MI 49117

Copyright © 1997 by Action Research Institute

Printed in the United States of America

All rights reserved,
Including the right of reproduction
In whole or in part in any form

Library of Congress Cataloging-in-Publication data

Keefe, William F.
Voices from the Sweetwater Seas:
A Great Lakes Anthology/William F. Keefe
Includes Index
1. Great Lakes - History; 2. Great Lakes
region - History, 20th Century; 3. Great Lakes
- Oral History; 4. Edmund Fitzgerald -
History; 5. Diving - Great Lakes region; 6.
Ships and Shipping - Great Lakes.

Library of Congress Catalogue Card Number:
97-73507
ISBN: 0-9635609-8-0

Our Cover: Caught by photographer Alan R. Kamuda as it broke the surface of Lake Superior, the bell of the SS *Edmund Fitzgerald* emerges into daylight nearly 20 years after the *Fitzgerald* sank. Recovered from a depth of some 530 feet, the bell became the centerpiece of a memorial to the 29 *Fitzgerald* crew members who lost their lives in the tragedy of November 10, 1975. The memorial is located in the Great Lakes Shipwreck Museum at Whitefish Point, Michigan. The diver in Mr. Kamuda's photo is Canadian Bruce Fuoco.
Authorization for the bell recovery came from the Northwestern Mutual Life Insurance Company, owner of the vessel at the time of the loss, and units and personnel of the Canadian Navy engineered the recovery.

My heartfelt thanks go to all those who helped, as interviewees, to make this book a reality. They have taken part, I believe, in a significant first for the Great Lakes: a compendium of interviews with the living as a means of probing the todays and yesterdays of this most marvelous and unique region of the world.

Special appreciation is due Rev. Richard W. Ingalls, rector of Mariners' Church of Detroit, and Capt. Fred D. Leete III. The help provided by both was unstinting and invaluable.

Among those who provided mechanical/conceptual assistance, my thanks go particularly to John Calo of New Buffalo, Michigan, computerist-desktop publisher extraordinaire.

And to my wife Carol, endless thanks for patience, help where needed, and overall encouragement.

W.F.K.
Summer, 1997

"Man hoisted sail before he saddled a horse. He poled and paddled along rivers and navigated the open seas before he traveled on wheels along a road. Watercraft were the first of all vehicles. With them the Stone Age world began to shrink..."

-- Thor Heyerdahl

About the Author...

Spending all his early summers on the shores of Lake Michigan in the area of Benton Harbor/St. Joseph, Bill Keefe absorbed the mystique of the Great Lakes by osmosis. Not totally by coincidence, one of his first adult jobs was as a summer laborer in the United States Steel-owned Carnegie-Illinois South Works in South Chicago. The mill sat on the southern shore of Lake Michigan.

A seven-year hitch in the U.S. Army followed Keefe's college career at Loyola University, Chicago, and took him away from his beloved lake from 1943 to 1950. The separation continued through four more years in the United States Information Agency. The bulk of the Army-U.S.I.A. years were spent in Germany.

By the late 1960s, Keefe had begun by degrees to renew his old acquaintanceship with the Lakes. After working as an editor, writer, consultant, and newspaper publisher for more than two decades, at the same time raising a family, Keefe went into full-time free-lance writing. He had been on his own more than 15 years when he took a part-time job as editor of a Great Lakes boaters' magazine. That experience brought him back into the Great Lakes orbit and he has yet to escape. His book, **The Five Sisters: 299 Things Every Great Lakes Buff Should Know,** *appeared in 1991 and went into a second printing shortly afterward.*

Mr. Keefe has published more than 20 books, among them:

Listen, Management!
Open Minds
Steel Summers

CONTENTS

INTRODUCTION   ix

I. CHARTERS, ODYSSEYS, RACES, GUNKHOLES   1

1 Timothy J. Kent   Deane H. Tank 33
14 Yvonne Hoag   Camilla B. Ross 41
22 Peter G. Code   Mark S. Nemschoff 49
Verlen Kruger 61

II. THE VIEW FROM BELOW   77

77 David L. Trotter   Valerie Olson-van Heest 91
Terry German 104

III. THE CREATIVE SPIRIT   117

117 Lee Murdock   David Irvine 142
129 Peter Rindlisbacher   Charles Vickery 149

IV. ASLEEP IN THE DEEP: 157
THE *EDMUND FITZGERALD*

158 Capt. Donald E. Erickson   Rev. Richard W. Ingalls 188
170 Capt. Jimmie H. Hobaugh   Ruth Hudson 198
179 Cheryl Rozman   Capt. Fred D. Leete III 205
Dwight "Bucko" Teeple 221

V. CRAFT MASTERS   229

229 Ray Boessel Jr.   Paul D. Brugger 245
236 Terry L. Searfoss   Winston Smith 254
Matthew L. Daley 258

VI. MOVERS AND SHAKERS   269

269 David P. Kensler   Henry A. Spang 290
276 Robert A. Manglitz   Dan McGee 299
284 James Hogan   John Tanner 310
                  Ralph C. Frese 320

Appendix A: Our Interviewees   335
Appendix B: In Memoriam: The Crew of the
                  SS *Edmund Fitzgerald*   337
          Index   339

Introduction

Searchers after history justifiably haunt libraries and archives. For them, an attic crammed with Grandma's letters may be a temple; a primary source may be a treasure and a dusty book a thesaurus of unimpeachable wisdom. They may wander through entire catacombs of book stacks and file cabinets. A footnote may have the patina of Absolute Truth.

Is there another way to research history? How about the words and thoughts of the living? Are they not, once enunciated or put to paper, equally part of the human record? Are their words, spoken or written, any less reliable than dusty tomes--simply because the living are *now* and the late ones were then?

My bias, obviously, is toward the belief that both forms of historic research are valid and fruitful. In that spirit I offer this book. My deep sense is that the remarkable cast of personalities whose words are recorded here possesses a marvelous power: to reflect the many-splendoured phenomenon that is the Great Lakes. Read carefully, the interviews reflect that phenomenon with all its mysteries and attractions, its mood swings and moments of wrath, its traceries of symbol and its wild prodigalities.

The Lakes have taken lives and blessed lives, opened paths to adventure and commerce, inspired artists and poets, provided sustenance. They have begotten myths and legends whose roots are centuries old; they have whispered secrets into the ears and imaginations of the earliest--and the latest--peoples who have thronged to their shores.

The Lakes are a geologic/geographic phenomenon. Not only the researcher feels their magnetism. "Les Lacs Grands" to the early explorers who called them home, they conjure up so many images that the mind demurs. For most of us they represent enchantment, a stage beyond excitement. Who among us cannot recall the child's thrill felt on approaching one of the Lakes, then of finally *seeing* it? The lucky ones then got to touch, to feel, to immerse a toe, a leg, the whole *corpus*. The blessed ones got to ride the water using an inner-tube, a canoe, a Rinker powerboat, a 30-foot sloop, the 410-foot *Badger*, a 1,000-foot Lakes freighter.

None of this is abnormal or unusual. Throughout history man has gravitated to water. The larger the patch of water, the more we humans have swarmed toward it, tried to embrace it, used it as a highway, and written poems and songs about it. We have devised ways to make it safe to drink. We have not completely developed the key to mastering all its moods--though from time to time we have entertained the conceit that we have.

If our voyages, cruises, passages, navigations and circumnavigations, and sailings had left tracks, the world's great bodies of water would be as scratched, lined, and scarred as a hen-yard. The Great Lakes would be as scarred as any others.

The mystique of the sweetwater seas lies like a magical presence over all of middle America. Smaller lakes in the eight Great Lakes states acquire dignity; Ontario's estimated 400,000 inland lakes sparkle more brightly.

With this book we salute the Great Lakes in what we believe is a unique way: through the eyes and ears, the voices and observations, the works and experiences and achievements of more than 30 Lakes aficionados. One way or another the speakers here have left their marks on one or more of the Lakes or their connecting waterways, bordering dunes and bluffs, shore- or environment-related communities, even their shipwrecks.

Hopefully you'll look at the Lakes differently, with new eyes, after reading this book. You'll understand the hopes and fears, the dreams and ambitions that lie hidden in the ever surging waters. You'll picture the images, young and old, of those who have perished in the waters. You'll hear the whistle of the *Lady Elgin* as she sinks beneath wine-dark waves in 1860 and hear Captain McSorley of the *Edmund Fitzgerald* as he speaks his last words:

We are holding our own.

Most of all, perhaps, you'll see why great cities from Toronto, the old York, in the east to Duluth in the West, have sprung up along the shores of the sweetwater seas. The fact of the matter, as some of the interviewees attest, is that the Great Lakes are a concept and force, a geographic basin and a cultural entity. Canadian side or American side, they provide the drama, the vital force, the water connections that humans have used since time immemorial for travel and trade, for settlement and growth.

With your new eyes you'll see the Lakes' 10,000 years of history unrolling before you in the spray of a wave, in the glint of summer sunlight off water, in the cry of a gull.

Happy reading.

I

Charters, Odysseys, Races, Gunkholes

Should you ask me, whence these
    stories?
      Whence these legends and
    traditions,
With the odors of the forest,
      With the dew and damp of
    meadows,
With the curling smoke of
    wigwams,
      With the rushing of great
    rivers,
With their frequent repetitions,
      And their wild reverberations,
As of thunder in the mountains
      I should answer, I should tell
    you,
From the forests and the prairies,
      From the great lakes of the
    Northland,
From the land of the Ojibways.

        -- "A Night-Memory," a trans-
        lation from the Ojibway

"A TAHQUAMENON TALE"

---

2   Charters, Odysseys, Races, Gunkholes

"The remaining days passed all too quickly, filled with wood gathering, cooking, games, crafts, evening fires, soaking up the sun and history... One afternoon, as I sat in the warm sun on the riverbank..., I carved a spoon from a moose antler tine...

"On the last day of our stay at this camp, I arose early with (our dog) Jacques. We made our way in the quiet of early dawn over the soft bed of moss which covered the forest floor, past thousands of tiny delicate white flowers, to the large fallen tree which had been our source of firewood during our entire stay. I reviewed its years of slow growth from a tiny twig to a young sapling to a mature tree, and then considered the fierce wind which must have swept through a few years ago, breaking the large tree off at about my head height and partially uprooting several others nearby, which now leaned at an acute angle to the north.

"I thanked the spirit of the broken tree for providing us with its branches for fires that cooked our meals, warmed us each evening, and gave a cheerful light for our times of stories, songs, and games.

"Then, I turned and reluctantly stepped back into the twentieth century."

> -- Timothy J. Kent, in *Voyageur News*,
> Fall, 1990

TIMOTHY J. KENT

(1992)

For Tim Kent, the task of meshing two full-time careers for more than 20 years became unduly burdensome by 1995. His writer-historian persona won out over the musical. Tim played his last concert in the trumpet section of the Chicago Symphony Orchestra on November 3, 1996. The next day he began life with one full-time job, about 10 major projects on his drawing board, and a vaulting determination to finish all the work he had plotted for himself with his massed files of research. First on his history-archeology book-writing agenda: Birch-Bark Canoes of the Fur Trade, *a two-volume labor of love that was scheduled to go to press in the spring of 1997.*

The title suggests where Tim's interests have lain throughout his 18-year CSO career. Within the framework of the orchestra's inexorable schedule, he had spent thousands of hours of free time, including vacations, in researching the people, artifacts, vehicles, travel and life habits, clothing, and other minutiae of the fur-trade-era culture that developed in the late 1500s in North America and flourished until the middle 1800s. The research included annual vacation reenactments, with wife Doree and sons Kevin and Ben, of the life-ways of a French Canadian trader of the late 1600s. In addition to such "living history" research he took another block of vacation time each year for annual family canoe voyages over successive segments of the mainline fur trade route between Montreal in the east and Fort Chipewyan on Lake Athabasca, Alberta, in the west. In the reenactments he walked the period walk and talked the period talk to the fullest extent possible: he ate the traditional food, sang voyageurs' songs, played Indian games. While journeying over the fur trade route in annual stages, he wore modern garb and carried modern, state of the art gear, including a hollow-fill sleeping bag and a wetsuit for protection against wave and weather.

In 1992, in the tenth year of his stage-by-stage revisitation of the fur trade route, he has traveled 1,400 miles, having reached the Saskatchewan River, and has "only" 1,700 miles to go in the next seven summers, covering 150 to 300 miles each summer...

* * *

It seems right now as if your mortgage-paying work is interfering with your life's work. Is that an accurate impression?

I would say so. Scholars in scientific and historical fields search for some corner of their area of expertise that hasn't been already mined. Then they go for it. It so happens that I've found eight such corners, all pertaining to early watercraft, fur trade history, and archeology. I may find more. I spend all my free time researching them.

4 Charters, Odysseys, Races, Gunkholes

Can you tell us about one of these corners--avenues of research?

I think my dugout project is of interest. I started it by writing to 4,900 museums in the United States and Canada, to locate as many surviving dugout canoes as possible. I've located about 470 and have studied in detail about 300 of them so far. So the research has gone far beyond just writing to museums.

This kind of research gets me into some interesting places. I've run my letter of inquiry in hundreds of publications, museum quarterlies, historical societies' newsletters, the publications of marine and maritime groups, and so forth. I've found dugout canoes in a barn in Iowa. Another was beached at a research station on Chilko Lake, deep in the interior of British Columbia. The oldest that I've found has been carbon-dated as originating about 2,400 B.C. I'm not pursuing any that were built after about 1930.

You have a record of each dugout canoe?

A precise, detailed one. I take measurements--length, beam, depth, the tapers, everything. I also take detailed photos and determine how the canoe was made. You can tell what tools were used by the tool marks. With the profile I have on each canoe, a woodworker could make a nearly exact copy.

I've been at this project for about five years and have at least five more to go. Some of the hardest miles are behind me. I heard of one canoe that had survived through four generations of an Indian family in Sheboygan, Wisconsin. The canoe passed into the hands of a 16-year-old in 1929. From then until four or five years ago, in about 1987, this man kept the canoe in his father's loft. I heard that it was for sale and within a week it was delivered to me.

Tim Kent traces his route from Montreal to Lake Athabasca on a map that he drew himself.

Have you any others?

One other. A museum official in Michigan called me and said some folks had found a dugout half-buried on a beach. It was still there, *in situ*. The museum had no room for it--did I want it? The curator was anxious to have someone preserve it. I went there and found it. The lake had washed away the sand that had covered it.

People start thinking the dugout is more important than they had ever guessed when they see me at work. (Laughs.) I come in with my briefcase and measuring tapes and tools. When I'm done, I know how the canoe was made, whether the builders bored holes in the wood to determine the thickness of the hull--everything. I also record whether the canoe was repaired along the way and what wood was used to build the craft.

How do you identify the wood?

I remove a minute sample from each canoe and have it microscopically identified by a wood scientist. I received a report recently on 97 fragments of wood from dugouts that I had found in the Great Lakes region. There were 19 different woods in the samples. The most common is eastern white pine, but there were also red and white oak, cedar, aspen, and maple, among others. Farther to the West, dugouts have turned up that were made out of cottonwood and black walnut. The builders often used trees that grew along rivers and lakes convenient to the building sites.

Where do you find most of the surviving dugouts?

I've found them across Canada and the United States. But the greatest number have turned up in Michigan--about 80 of the 470 I've located. In size the dugouts I've found range from 36 feet in length to eight feet.

The myths about dugouts are everywhere. People think they weren't portaged--too heavy and klunky and thick. That's often not true. Also, it seems to be a common belief that the dugout gave way to birch-bark and skin canoes. But there's strong evidence showing that the birch-bark canoe and the dugout were in use by different Indian groups at the same time--for different purposes.

All this, for me, amounts to trying to find out what people really did, not what we think they did. For instance, repairs--nailed-on tin sheets or tar applied to the cracks of a canoe--might mean the craft isn't an authentic native dugout. But if you were to go back in time and visit a latter-nineteenth century Indian village, and you saw five dugouts pulled up on the river bank, my research indicates that more than one of them would probably be loaded with tin patches, nailed on.

Some of these canoes must interest you more than others.

The ones I'm most interested in are those that have been carbon-dated and are known to be prehistoric. With these I go over the surface with a fine-tooth comb for evidence of tool use. These older canoes were made by the burning and scraping method. This was the method that was documented by some of the earliest observers, including the explorer (Giovanni di) Verrazano in 1524. In the 1580s, John White documented dugout manufacturing methods very well.

You've got a book coming out on the canoe in the fur trade--but these are birch-bark canoes that you're talking about in the book.

Yes, all this research proceeds at the same time.

What are the other "corners" that you've discovered and will write books on?

One will deal with the story of our annual travels along the mainline fur trade route across Canada. Another subject is the implements, tools, weapons, and other items found in the 1600s fur trade. A third will be a collection of biographies of employees of the French fur trade who were my ancestors. I've traced about 725 of my French forebears, back to more than 120 communities in France. The other subjects I've been researching include early sailing canoes and a detailed account of the founding of Detroit.

Can you talk about the annual trips along the fur trade route from Montreal? You can't really plan those from travel brochures...

I sometimes wish we could. (Laughs.) The planning for any given trip starts about seven or eight months before departure. First I'll study some of the approximately 900 books, atlases, personal journals, and other publications in my home library. Reading the journals of the fur traders of the 1600s and 1700s, I locate on modern topographical maps the lakes, rivers, portages, and rapids that they encountered. I record the original Indian and French names of each.

I figure out how long each portage was and the locations of the trading posts, rendezvous centers, and major Indian village sites. Next year, 1993, we'll be doing the tenth annual installment. As usual we'll travel in our 17-foot fiberglass canoe for up to two weeks, covering 200 to 300 miles. Since we've covered about 1,400 miles in nine years, we have about 1,700 to go. Some of the future mileage could be really tough because it includes lakes Superior and Winnipeg.

You just attack them in order, as you get to them?

No, we'll leap-frog the biggest lakes for the time being. They get a little dangerous because of the winds and waves. The amount of time you can spend windbound on a lakes canoe trip can be discouraging if you live by the schedule of our twentieth century civilization and have maybe a month's vacation to do your traveling. We'll come back in four years and paddle Huron, Superior, and Winnipeg. We'll have a canvas cover on the canoe so we'll be able to start out in heavy surf and spend less time windbound.

Right now we're paddling across the area 600 to 700 miles north of Montana--where our next three segments will take place, two in Saskatchewan and the other in Alberta. To plan these trips, I start by studying the roads. In the stretch of about 1,100 miles between Lakes Winnipeg and Athabasca there are only five or six roads that run far enough north to intersect with the canoe route. Since we normally drive to the put-in places, these intersection points determine the lengths of the segments that we paddle each year.

This past summer we found a Cree-Scottish man who runs a fly-in fishing camp. He became our shuttle driver. We drove a day and a half to get to his place, then he and his son rode with us another six hours to where we put our canoe into the water. He and his son then took our van back to where we planned to end the trip--at his camp, 270 miles away. We covered that distance in about seven and a half days, paddling about 36 miles a day.

You've seen a lot of rivers.

8   Charters, Odysseys, Races, Gunkholes

We really have. The Ottawa, Mattawa, French, Rainy, Winnipeg, Saskatchewan, Churchill, and Athabasca rivers are all on the mainline route. Each one has its own character. On the trip this past summer we ran into about 25 obstructions, and had to portage around them. It seemed like we were out of the canoe almost as much as we were in it.

Worse than that, the muddy banks of the Saskatchewan were a problem. For something like a hundred miles the mud made landing almost impossible. The mud comes from the silt that drains into the rivers as it flows from the Rockies across the plains and prairies.

You're carrying your own provisions--there can't be many supermarkets out there?

We prepare and take our own food, all of it. Doree dries meat, vegetables, fruits. We make our own special mixture of breakfast and snack foods using nuts, grain, seeds, fruits, and honey.

Your and your family do the "living history" recreations in fur-trade-era clothes, living the life of a woodland family?

Right. Traveling over the fur trade route we use modern gear, with life preservers and everything else we might need. That's been an August vacation for us because the water is warmest at that time. Also, the insect population is usually reduced a little by then. And the weather is user-friendly.

The living history trips have been taking place in June. We pick a wilderness site and paddle to it in our 16-foot birch-bark canoe. On these trips our whole effort is designed to re-create the life of a 1600's French-Canadian fur trader and his woodland Indian wife and family.

What's the clothing?

The family at that time would have been wearing moccasins, leggings, and chemises or shirts, a mixture of French and native clothing. So do we. I've made all the clothes. We also eat the foods that they would have eaten. My family has learned a lot of voyageur songs, so we sing those from time to time. To cook, or to do other chores, we use the tools and implements that the traders would have used.

This is research for me. Last June we camped in a quiet spot about

Tim and wife Doree, 25th anniversary, 1995.

Weary reenactors? Tim and sons Kevin and Ben on the Mattawa River, Ontario, in 1984.

10   Charters, Odysseys, Races, Gunkholes

50 miles from Duluth, Minnesota. For breakfast we brewed tea from dried raspberry twigs. We had what the French-Canadians called *gallette,* a kind of fried corn-meal cake. Kevin and Ben really love that treat.

The June outing lasts about a week. Each year, we focus on a different aspect of the life of the 1600's fur trade period. If anyone from that era could visit us, he or she wouldn't find much out of order. It's all authentic, down to the camp layouts, the ornaments, the spices. For the first four years we didn't use salt because I hadn't documented the importation of salt by the traders. Now we can salt our food; salt appeared on a 1688 list of trade goods that were taken into Illinois country. We also waited until we could make the *gallette* in an old, traditional frying pan of copper, with the tinning still on the inside.

I've tanned some of the hides for our clothing by the traditional, prehistoric method of brain-tanning. To do this you stretch the hide on a frame and rub it hundreds of times with a pole. Then you work the brains and sometimes the liver of the animal into it.

We smoke it after the tanning process and it never goes rancid. To sew the clothes together I use sinew threads that I make by pounding and separating the fibers from the tendon that runs up the rear leg of an elk.

You're sleeping under the sky, cooking with primitive utensils?

We sleep in black-bear and buffalo robes, under a canoe-and-canvas lean-to. We cook in traditional native containers of birch-bark, wood, rawhide, and clay, either directly over a fire or using hot stones heated in the fire. We also use copper and brass pots and pans like those that were brought into the fur country in the 1600's by the French.

I've studied over 50 archeological site reports and hundreds of early French documents to make sure every item is authentic. If I can't document it, we don't use it.

You make no exceptions to your rule of authenticity?

For safety we choose to make a couple. For example, we bring along a modern first aid kit. Otherwise, we're using nothing but what the fur trader would have used--things common in the Indian culture plus the overlay of items introduced by the French.

Some of these research themes must be more difficult, or interesting, than others.

Right. Last year (1991) we were comparing woodworking technologies. We started with those common to the prehistoric period and then studied what the French would have brought. I really enjoyed that.

In the spring, before the reenactment, I made a complete, prehistoric toolkit--what the woodland Indians would have had before the arrival of Europeans and their tools. The native tools were made of bone, stone, shell, and copper. Some were also fashioned out of beaver teeth. I had puzzled for years over early tools made from some of these materials--how could you make a wood-scraper out of a mussel shell? While making the Indian tools I found out how breakable some of the materials are.

On our trip we did a series of woodworking experiments on green and dried wood, and on the burn-and-scrape method, using the whole gamut of tools. It was a real kick to learn that every one of the tools, made of different materials, was equally effective in scraping away charred wood. The thin little mussel shell did just as good a job as a heavy antler scraper or a stone axe.

You're recording all these observations and findings?

Absolutely. Not only recording facts and details, but writing up the entire living history experience. My accounts are published annually in publications such as the *Voyageur News* or *Michigan Habitant Heritage*.

During the reenactments, we all have names that a trader's family might have had--native names. Doree is Sunning Otter and Kevin is Golden Eagle. Ben is Red-Tailed Hawk. I'm Silver Fox. I write the reports in the third person, as if I were an observer reporting on the day-to-day life of the family.

Can you give us a picture of what happens when, for example, you're preparing breakfast?

Sure. Sunning Otter uses firesteel and a razor-sharp piece of flint to start a fire. When the firesteel strikes the edge of the flint, tiny, orange-hot sparks of steel fall onto a piece of linen charcloth that she

12   Charters, Odysseys, Races, Gunkholes

holds wrapped around the flint. The sparks smoulder until she blows on them. Then they burst into flame and she plunges the fireball into a little teepee of twigs and kindling. In no time she has a fire going.

Remember, this is the 1600's, perhaps 1670, and I'm a trader. So I have earthen and brass pots and pans like they'd have in the French settlements. Among the Indians such utensils wouldn't last long in the early decades of the trade, as the people would cut them up and turn them into jewelry or ornaments and go on cooking with their more primitive utensils. We're having wild rice and jerky this morning, and you can smell it as it cooks, spiced with ginger root. Delicious stuff!

One of us goes to fill the water bottle from the handy supply at the riverbank. We add wintergreen leaves and set the bottle in the sun to steep the tea.

Soup's on?

Yes. We bring out drinking cups of wood and box turtle shells and dishes of both snapping turtle shells and birch-bark. Otter spoons out the hot breakfast food with a twisted ladle carved from a tree root. Each of us has a clamshell spoon, and there's a salt container of cowhorn.

You're re-creating an entire way of life...

That's our goal.

(1997)

_____

_____

It's five years later. The Kent family has stayed with the annual reenactments. They have also continued the yearly journeys along the route followed by the voyageurs. Tim is deep into final preparations for the publication of his book, actually a two-volume set on the birch-bark canoes of the fur trade. It will be out later this year of grace 1997. Holding down one full-time job agrees with him. He has a new home in Ossineke, Michigan, where he grew up...

* * *

You reached Lake Athabasca on schedule?

Two summers ago. If you remember, we were going to leap-frog the larger lakes--Huron, Superior, and Winnipeg. This past summer we paddled across the north shore of Lake Huron.

Without serious problems?

Overall, it was a great trip, with the usual dosage of high drama and tense moments, with only one capsize in heavy surf. We did it exactly on the schedule the voyageurs used. We didn't leave our camps at 1:00 or 1:30 in the morning, but set an alarm for 3:30.

We had beautiful moonlit nights and early mornings for paddling. We covered the 200 miles in about seven and a half paddling days. On a couple of other days we were windbound on islands that had great crops of blueberries ready for our harvesting. We traveled east, starting at the Sault (Sault Ste. Marie), and paddled all the way to Killarney, Ontario.

Looking back, it took 12 segments, 12 summers, to do the river route from Montreal to Lake Athabasca. Now we're working on the three major lake segments. We have two summers to go.

On lakes Superior and Winnipeg.

In reverse order, yes. We'll cover Lake Winnipeg this coming summer (1997) and then Superior in 1998. Winnipeg could be worse than Superior. It's a shallow lake, near the edge of the prairies. So the winds coming off the prairie can whip things up in minutes.

The leg to Lake Athabasca was your 1995 project?

Yes, on the Clearwater and Athabasca Rivers. We were flown over to the Clearwater by float plane. When we got to Fort Chipewyan, we called our pilot and he brought us back out. There are no roads that far north. The rivers serve as the roads.

Any more canoe trips planned after you finish the final two lakes?

14   Charters, Odysseys, Races, Gunkholes

No plans yet. The paddling of the mainline fur trade route has been such a nice ongoing project to work at year after year that we haven't given any thought to what we'll do once it's done. But the big thing that's new for us is that I no longer have to work within the confines of the orchestra's schedule. I'm free to write, and research, and reenact on our schedule.

Have you discovered any more dugout canoes?

A few. Maybe 10 or 12. Last summer I got a note from a gentleman who runs a wilderness skills school in northeastern Wisconsin. He was just letting me know that two dugouts had been sold at an estate auction. They were acquired by the local Menominee tribe. That's good because the Menominee reservation was one of the centers of dugout production in the nineteenth century.

Now and then I get calls from people who want to reestablish the dugout. They want to learn wilderness skills. Some museums also sponsor dugout building projects. People ask me what kinds of trees were used, what kinds of tools.

Is music out of your life now?

I play the Indian flute. It used to interfere a little with my playing the trumpet. Now the flute is what I enjoy playing. As for the trumpet, I enjoy being a layman listener now.

YVONNE HOAG

(1996)

It's embarrassing to have your 38-foot Bayliner sitting cross-wise

*in a Welland Canal lock, but it's rarely fatal. If you're Yvonne Hoag,
it's one more learning experience on the way to earning the Great
Lakes Cruising Club's prestigious Admiral Bayfield Award.
Established in 1981, the award honors club members who have
"engaged in substantial cruising in all the Great Lakes." The first
woman to earn the award, Hoag received it during the GLCC's annual
meeting in October, 1995.*

*That occasion marked the culmination of four years in which Hoag
graduated from the ranks of boating spectators to the exalted status of
accomplished cruising captain. Her "Delphinus," the Bayliner 3870
in which she did her "course work," is a 1986 model, "very
comfortable, with twin diesels, a great galley, all the amenities."
Behind her at the presentation by GLCC Commodore Richard A.
Danly lay some 6,000 qualifying freshwater miles. Her odyssey had
taken her as far east as Clayton, New York in the St. Lawrence River
and as far west as Loon Harbor in Lake Superior. Her Great Lakes
Cruising Club burgee flew in an estimated 60 lake ports, anchorages,
gunkholes, and inlets. She remembers it all in sometimes painful,
sometimes laughable detail...*

* * *

We had joined the Cruising Club in 1982. We were trailering the
Bayliner, at that time, but I didn't have a thought about the Bayfield
Award. Not a clue. It may have been mentioned, but that was all. I
found out later that the mileage I piled up while crewing for my
husband counted toward the award. That included the mileage from
Vermilion, Ohio, where we bought the Bayliner, and across Lake Erie
and through the Detroit River to Lake Huron and up to Bay City. That
was our home port. Still is.

What touched off the race for the Bayfield?

I had been exposed to pleasure boats since 1960. We started out at
that time with a 25-foot inboard. Then it seemed we couldn't afford a
boat and a mortgage. So the boat went. But in 10 years we were back
into boating with a 1979 23-foot Sea Ray. We used it on inland lakes
as well as on the Great Lakes. After joining the Cruising Club we
would go to their rendezvous, their annual gatherings for members,
always in a different place.

That's the background. In 1991 I was reviewing the Cruising Club directory and discovered that no woman had achieved the Bayfield. Well, I thought, that's a worthy goal. I decided to see if I could do it. A long time before, way back about 1959 or 1960, I had taken a Coast Guard Auxiliary boating course. I had forgotten everything I had learned. And we now owned the Bayliner.

During all those years my husband handled the boat. All I did was work as a chief cook and bottle-washer, and anchor dropper. He did all the navigation, all the piloting. In 1991 the boat was in storage. I decided to take it out and go for the Bayfield.

Did you prep for it?

I knew I needed more education. I couldn't do it by myself; the boat was too big. I took the course in boat-handling that the Saginaw Bay Power Squadron was offering. A couple of friends who were boaters heard what I was planning and told me, "Well, Von, we'll crew for you." That encouraged me. The couple were Don and Doris Evans, and they had cruised thousands of miles on the Great Lakes. Don helped me with the navigation and Doris became the chief cook. I told her, I'm out of the galley, it's yours, and I'll eat anything you put in front of me.

Yvonne Hoag

On the first of June, 1992, the *Delphinus* left the Saginaw Bay Yacht Club for what we hoped would be a cruise on each of the five Great Lakes. I wanted to do it all in one summer. I had only docked the boat four times, and was finding it pretty intimidating. Don had had to rescue me several times.

You had laid out the route you were going to follow.

We were basically following the route that the Evanses had followed in earning the Bayfield. That meant Huron and Erie first. According to the Cruising Club rules, you had to stay in each lake at least a week. You had to stop at three ports or anchorages. You had to do at least 5,000 miles. There are a couple of other rules.

Murphy's Law was hard at work right away. At Mentor-on-the-Bay in Lake Erie my water system failed. I found out how marvelous it is to have port captains listed in the Cruising Club directory. I called Boat U.S. and, yes, they did have a water pump my size. I had to have it shipped somewhere, so I called the port captain at our next port of call, the city of Erie. He graciously agreed to have the pump shipped overnight. Would I contact him when I reached Erie?

I would, and did. The pump arrived at the marina next day. We were on our way again--back in business.

On the way to the Welland Canal...

Yes. There's nothing like getting your boat kitty-corner in the Welland Canal. You could write a song about it. We had a very large anchor that had been installed at least a couple of years earlier. I swear it would hold a 90-foot yacht. It became difficult, even with our power windlass, to hoist it. But some way Don managed to do it.

I could see the locksman--he was standing there, and our boat was sitting cross-wise, and he was thinking, "What does this woman think she's doing?" But I was thinking of the engines, both port and starboard. I did this and that with the throttles--Oh, it was a hands-on learning experience.

You were glad to win that battle.

Very. But we still had to do a lot of improvising. At Cape Vincent, for example, they were out of diesel fuel. We went on to Clayton, New York to find fuel.

The scenic beauties of the trip made up for some of the problems. The Trent Severn Waterway is just a marvelous memory. I'd love to do it again. And emerging in Georgian Bay we stopped in Midland, Ontario, another great experience. Midland is the sister city of my hometown of Midland, Michigan.

You were completely outfitted with charts?

18 Charters, Odysseys, Races, Gunkholes

You have to be, especially once you get into the 30,000 rocks and shoals and islands of Georgian Bay. You sort of thread your way among the obstacles. We had a taste highlight in Killarney. When you go there, you've got to try the famous fish from the Red School Bus. It's a tradition--every afternoon in season the bus opens up and they sell the world's best fish and chips. Sometimes the fish is perch, sometimes it's lake trout. It's whatever their nets bring in that day, I think.

Your luck had changed.

We thought so, but Lake Superior was a different challenge. I had no trouble with the Soo Locks, not after all I had been through in the Welland Locks. But after we had had a required stay in Houghton, we were greeted by six-foot seas. That wasn't for me, novice that I was, and we went east through Portage River into Lake Superior. I was planning to re-fuel in Copper Harbor. However, there was no fuel in Copper Harbor and we were running low. I had a decision to make--do we try to get a fuel truck to deliver in Copper Harbor or do we go on? I looked at the fuel gauge and decided to go on. We're headed for Canada and had three-quarters of a tank of fuel. But we had flat water and great weather.

You're encountering other boaters?

No, almost none. I felt totally isolated. Occasionally we would see a sailboat. We might be tucked in, or just rounding one of the islands in the Slate Islands. We got some heavier seas again. The waves were pounding on the shore and here comes a caribou calf, splashing up and down, having a ball. We never really saw the mother, except for her legs, because of the dense foliage. We watched for about 20 minutes.

I'm forgetting something. Starting in about the North Channel my motors had started dying periodically. We did everything we could think of to clear them, but when we got to Mamainse Harbor we hadn't solved that problem and we were almost out of fuel. All this shows my inexperience. Or so I thought.

You're on the Canadian side.

Yes. Mamainse was about as lonely as some of the other harbors and gunkholes we had visited. But there were three fishing tugs in there, and there was a fish processing plant. Sitting on the dock we could see some 55 gallon drums of diesel fuel. We were just a little desperate, so I went to the manager of the plant and asked whether we could buy some of that fuel.. "Well," he said, "I'll check with my mechanic." He went out and checked and when he came back he said we could have some fuel.

It's a damp evening in August. I'll never forget seeing that kid coming down to the dock with a drum of fuel on a fork lift truck. Suddenly we're in a mad scramble for a funnel with a filter in it. There was none to be found. All three of us were looking, and throwing things around--no funnel. By the time we gave up he was starting to load the fuel into my starboard tank.

Saved by the barrel?

Not exactly. When I came up on deck, and was about to say, Don't tip the drum, he was already taking the forklift *and* the drum away, trying to get out of the foul weather.

There are things that make you forget your troubles. That evening I was walking Cyrus, my Labrador, and a lovely sailboat came into the harbor. I noticed that the boat was from Suttons Bay, Michigan. I have very dear friends who live there, and I knocked on the hull. A young woman came out. I told her I had the Bayliner down the dock a way, and she said, "Oh yes, I heard you on the radio, coming in." We got to talking and it turned out that she was from Midland, Michigan. The world got smaller and smaller. We had common acquaintances. Her husband came up and we got to talking. His father

The *Delphinus* boasts a great galley and all the amenities, says Captain Hoag. But learning to pilot the craft takes immense concentration. (Photo: Sandra Swanson)

20   Charters, Odysseys, Races, Gunkholes

and I had played clarinet together in the Mason, Michigan, High School band. That went back a few years.

Old Home Week?

Exactly. The next morning we wanted to get a fairly early start. We get out of the harbor, and travel maybe a third of a mile, and the engines begin to miss, sputter, and then my starboard engine died. We finally got the anchor down and were trying to figure out what had happened. But by that time the wind had blown us back close to the shoals near the entry to the harbor. I got on the radio and contacted the Canadian Coast Guard. I also called the fish plant and got the manager. I had both engines on the one tank of fuel that we had bought the night before, but both of them had gone dead.

Well, they towed us in, and we worked, we pumped fuel, we found everything absolutely clean. We changed all the filters. We rocked the boat. We probably took out 10 gallons and there was no sign of sludge, no sign of dirt. Finally, to make a long story short, we got it solved, and the engines started running great. But we had spent so much time that it was getting late in the day. We stayed over night. Lo and behold, that evening another boat came in, a gorgeous yacht, a Grand Bank, probably a 45- or 48-footer. We can see that it too is from Michigan, and the party got bigger. We had not two, but three boats with Midland connections. The new arrival was owned by Michael Dow of Dow Chemical.

You hadn't forgotten the Bayfield Award?

Not at all. The next morning we took off again, and this time I got a little farther before the engines started to sputter and die. The sailboat people had said to me, "We'll follow for a ways. I always wanted to tow a power boat with a sailboat." Anyway, the same thing happened again. We went back in. A fuel truck had come in and we got some more fuel.

We thought we had dodged some kind of bullet. We got down through the Soo Locks and on to Detour, where we topped off the tanks. I had planned to do all five lakes, as I mentioned, but I decided to head back to Saginaw Bay. We had some more problems on the way.

Did you ever figure it out?

Yes. We had the tanks cleaned out thoroughly when we got back to our home base. There were three little bats stuck in the fuel line-- dead, of course. How they got there I have no idea.

That was '92. I had no chance to get back on the Lakes again that year, so I decided to try again the next year and cruise the one Lake I had missed, Michigan. I had done Huron, Erie, Ontario, and Superior.

You could say "mostly Superior."

I think you could. In 1993 I again had expert help. Two different crews, in fact. Bill and Patricia Taylor, and John and Esther Frost. Bill and Pat are members of the Great Lakes Cruising Club. They helped me with plotting, doing the navigating, standing watches at the helm. But I have to confess, after doing those 6,000 miles, 2,000 of them in 1992, I'm a fair-weather sailor. We're all retirees--I retired from Dow Chemical after 32 years. In my last assignment I worked in an advisory capacity on Indian matters.

You've piloted the boat all alone since qualifying for the Bayfield?

Yes. I took it to the 1995 Cruising Club rendezvous at Rouse, Ontario. There--they always have someone who acts as harbor-master and others in dinghies who escort the boats to their anchorages--and they helped me. They even helped me set my Bruce anchor, and I chose a spot in the northeast corner. And then, when the big storm of '95 came roaring through, I sat there watching, fascinated--I never saw such a thing in my life. My Bruce never moved.

It woke me up. I came up to see the most awe-inspiring, awesome sight ever witnessed--it was like something out of a movie. Later I was just thankful that my anchor had held. There were no injuries, but the storm damaged some boats. Some were blown backwards. Friends of mine in a sailboat were blown right across the harbor without touching another boat. A roll call the next day showed that everyone had fared quite well.

Even though you were in a crowded harbor...

Yes--about 100 boats of all sizes and descriptions. From there I

22   Charters, Odysseys, Races, Gunkholes

went on to Little Current, and had the misfortune to step off my boat onto a floating finger dock. The wake from a passing boat was enough to set the dock in motion. My foot slipped and I hit my left quadricep and managed to peel it off. I ended up being taken by taxi the following day to Sudbury to an orthopedic surgeon. He told me that I still had three quadriceps left.

I was concerned because I'm a downhill slalom racer. But he said with therapy and exercise I should be able to manage quite well. That's the way it's turned out. I even found friends to help me get from Little Current to Sault Ste. Marie, where I was to meet other friends.

You're Captain Hoag now.

Women ask me, "How did you do it? I've wanted to cruise like that." And I tell them, Just do it. I don't know whether I've broken any kind of barrier, but it certainly feels like I have.

And came out smelling like a rose.

Yes, almost. I did have to have Cyrus put to sleep. He was well known at the Cruising Club rendezvous. He would sit up on command and salute. He also knew port and starboard. He was featured in a layout on the Cruising Club once. I think the magazine was *Cruising World.*

Cyrus is still remembered every year in the infamous dog show that they hold every year at the rendezvous. That's been done for two years now. It brings back memories.

PETER G. CODE

(1997)

The headline was typically succinct. "CANADIAN ROWERS," it read, "COLLECT FOUR GOLD, TWO SILVER, AND FOUR BRONZE IN THE U.S. ROWING CHAMPIONSHIPS AT INDIANAPOLIS." The body of the article told how, among other things, the Canadian men's lightweight quadruple sculls team won one of the golds. Peter G. Code, whose name appears as one of the four-man crew, keeps the clipping pinned to the wall of his boat-repair workshop, The Skiff Shop, a 20-x-60-foot room located "about 75 feet from Lake Ontario" in Toronto.

The persona that took part in those 1989 U.S. Championships was his competitive side, Peter Code admits. His creative side drives him to build and repair small boats and larger yachts while his professorial side impels him to give classes in traditional boat-building under the aegis of The Marine Museum of Upper Canada. One of his proudest possessions travels with him to boat shows in the United States and Canada: a genuine replica of an 1890 St. Lawrence skiff that he constructed from scratch. That boat is one of more than a dozen that he's built either alone or while coaching students in boat-construction techniques. He talks about boat-building and re-lives some of the challenges of international scull racing...

* * *

You got professionally interested in boat-building years ago?

Not really. In 1991 I spent most of the year in Victoria, British Columbia. I was out there training with the Canadian National Rowing Team. After competing that summer in the Pan American Games, I ended up back there in Victoria. I found out that the Northwest School of Wooden Boatbuilding was just across the way in Townsend, Washington. I went over the next day, on the ferry, and put down a deposit.

That was a six-month course, and they took a traditional approach to wooden boat-building. That means they taught processes and practices that dated back before the invention of marine epoxies, before plywoods. Their techniques would have been common in the years 1850 to 1950, approximately.

This was full-time schooling--five days a week?

A boat takes shape in the Skiff Shop under the skilled ministrations of Peter Code.

In a practice session, Code demonstrates the form that took him to international competitions.

More like seven. (Laughs.) The school was officially in session from Monday to Friday, 8:00 to 5:00. But we worked evenings and weekends as often as not. You wanted to get as much as you could out of the course even if you didn't plan to use the knowledge professionally. There was a lawyer from South Bend, Indiana, who was retiring and wanted to build boats after he retired. Some of the other students were fishermen who wanted to learn to repair their boats. The chief instructor was Jeff Hammond, who's very well known in the field. He was an inspiration for all of us.

You actually built boats?

We built a Lawley tender while I was there. That's a ship's boat, a lightweight, lapstrake boat, made of cedar in our case. That was an exposure to boat-building on a small scale. The lapstrake hull construction makes it stronger. The planks don't lie side by side, but one overlaps the one next to it. You see these in museums, and you can see the edges of the planks, almost like a clapboard house wall. You get longitudinal reinforcement with this kind of construction.

A lot of lifeboats are lapstrakes. Because the planks overlap, they tighten in water, or *take up*, much more quickly than the regular hull form. That means they can sit on a ship's deck for days or weeks, and then when launched they swell up or seal up rapidly. You don't have to bail as long. The lapstrake method hasn't changed that much since the Viking days. Boat builders often look back and study those old boats to see how they were made. They're very important in the evolution of the small boat.

I think just as importantly we learned things like lofting. That's taking a drawing or boat design that's roughly two feet by three feet on five or six sheets of paper, then making a full-sized boat exactly as the designer intended. You're also producing the picture or design from different angles. There's a profile view of the boat, there's a plan view from overhead, and then there are what we call sections. These are basically cutaway views of the boat. When he's done, the builder has what may be a 30-foot picture from which he can make a set of molds for the finished boat.

Does your interest in building boats come out of your rowing, or was it planted earlier?

I got involved in competitive rowing about 15 years ago. But I had had experience with small rowing craft years before that, probably at a summer place in the Muskoka Lakes district north of Toronto. Then in the early '80's I joined the Argonaut Rowing Club, here in Toronto, and started my own small business repairing, refinishing, and restoring wooden racing shells. It expanded from there, and I got into competitive racing with the Rowing Club.

I did find that because I had done little things with boats--I could paint and varnish, for example--I was far ahead of others who were doing repairs. I sort of became the Club's unofficial repairman. That's been pretty much the case for the 15 years that I've been here. The Rowing Club is in downtown Toronto, and has about 300 members. It's been active for about 125 years, and they've been in competitive rowing all that time.

Rowing singles, doubles, quads?

Mostly single sculls. I've owned five different shells. Three were wooden ones built by a manufacturer in London, Ontario. Now I've switched to a carbon fiber boat. The material makes this boat more rigid, and that's an advantage. You've got a boat that's 26 feet long, about 10 inches wide, and weighs about 29 pounds.

26   Charters, Odysseys, Races, Gunkholes

The stiffness or rigidity has a lot to do with speed. These boats are like pencils, long and narrow, and the races cover a standard distance of 2,000 meters. The boats aren't very seaworthy, so we find that trying to race on Lake Ontario is very undependable. You need what we call flat water. We can practice behind a breakwall here at the club, but the area isn't big enough for a six-lane-wide race course. That means we have to go to smaller towns in Ontario for the actual racing. We usually race through June, July, and August.

Then you're done for the year?

We may have what they call *head races* in the fall, and these can be longer than 2,000 meters. There's also a fall regatta in Boston, on the Charles River called "The Head of the Charles." I've been competing in that on a pretty regular basis.

Any trophies? Medals?

In 1987 I was on the team that won the Ontario championship in double sculls. That same year I got the Argonaut Rowing Club's Sculler of the Year award. They also awarded me what they call the Jim Millar Trophy for contributions to club activities. In 1988 I was half the team that won the Canadian championship in double sculls.

That was your biggest victory?

I don't think so. I think the gold medal we won in the quads at Indianapolis was the high point. I had just gotten into international rowing competition. You have to picture this. We had been brought together as a team about six days before we were due to race. They had tryouts about June 5 in single sculls, then they put us together for the quad.

My recollection of the first time we raced in Indianapolis is that it was extremely hot and humid. We had a very bad first race and were sent afterward to what they call a *repachage*. That's a second chance. By the rules of international rowing, you have that opportunity to make up for a poor performance. We won the second-chance race and were able to advance to the finals.

What changed between the first round and the repachage?

One of the things with a boat crew is that you have to communicate well and do everything together. In the first race we weren't able to communicate--and that meant we couldn't sprint at the same time. The communication between the bow-man and the rest of us was lacking.

The bow-man is the key. It's a very difficult job. He sits in the bow, naturally, and has to row. He has one of the four pairs of oars. But he also steers, using one foot, to keep the boat in a buoyed lane that is 12 to 15 yards wide. It's a real trick. Finally, the bow-man has to call strategy--tell us when to sprint, that kind of thing.

When it's working right, you feel as if there's no one else in the boat. The boat feels light. Fast. That's what happened in the *repachage* and in the finals. We got it together. We talked it over after that first race, discussing strategy.

Is that common?

I think so. You look for reasons why you lost. We were out of sync. If you all go identically together, the boat actually rises up in the water. It doesn't plane, but it sort of skims. If that's lacking, you take too many strokes per minute and just sort of splash around. You never become really efficient. That happened in the first race.

The race course was laid out in some kind of reservoir, inside an Indiana state park. But it's a natural reservoir, so there are trees around it. Near the shore there were stumps and logs, so we had to be careful with the boat. The shells that we were using were built in Zurich, Switzerland. They are made of a single layer of wood--I learned that was Honduras cedar--and are extremely fragile. They're 42 feet long and weigh about 125 pounds.

You won the repachage *and then came up for the finals?*

Yes. In the finals there were the usual six boats. There had been about 15 crews competing at the start. Several were from the United States, including a few from the top U.S. rowing clubs. There was an official U.S. team plus a crew from Mexico and our Canadian crew.

Everything is controlled in these races by the International Racing Association rules. Everyone's in uniform--we wore red and white, with maple leaves on our chests. Even our oars have our colors and the maple leaf. If you don't wear absolutely identical uniforms you're disqualified. They don't even allow hats or caps. You can't have an

28   Charters, Odysseys, Races, Gunkholes

undershirt hanging out. In 1989 there were strict rules about wearing advertising of any kind, but that may be changing a little.

What were the water conditions?

It was glass-calm. There was some wind for the earlier races, but for the finals it was flat. That made it easier to steer, and of course in steering the trick is to make as few adjustments as possible. Steering too much slows you down. If there's a cross-wind or diagonal winds, it plays havoc with your steering. If you add in the possibility of poor rudder work, you can lose a race before it starts.

You can visualize it. The lanes at Indianapolis were about 40 feet wide. You seem to have a lot of room beyond the ends of the oars, but you don't. If you're having a bad day, or if there's a strong wind, the lane could be twice as wide and it wouldn't be enough. Remember that the oars are 298 centimeters long--nine feet, nine inches. They rest in an aluminum oarlock built onto an outrigger. You've got about 60 inches between each set of oarlocks. That's your whole working space.

What was your time in the finals?

We did the 2,000 meters in six minutes and I believe four seconds. That's very fast. The world record in the quads was probably a couple of seconds under six minutes. That record goes down about a second and a half a year as boats get more rigid and lighter. The record is probably five-fifty-four, or five minutes 54 seconds.

You receive your medals right after the race?

We pulled in at the finish line, which is very close to shore. There's a dock there, and a grandstand and a beach. They awarded the gold, silver, and bronze medals instantly.

Then it was on to other international races?

Not right away. We had another six weeks of training in Canada. The crew broke up for a week because we had to drive to Victoria, British Columbia. Three of us jumped in my truck and we drove out to train on Vancouver Island. One member of our crew was from that area and had to stay out there to work.

After that training we had had another trip back to Ontario and Quebec. Midway through that six-week stretch we had to race in the Canadian Championships. We won that, then we raced at the Royal Canadian Henley at St. Catherines. Those two races were a week apart, August 1 and August 8. We had another 10 days of training in Victoria, then flew all the way to Yugoslavia. With a stop in Toronto to pick up other members of the Canadian team, we were traveling 24 hours.

In Yugoslavia you're up against European and other international scullers?

I think there were a dozen European countries represented. These were the 1989 World Championships. We finished eighth. The only consolation was that the Americans finished ninth. (Laughs.)

There was a story there. We weren't doing well. I think we were in the third or fourth position, and were having a hard time. The American crew was ahead of us--just on my left-hand; then we started to get it together, and were at least keeping them from getting ahead of us any further. It went on that way for hundreds of meters.

It was very cold--this was Bled, Yugoslavia--and windy. Suddenly the American boat hit a lane marker. When that happens, you can usually hear the blade strike. They had been having steering problems, and were being pushed into our lane. When they struck the buoy it

Dressed for a race: Holding two of their oars and wearing the prescribed uniforms, members of the Canadian National Rowing Team pose with their coach, Doug White (center). Team members are (left to right) Lewis Hancock, Keith Battersby, Peter Code, and Eric Therrien.

was very disruptive. You're racing at 36 or 37 strokes a minute. Their boat slowed down drastically. We all heard them hit, and then our bow-man made a call, an aggression call, and we took off and passed them--and came in ahead of them.

The Europeans won?

They really outclassed us, and in retrospect that wasn't a big surprise at all. That was the first year the light-weight quad sculls had been included in the World Championships. But European clubs had been expert in that class for dozens of years. They had a huge pool of scullers to choose from.

You've done international racing later?

I was with the Canadian National Rowing Team again in 1991. We competed in the Pan American Games in Cuba. We didn't win any medals, but it was an experience. In 1989 and 1991 we were breaking ground. Now Canadian and American scullers have a much higher profile than they did then. It's been an international sport for years and years, but we've gotten into it only in recent years. As one footnote, my coach, Stephen Sandor, raced in the 1956 Olympics, rowing for Hungary.

Are you still racing competitively?

Definitely. I can row in the master's B category now, which is for people 35 to 41. But I can also row in the A group, for people 29 to 35.

I went to Budapest last fall and took part in a masters' international regatta. Some friends from our rowing club, the Argonaut, went along. I had four races there in A single, B single and then in some mixed-sex boats, doubles and quads. So I was in four levels of rowing there.

Tell us about your boat-repair shop?

I call it The Skiff Shop. It's just off Lake Ontario. But I also repair yachts at the Royal Canadian Yacht Club here in Toronto. They have about 20 wooden yachts up to 50 feet in length. Repairing them is a science.

The wood rots if you don't take care of it--the frames, planks, and decks require constant maintenance once they get old. I know about this kind of maintenance partly because I own a Dragon, a 30-foot wooden racing sailboat.

The woods you use in repair work are critical. Planking on most boats in this area is mahogany. Some boats are planked with cedar, which has different characteristics. Whatever the original wood is, you try to put in what you take out. You wouldn't replace mahogany with cedar, for example.

Now you're working with the Marine Museum of Upper Canada?

I talked with John Summers, the curator at the museum. It seemed that there was pretty strong interest in getting some boat-building activity in Toronto. To start with, we built a seven and a half-foot yacht tender. We wanted to build a boat in order to teach others how to build one. We finished that boat three winters ago, in '94-'95, and started classes the following winter.

We expanded a little the next year, adding half-model making and boat repair and restoration. Then we added hand-tool sharpening. There's been a good response from the public. In fact, we're hoping to finish seven boats by June of 1997. One of the most interesting is a 13-foot lapstrake canoe. We'll be working on that, with different classes, for several years.

What happens to the boats once they're built?

They don't go into the museum. Usually the people in the class buy them for their own personal use. There's an element of builder's pride there. They really have learned how a traditional wooden boat is made, in that process finding out about the wooden boat terminology and plan-reading. They end up with planking and fastening.

They could go home and build their own boats.

A lot of them do.

What's your proudest boat-building achievement?

I'd say the St. Lawrence skiff. I have it here in the shop. John

32   Charters, Odysseys, Races, Gunkholes

Summers told me about this boat. It was used mainly between 1880 and 1920--a boat that was extensively used for fishing. That meant usually that a guide was in the boat. But the skiff was also used for basic transportation, taking people to the residences, holiday lodges, and recreation areas on the St. Lawrence River and Upper Lake Ontario.

This boat ranged in size from 15 to 20 feet. The one I built is 18 and a half feet long, a copy of a skiff that was built by Moses Sauvé, in Brockville, Ontario. He was a professional boat-builder in the late 1800's. I got the measurements off a skiff that Sauvé built, one that's over 100 years old and is still used on a regular basis.

Yours is historically accurate?

Every inch. And I built it using the old techniques, keeping the same dimensions. I used the same woods as were in the original--cedar planking, white ash keel, and oak frame. Butternut decks.

It's a very fast boat, very seaworthy. These boats had to be seaworthy because the St. Lawrence can get very rough, especially on large expanses of water. Also, you're fighting a current. With a slow boat you'd never get anywhere.

What do you do with the skiff?

I take it to boat shows. It's my demo. I've been to Clayton, New York, this year, for a boat show and to Gravenhurst, Ontario. Also, I displayed it at the Newcastle Wooden Boat Weekend, another annual event. In January I had it on display at the Toronto International Boat Show.

Would you say that the age of the woodie is back, or that it never died?

It survives. Many marine museums in the United States are running classes like mine on small, traditional boats. People are starting to collect them. I can see the interest in my classes--I've had students from age 13 to 70.

DEANE H. TANK

(1997)

Sail once in a Chicago-Mackinac race, says Deane H. Tank, Ph.D., and you're hooked. "The Mac is a very demanding sailing challenge," comments Tank, understating the case. "Lake Michigan routinely experiences abrupt changes in weather conditions..." The holder of a doctoral degree in education, president in early 1997 of the Chicago Maritime Society, and instructor in the philosophy of education at Chicago's DePaul University, is living, sailing proof of his own thesis: In 1996 he took part in his 37th consecutive Mac. He sailed in his first in 1960.

For Tank, the inner mystique of the Mac lies in its imponderables: the team approaches to strategy and tactics, the meteorological anomalies that hurl endless surprises at the sailors, and the victories and losses that seem sometimes to occur without much nautical rhyme or reason. It's also true that each race develops its own character, or personality, almost with the report of the first starting gun. Example: '96 was relatively predictable where '95 was a full boat of unforeseen extremes.

None of this means that Tank has spent a single minute of boredom while sailing those 37 races. Quite the contrary. He can wax lyrical on all of them, perhaps most analytically on the '95 and '96 races.

* * *

Give us a little background? Does the Chicago Maritime Society have anything to do with the racing?

Not really. You could call them a conjunction of interests for me. I've been sailing since I acquired my first sailboat at the age of 9. But the Maritime Society is a more recent, and more time-consuming and engaging, project. We've come far in the few years since our founding in 1982.

34   Charters, Odysseys, Races, Gunkholes

Name some Society activities?

As a sampling, we've assembled some 11 exhibits and seven museum-type displays on subjects ranging from the *Eastland* disaster to Maritime Art, and from the aircraft carrier *Wolverine* to the "Christmas Tree Ship," the *Rouse Simmons*. The exhibits move from site to site. Obviously, they serve an educational purpose, giving people insights into Chicago's and the Great Lakes' maritime heritage. The exhibits go to schools, public buildings, airports, and institutions.

The CMS serves as the primary repository of maritime artifacts and research materials in Chicago. The collection includes, in round numbers, 3,500 books, articles, artworks, photos, and various kinds of documents. We also have a genuine treasurehouse of about 130 small watercraft including canoes of ancient and more recent vintage. Some of them are over 100 years old. A member of our board of directors, Ralph Frese, assembled the collection over more than 40 years.

We've got a couple of book projects under way and are hoping to finish them this year. One is a history of the Great Lakes schooner. We call it *Chicago's Era of Sailing Schooners*. It'll cover roughly the period from the early 1800's to about 1920. The schooner in that period was a workhorse of Great Lakes water-borne commerce. The other book will be a compilation of articles on Chicago's maritime history. We're expecting these books to be well received.

I'm editing another book that has nothing to do with the CMS. It'll be a history of the Mac race that will help celebrate the 100th anniversary of the first Mac next year. I'm working on that as a member of the Island Goat Society, a group of people who have sailed 25 or more Chicago Macs.

Will the Maritime Society have a museum open to the public?

We started one in 1987 and it closed in 1994. One of our great ambitions is to reopen in a more favorable location. Our displays and exhibits are all in preparation for a public museum. Chicago without a maritime museum is like a sailboat without masts.

The CMS has an army of volunteer members engaged in different projects that serve the public. We've put together a rowing and paddling course for local Sea Explorers Scouts. We provide the instructors and canoes plus funding, posters and just about everything else they need. We invite the public to come and learn.

Are your canoes and other watercraft on exhibit locally?

Depending on the space, some of them are traveling and on exhibit practically all the time. A half-dozen will shortly be entertaining crowds at Navy Pier. We can assemble more than 20 to show the historical progression of canoe construction technology from early times to the present.

Almost as interesting, we think, is our collection of model ships. They must be worth two hundred thousand dollars. Some are replicas of Great Lakes ships like the *David Dows*, which sank off Chicago in 1889 (see Olson-van Heest interview). Another model is the old passenger-sidewheeler *Comet* and a third is the Great Lakes whaleback *Christopher Columbus*.

Deane H. Tank

You tie all this together--and race in your own boat?

I own a cruising sailing yacht, the *Prelude*. But I'm not racing in my own boat these days--though I've owned six or so boats that I've raced in the past. In recent Mac races I've been aboard the *Iskra*, which means "Spark" in Ukrainian. Boris Jarymowycz is the owner and skipper.

Describe the Iskra *and her crew?*

The boat's a marvel, a wild, fast, sleek Mumm 36. The boat almost literally skims over the water. It has extraordinary upwind tacking characteristics, meaning that it can sail close to the wind.

We have a fine crew. Besides Boris and me, there are Boris's son Bo, Steve Lovendahl, Skip Ryan, and our three Johns: John Ludvik, John Wallen, and John Hartford. Every one of them has special sailing

36   Charters, Odysseys, Races, Gunkholes

skills.   Skip knows navigation and tactics, for example.   Steve is a wizard at sail trim and tactics.   "Big John" Ludvik knows yacht operations and dinner preparation, which makes him one of the most valued crew members.   "Middle John" Wallen handles sails and "Little John" Hartford is also an excellent sail handler.   Four of us do the helm work--myself, Boris, Steve, and Art.   Over 100 Macs are represented by the crew.

The Mac must be quite a spectacle.

You've got to see the start of a Mac to believe it.*   It's an impressive sight.   The yachts come in all sizes, though most are over 30 feet in length.   They gather in Chicago from ports all around the Great Lakes.   They also arrive by truck from the east and west coasts. Every year a number come from the Bayview Yacht Club in Detroit. Last year, '96, we had 243 yachts in the PHRF class and 32 in the IMS class.   The letters identify the two handicapping systems, the Pacific Handicap Rules Federation and the International Measurement System.

You blast off on Saturday?

Invariably.   The race starts Saturday about 12:00 noon, no matter what the weather is.   There's an official boat at each end of the starting line, out in the lake off the end of Madison Street.   The yachts staart in groups up to about 4:00 p.m.   In the minutes before each group starts the yachts are maneuvering, trying to position themselves for a good start.   They start in 13 separate sections.

The boats come into the race pretty equally matched because of the handicapping.   One mistake, like a foulup in sail handling, can doom your start.   When the last starter's gun goes off they're all off, racing over the 333 miles to Mackinac Island.

Our "steed," the *Iskra*, sounds like it ought to be rated with the 36-footers.   But because it's so naturally light and fast, they handicap it with yachts that are 40 and more feet in length.   That means that to win we have to reach the finish line a heck of a lot earlier than others of the

*A similar race brings together up to 300 yachts for the Port Huron-Mackinac Race sponsored annually by Detroit's Bayview Yacht Club.   First run in 1925, the race covers 259 miles.   The racers may carry crews of five or six to 20 or more.

same length. Since she's a strictly racing yacht, not a cruising yacht, she has only the minimum in the way of creature comforts. Where other yachts have big galleys and roomy cabins, *Iskra* has a two-burner stove and can sleep four comfortably while under way. I know about the stove because I cook breakfast in the mornings during a race.

This past year we had a moderate breeze when we started, and took a course northward up the west shore of Lake Michigan. The *Iskra* is designed to be crew-ballasted. That means that some members of the crew have to sit on the side of the boat to counteract the pressure of the breeze. I've heard of races in which crew members went all the way to Mackinac--two days or more--without leaving their deck stations. They ate and slept hanging on, helping to keep the craft more or less stable.

The crew has other duties while racing?

They're usually as busy as one-armed paper-hangers. They have to manage the sails, constantly keeping them in perfect trim and, of course, changing them to meet the wind conditions. People who know how to work the foresails, like the spinnaker, are worth their weight in gold. Our Little John concentrated on the foredeck.

Note a difference between '95 and '96. In '95 the boats started in 97-degree heat. Some had hardly reached Waukegan when a storm struck. We could see it coming when we saw white caps building out west of us. A lot of boats sort of went over on their sides the moment it hit. We were able to hang on and make good time. The strange thing was that the squall lasted about an hour, which is very unusual. That makes it about as sustained and violent a squall as you'd ever encounter on Lake Michigan.

In '96 the wind gradually faded. You could tell by Saturday night that no one would set any records. That continued pretty much through the night and into Sunday morning. You'd think that would make it easier on the crew. But it gets harder actually. You do everything you can think of to keep the boat moving. You change sail leads or change sails. That goes on endlessly, with all kinds of sweat and strain. Because you're hardly making headway, the flies can attack by the thousands. Sometimes they turn the deck black, there are so many of them.

Saturday night we had one bright spot. Big John performed an

38 Charters, Odysseys, Races, Gunkholes

Sails billowing, and with Chicago's skyline as a backdrop, the *Iskra* heads for the open lake. The Chicago-Mackinac Race took place for the first time in 1898. (Photo courtesy Boris Jarymowycz)

amazing culinary feat on that stove while it careened back and forth, serving a tasty three-course oriental meal. But light airs prevailed until Sunday morning, when we got an overdue easterly breeze and started moving again toward Mackinac Island.

Strategy intact?

Not exactly. Our confidence in our strategy was eroding when we saw Milwaukee Sunday morning. It was close enough, as someone said, to order beer and brats. By afternoon, we could see very few boats. Our hopeful conclusion was that the other boats had dropped behind us, having crossed the lake on a less favorable tack

Our breeze from the east finally shifted around to the southwest and pushed *Iskra* at exciting speed past Point Betsie, the Manitou Light, and Beaver Island. By Monday we were surfing along at 15 knots--nearly 20 miles per hour, very fast for a small sailing yacht. We passed under the Mackinac Bridge, then crossed the finish line racing fast, with the spinnaker up.

On to victory?

We did lousy. We didn't know that those yachts that had taken tacks earlier out into the lake had found more breeze and finished ahead of us. There were a crowd of people and a party at the Pink Pony Bar when we got there. I think we were twelfth in our division. There's an overall prize, and we must have been fiftieth overall. If you're not in the top three or four, it doesn't really matter how you finish.

Just to give you an idea of how these things work with the handicap system, a relatively slow boat won the PHRF overall trophy. That was the 40-foot *Bantu*, owned by Tom Kuber of the Menominee-Marinette Yacht Club. Second in PHRF was *Different Drummer*, a 33-foot Tartan 10 owned by Chris Goff of Lake Bluff, Illinois.

Did you review your '96 strategy?

There's always a big study after it's over. We knew that the shore has a profound effect on the breeze. It's very technical, but I think we underestimated how far out in the lake the shore could affect the wind. That's especially true at dusk or at daybreak. That could have been

Spinnaker flying, a Mac racer crosses the finish line at Round Island Light. The Chicago-Mac Race takes place annually in July. (Photo courtesy Beverly A. Ford)

one thing that tripped us up. We were several miles offshore on the Michigan side, but it must have been too close. That's all we can figure.

Have you ever won a Mac?

No. I overlapped the winner once. The bow of the winning boat and the bow of the second boat were less than six or seven feet ahead of us. You don't forget a finish like that. It was an exciting experience.

Remember other Mac high points?

A lot of them. There was a monster storm in 1970, for example. Ted Turner, the media magnate, had a large yacht, *American Eagle*, in that race, a 12-meter boat that had been in the America's Cup. They had 167 starters that year and 60-knot headwinds. Eighty-eight boats had to drop out.

In the '70 race we broke some gear. We also had a crew member injured, and had to take him to a hospital in Frankfort, Michigan. We couldn't continue after that.

A lot of people remember '95. The boat that set the all-time Mac Record, the *Pied Piper*, a Santa Cruz 70, was dismasted in '95--a first for Dick Jennings, the boat's owner. That was Jennings' 35th Mac. In a lifetime of racing all over the world he had never lost a mast. That'll give you an idea of what the winds were. We came in intact, so we were lucky.

What is the fastest elapsed or actual time record?

Twenty five hours and 50 minutes. Jennings set it in the *Pied Piper* in 1987.

You'll be on the Iskra *again in '97?*

That's my target. From what I hear they're ready to go. I'm also planning on making the 100th anniversary race in 1998--not the 100th race but the 100th anniversary race. The race took place for the first time in 1898, then it lapsed for five years and was again suspended for four years during and after World War I.

The book by the Island Goat Society, Tales of the Mackinac Race, *will tell about it?*

Yes. We'll cover the period from 1925 on. There's another book that covered the races up to 1925. We've collected many fine Mac stories and photographs that should be great reading for anyone interested in the race.

CAMILLA B. ROSS

(1994)

"This job combines the challenges of river boat captaincy with the fascination of the rich historical and architectural heritage of Chicago."

So says Camilla B. Ross of Hinsdale, Illinois in nutshelling her job as a captain with the Chicago From The Lake tour-boat firm. Completing seven years with the firm in 1996, Ross pilots the 72 ton Fort Dearborn *on architectural tours of the Chicago River or the 36 ton* Marquette *on Lake Michigan and the Chicago River. On Lake*

Michigan it's a historical tour. She's moonlighted, taking day sails on Navy vessels from Chicago's Navy Pier or piloting the state-of-the-art nightclub/restaurant ship Odyssey II. *An active downhill skier, competitive runner, and supporter of the nuclear submarine* USS Chicago, *she has earned her license to pilot ships up to 500 tons.*

* * *

We have two types of tours on the river, architectural and historical. On the architectural tour we have a docent, a knowledgeable person, talking about the buildings, about the architects, about some of the engineering principles that have gone into construction of these buildings. These docents present this information through an entire hour and one-half trip.

The boats are moored in Ogden Slip--we go out of the slip and into the main branch of the Chicago River, heading west. Then it's up the north branch, and we spin (u-turn) at Goose Island, or Ogden Island as it's called officially. We go back down the North Branch--the Kinzie Street Bridge opens for us; it's the only bridge that has to open--and go down the South Branch as far as River City. We spin there, and have a beautiful view of the Chicago Skyline. As a matter of fact, Chicago from the river is exceptionally attractive, as opposed to New York, say, where you're looking up from the street. When you're on the river, on our boats, you get a much better perspective on the buildings--and you can see the buildings one alongside another and see how the architects have used--how they blend one building into the next to honor the architect of the adjacent building.

After we go down the main branch, of course, we're passing the Centennial Fountain. Its water arch over the river represents the gateway from the Great Lakes to the Inland Waterway. It's really quite impressive.

The people, when they leave the tour vessel, are usually quite pleased with the hour and a half that they've spent. You can tell that because they're smiling when they get off. And they say they're going to tell their friends. We play classical music, usually Mozart, during the boarding and debarking. I particularly like to play Handel's "Water Music"--it was written for King George on the Thames. You'd be surprised how many people recognize it. That adds to the fun of it.

We don't have good location. You know, a lot of people have never heard of North Pier. They know Navy Pier but not North Pier.

But we can compete by delivering an excellent product. Like I mentioned, we have very good docents. The boats are clean. We provide hot coffee, Starbuck's coffee as a matter of fact, and lemonade and a slice of fresh lemon. We have cookies or muffins depending on the time of day. It's all presented very nicely.

Actually I think I'm lucky. I'm lucky to be working for this particular company. We've got the best product on the river. I love what I'm doing, and I don't tell them that I'd do it for nothing. I get paid for what I like to do anyway. Well, that describes the architectural tour.

How about the historical?

That goes out through the locks into Lake Michigan. She goes into Monroe Street harbor and by Buckingham Fountain, the (Field) Museum of Natural History, the (Shedd) Aquarium, and the (Adler) Planetarium. The boat could be the *Innisfree*, it could be the *Marquette*. Any of the three boats could do any of the tours. The largest of the boats is the *Fort Dearborn*, 72 tons. The next one is the *Innisfree*, 48 tons; the *Marquette* is 36 tons.

On the historical tour the emphasis of the presentation is different. We're emphasizing the history of Chicago as opposed to the architecture of Chicago. And that doesn't mean we eliminate all discussion of architecture, because in fact the two are quite closely related. The historical tour comes back through the locks and heads up--actually down—the Chicago River, and we try to get as far as Wolf Point.

We always get down to Michigan Avenue, to the main intersection there, for the architecture. It's one of the best places for architecture in the whole world. You've got so many different types of architecture represented.

We have four tours a day. Both types of tour. Some of the docents are architects, or architectural students. Some aren't, but all are knowledgeable.

We open the first of May and close the 31st of October. But the October schedule is reduced somewhat. That's because of both weather and fewer tourists.

In May the weather can be very changeable. On a day like today we'd have a lot of business. On a day like Thursday, unbelievable. That day I had 56 lovely ladies, average age about 60, and we had

The tour boat *Fort Dearborn* glides along the main branch of the Chicago River under the expert guidance of Capt. Camilla Ross. The 65-foot *Fort Dearborn* can accommodate 200 sightseers.

winds gusting up to 40 miles an hour. We had little water spouts right at the end of the slip. I'm taking the *Innisfree* through that. I had to tell my crew to tie everything down. These ladies, after an hour and a half of being blown around, loved the trip. That says something about what we've got.

I'll tell you, bringing that lady in was a challenge. And I like that.

Can you talk about your work on the Oddyssey II? The restaurant ship?

I was in the right place at the right time. I really lucked out. This was last year. The *Oddyssey II* had just been brought in to replace *Oddyssey* I. I never dreamed I'd have a chance to captain that vessel. It turned out that one of her captains, an Argentinian, a wonderful young man from the Argentinian Naval Academy, had sailed tall ships around the world. Very personable. But he didn't have his Coast Guard license yet. So there was that short period of time when they had to have a licensed captain. They needed a skilled person, so they asked me if I wanted to do that. Of course I wanted to do it.

I really didn't think I'd be doing much more than just sitting there. But the first time out, he took it off the pier, and as soon as we got away from the pier it was mine. Like I said, you don't need drugs to get a high. I took her out around Navy Pier and over to the Oak Street cut. Spun down there at Montrose. Did it again. Second time same thing. I wanted to take her off the dock, she's got bow-thrusters. Oh, man!

I had a couple of more opportunities after that. And each was just a marvelous experience--this ship 40 feet wide, bridge with big easy chairs, all the instrumentation, beautiful radar and all that stuff, and of course I was the captain, and the people on the bridge would ask the captain questions. It was a super experience--the young guy was able to get his license and that was that. I did it five times.

You don't give any of the talks on the tour boats?

As a matter of fact, when I first started I was crew and it wasn't set up quite the same way. So I was the docent. I learned a lot by listening. Then I added my own--I'm a Chicagoan and proud of it. I like Chicago, I think Chicago is a wonderful place. Then I've traveled around and could compare--I'm not like a blind native. Our waterfront is spectacular. And besides, O'Hare Field is half an hour away and that's access to the whole world. What could be better? Anyway, I like Chicago and I was able to convey that to the people who were listening. Some of them even asked if I was an architect.

Now I don't talk. I pilot the boat. Some of our opposition will just say, Now this is the Post Office, the--whatever they see, the Wrigley Building. Unfortunately, we once had an association with the Chicago Architectural Foundation. Now that's gone. To compensate for that, we emphasize again the courteous, competent crew, clean boats, the excellent docents we have.

On the *Fort Dearborn* I have two crew. On the *Innisfree*, one. But I'm associated with the kind of people I like. I say, what could be better? I wallow in a sea of handsome young men. They say, you dirty old sailor. That's a sailor joke, so you wouldn't appreciate it.

You've got family?

A son, Karl with a K. Wife Brenda. Two grandkids. Someone wanted to write a headline, "Local Grandma Pilots 70-ton Tour Boat." Then there was my father. Want to hear a five minute story on this?

46 Charters, Odysseys, Races, Gunkholes

I certainly do.

We had an older brother's 40th wedding anniversary, and when we get together we talk about ships. Of course the fact that my Dad was a chief petty officer on the battleship *Massachusetts* came up. Somebody at the party said, Oh that battleship is at Falls River, Massachusetts, now, on display. I said: That's funny. I thought she was sunk. Target practice. I let it go at that. I'm taking care of Dad too. At any rate, I took him down to Florida and I got hold of the AAA to find out about this Falls River place, because if it were in fact my Dad's ship I would return from Florida via Mass so he could get into his chief's quarters, just to be nice. And I called up there, and we started talking about WWI, and they said, Oh, you've got to talk to a historian. And the historian says, oh no, the battleship you're talking about isn't at Falls River, this is Battleship *Massachusetts Two*. There was a previous battleship of the same name and indeed she was sunk. And they were kind enough to send my Dad, you know, pictures and all that kind of stuff. And that was the last I thought I would hear of that. And then I get a letter--Dad gets a letter--from the Underwater Archeological Department of the State of Florida. And they're trying to make an underwater preserve in the state of Florida on this battleship--because in fact it was sunk, it was scuttled, in Pensacola Bay. And Dad was the last surviving member of the crew of that battleship.

They had tried everywhere to find somebody and Dad was the one. And they asked if I could bring him to Tallahassee for an interview. And I did. It was a really moving experience. Cause Dad literally saved that ship once from sinking. His knowledge in the engine room. That's why he got promoted to chief P.O. And he was telling that story, and they had a model of the battleship, and his eyes lit up, and they wanted him to come down for the inauguration of this park. Unfortunately the inauguration was delayed essentially a year, and in that time Dad had a stroke so he couldn't understand what was going on. He recovered physically, but not mentally.

And I got the honor, and a younger brother, who's a pilot for Delta, was an Annapolis man--we were invited down there, for this inauguration. And Dad was a photographer, not a professional photographer; he took pictures of this battleship, of the crew playing craps, of the Christmas party--it brought this ship to life, you know? And I took this album down for a meeting in Pensacola. Their eyes lit up, and they had the official photographer from the Blue Angels. He copied all those pictures, and they're now in the Landside Museum. So we were there for the inauguration; I made a little speech. And then we went off by ship to the battleship; and my brother and I threw wreaths out there in honor of my Dad and his shipmates. Seventy five years, three quarters of a century before that, my Dad walked the decks of that ship. It was a very emotional experience. And like I say, I'm really a very fortunate person--I got on TV down there, and I got t-shirts for all the nieces and nephews and grandchildren. Wonderful experience.

Amazing experience.

But my mom's three first cousins were ship captains on the Great Lakes, Atlantic, and Pacific. So I feel like I've got water in my veins. And one of my Norwegian ancestors was a square-rig guy. And my grandkids were both baptized up in Door County, Wisconsin in a little white church, and two charter members were my grandfather and grandmother. The one that this kid is named after (Thure) was a charter member of that little church.

You have ocean and lake water running in your veins. When did you start realizing that?

That's interesting too, because my husband was born in Scotland, a real Scot, and his father--I don't know whether you're aware that the Scottish people provided engineers for around the world. You know Scots were the best shipbuilders. The British people were often the deck officers, but the Scots were the engineers. *Like in Star Trek, it's not a fluke that Scottie is the engineer in Star Trek.* I mean that's historical fact. So anyway, my husband's father was an electrician and worked on ships. So he had ships on the brain. And he brought home ship magazines. My husband, little husband, looked at all the sea magazines, and wanted boats, from little boy on. Power boats. When we first got into--well, we were married and we thought, well it would be interesting to have a boat. He was interested in a boat.

So, okay, we started out. On Fox Lake. A cabin cruiser on the Illinois. Houseboat all the way from LaCrosse up to Minneapolis. Canoeing up at Quetico. And then it was really great--we went to all the boat shows, felt all the boats. And there was a Triton. Twenty-eight foot sailor. And we decided we would charter that boat. It turned

48   Charters, Odysseys, Races, Gunkholes

out that that boat was here in Michigan City. Accident. And so this guy didn't want to charter this boat, we realized, to anyone who didn't know what they were doing. My husband, being very well read, a professor at IIT, he always read everything nautical, other things. He sounded like he really knew the business. If you talked to him you'd think he was a sailor. But he wasn't. So these people that had the Triton invited us out here to go sailing. It was really funny, he wasn't a sailor, I'm not, and she was tied up on the sea wall. And we got on board, and the captain says, Make ready for sea, Ross. And Ross sits down, clears his throat, and says, "I'd like you to show my wife how to do this. She has to be the crew." (Laughter.) Smart man. So the captain shows me how to do it, and we go out, and they gave Ross the tiller--I didn't even know the term at the time--and it was amazing that we didn't get into irons, but we didn't. And they never caught on to the fact that we didn't know a thing about sailboats. So they chartered this thing. And we got a good book and we went sailing, and we learned how to sail here. That was a wonderful kind of experience, you know. That did it. The year must have been like '64.

You had gone through all these other kinds of boats--.

Yes. And each one has a fantastic story. But we're not going to tell that. Anyway, we're still going to the boat shows. Ross knew all about boats, and there's this Alberg 30, and he says, That's a good boat. So we ended up buying that. And it was a wonderful thing because we enjoyed sailing. Every weekend was different. The best part, you know, was you'd turn off the engine as soon as you get out of here, course I don't tell that to my friends, but I still feel that. You've got the wind, the sails, and the sea--you know sailing is a marvelous experience. And I think once people get on a sailboat they get hooked. And I'm still hooked on that, but I love the challenge of the powerboat. And I'm not sorry. Not sorry I'm doing this. Being a captain on the Chicago River is a challenge. Like Thursday, I've got these 56 elderly ladies, we've got a big sandbarge coming, with a pusher (tug)--but people don't understand what potential danger there is. And what skills people have to have to handle that.

You had a life before piloting.

Yes, I graduated from Carthage College (Illinois) in 1952. I applied to the University of Chicago and got admitted. I earned a master's degree and then a doctorate in organic chemistry. I wanted to teach, but then decided to get some experience in the industrial world. That way, I could prepare my students for that world.

I took a temporary job with Union Carbide Corporation. Twenty-eight years later I retired. I taught chemistry part-time at William Rainey Harper College in Palatine (Illinois) so that I could care for my husband, George. He was suffering from ALS, Lou Gehrig's disease. He died in 1987.

Funny about the Alberg. Ross wanted that boat, and he wanted to convince me that he wanted it. Of course I wasn't very hard to convince. So I said, Ross, we'll get this boat providing I can name it. He said, That's reasonable. And since he was a man of his word, when I said I'm going to name it George, he didn't like the idea, but nonetheless...The boat was trucked to Chicago from Ajax, Ontario, and we came down the river and through the locks and came into the Chicago Yacht Club and we had to go to the harbormaster there to sign up. The man asked my husband, What's the name of the boat? And my husband said, *George*. The man said, *George*? Yes, *George*. He said, How do you spell that? (Laughter.)

Now I wear a white shirt, and I've got my captain's epaulettes on it. At night, you wear black pants and a black tie, but I generally don't work at night. In the daytime I wear khaki pants. The white shirt. No tie. And the epaulettes.

MARK S. NEMSCHOFF

(1997)

Mark Nemschoff likes a challenge even if it's only implicit. In 1983, when Michael Reagan, son of the 40th president of the United

50   Charters, Odysseys, Races, Gunkholes

States, piloted a speedboat from Chicago to Detroit and called it a record, some mental antenna in Nemschoff began to vibrate. "That seemed like something I could do," Nemschoff recalls. The American Power Boat Association had established the Chicago-Detroit run as an officially sanctioned event that same year, mostly as a publicity stunt. Reagan's time of 12 hours, 34 minutes, and 42 seconds stood as a record because no one else had tried to win the newly minted Ralph Evinrude Challenge Trophy.

The Reagan time withstood several challenges over the next few years. Nemschoff's mental oscillations quieted somewhat. But in 1990 martial arts/action film star Chuck Norris drove a caterpillar diesel-engine boat over the 620-mile Chicago-Detroit course in 12:8:42, breaking Michael Reagan's record by some 26 minutes. Nemschoff's vibes became a drumbeat. The earlier assaults on the course had included refueling stops in Mackinaw City. Why not do the distance nonstop?--that was the question. Nemschoff went looking for a diesel-powered craft that could take the beatings that Lakes Michigan and Huron could administer and average more than Norris's 55 miles an hour.

Nemschoff ended up in Italy in 1995 with a boat, the Tecno 40, that had come out of the FB Design boat works run by Italian racer/designer Fabio Buzzi in Annone Brianza. Sponsored by Kohler Power Systems of Kohler, Wisconsin, the fiberglass Tecno 40 was powered by twin 750 horsepower turbocharged Seatek engines featuring high performance Trimax drives. But the story is Mark Nemschoff's...

* * *

You saw the Chuck Norris run?

I watched one of those racing magazine shows on TV, and they had something on there about Norris setting a new record. I videotaped it, and it had some footage that had been taken from a helicopter. I was intrigued by it. I knew I had to start working on it. That was August of 1990, and I ended up doing the record in July of '95, so it was a five-year deal. The first few years I worked on it I was very, very quiet about it because I knew that anyone who heard that I was working on it would think I was crazy.

You were looking for the right boat, actually.

Yes, and not only the boat, but the whole package. I was starting from ground zero. I have an engineering background, so I understand what it takes to do these things--to a certain extent. But I have a business to run--Nemschoff Chairs, Inc. in Sheboygan--and had never done any real boat racing before. I had done some auto racing, and had been an avid boater for a number of years, and I knew this was jumping into an entirely different league.

Most of the people I talked to did think I was crazy, because who am I? Who's Mark Nemschoff? They'd say, "He doesn't have a name in boat racing." Anyway, I traveled around, searching, met Reggie Fountain, the boat-builder, and got the name of Fabio Buzzi. This would be in February of '94. The phone rang here in my office, and it was Buzzi. "I was told to call you," he says. "You think you want to do one of these records?"

He and I became good friends. He's a phenomenal guy. Incredible. He actually designs the boats, the drive systems, the engines, everything. He's been racing for 35 years. He understands what makes these boats go.

You looked at a number of his boats?

In various parts of Europe, not only in his shop. He's not a mass producer. He knows where every one of his boats is, who owns it, what condition it's in, what it'll do.

On the surface a run like Chicago-Detroit is simple. You fill the fuel tanks and away you go. Maybe you stop for fuel, maybe you don't. But you can engineer the boat in a lot of different ways. With high performance boats, horsepower and weight are both big factors. The more horsepower you have, the more fuel you need. The more fuel you're carrying, the more weight you're hauling and the slower the boat will go. Therefore you need more horsepower.

You're working within this envelope. Actually we added fuel capacity to the Tecno 40 so that we could go nonstop. Nobody had ever done that before. We had a top speed of 81 miles an hour. We could have averaged 58 or 60 miles an hour and broken the Norris record.

When did you first drive the Tecno 40?

52   Charters, Odysseys, Races, Gunkholes

The Nemschoff Team accepts the World Championship honors it won in Key West in 1996. Team members include (in C-41 shirts, left to right) Richard Jones, Douglas Hahn, Paul Nemschoff, and Mark Nemschoff. The Nemschoff team won the title in Offshore C class racing. (Photo courtesy Mark Nemschoff Sports Ltd.)

About six weeks before we went for the Chicago-Detroit record. That's another problem with boat racing. You don't get to drive the boat very much. It's a big deal. You need a crew--it isn't like driving down to the marina and jumping in and turning the key and away you go.

Fabio actually rebuilt the boat for me. The boat was over there in Italy, and he convinced me that as long as I was over there I should run this race around Italy. It starts in Rimini and ends in Viareggio, 1,000 nautical miles.

That's the Mille Miglia.

Exactly. He supplied the crew. The two of them, plus my son Paul and I did it as a sort of warmup for the Great Lakes. You run through the night, traveling at 60, 65 knots. It took us 25 and a half hours. We stopped twice for fuel, but otherwise it was nonstop, a continuous race. Fabio tells me later, "I couldn't let you go out and do

Chicago to Detroit and not *know* that you could set a record."

After that we only had time to take the boat back to his shop, give it a quick once-over, put it on a ship, and send it over here. We got the boat here in Wisconsin about a week before we did the record.

Then you had to make all the arrangements, get your people together, set it up with the APBA, and so on?

Yes. Logistically it's tough. You do all that, and then you have to pick your day. The weather is a really important factor. Fabio had told me you never get good days for a record run, but I contradicted him. I had lived on the Great Lakes all my life and I knew there were good days and bad days. He looked at me like I was crazy. "You're a real smart guy," he said. "Let me see you pick a good day."

Four days before we did the run we were out on Lake Michigan. We were doing some photography and checking fuel usage, fuel economy, and so forth. And we threw a prop blade. Fabio was still in Italy even though he was going to be in our crew. I called him. "You could have some serious problems," he said. "You might have bent the shaft, or broken something in the transmission."

We didn't have a good replacement set of props, so Fabio got hold of the right people and had a good set of props made in one day. He arrived the day before we did the event. We already had the boat in the water--we had picked the date, July 24, 1995. We had to change the props with scuba tanks.

You got the weather you wanted.

It turned out that we had one of the best days that you could ever imagine. Even then, though, we delayed the start because it was foggy in Chicago. The shorelines were completely fogged in, and you couldn't see the tops of the taller buildings. It had rained during the night and everything was soaking wet.

You had a helicopter escort...

We were supposed to, but the helicopter couldn't take off because of the fog. We left without it, hoping that they'd catch up to us. They were supposedly taking off from Meigs Field. We were downtown in Chicago, of course, at Navy Pier. We finally started at about 5:24. We had planned to leave at 5:00.

The APBA had one of its people at the end of Navy Pier, checking our departure time. As we passed him, he was on a cellular phone to the Detroit-based official so they could synchronize their watches. The actual starting point is when you go through the gap in the breakwater, right off Navy Pier. At that point we were probably going 55, 60 miles an hour.

Did the helicopter follow at all--or give up?

We were going so fast that he had trouble catching us. They ended up flying across Michigan instead of up the Michigan shore, and they finally caught us over near Saginaw Bay. We had planned to have helicopter coverage the whole way, and of course we didn't. They finally put down at Harbor Beach, and they were out of fuel. They were waiting for us there at Harbor Beach in case we needed to stop for fuel.

Did you go inside the Manitou Islands?

Yes, we went on the inside, between the islands and the Michigan shore. Right up the Manitou Passage. See, I'm a performance power boater who has good friends at the Sheboygan Yacht Club, world-class sailors. And the sailors are the ones who know the weather, and they know the Great Lakes; those guys taught me how you can go really close to shore and take the most direct route. You can cut right across Gray's Reef rather than go up through the channel. But you'd better know where you're going when you do that.

Was there a point at which you knew you'd have a winning time?

You don't really know you're going to have a winning time until you see the finish line. The boat could break down. Luckily it didn't-- no more broken prop blades. We did lose our helm GPS (global positioning system), but it was relatively minor because we have two complete systems. And my son, after that race around Italy, has become very good at navigating and very good with this equipment. And so he had a complete system, and also we have an intercom system so we can talk to each other. Plus I know the geography well on the Great Lakes.

The only time that I was truly steering off the GPS was when we were going up the middle of Lake Michigan and couldn't see anything but fog to either side. You needed navigation systems at that time to be sure you were on course. My system didn't go out until well past the Mackinac Bridge, and at that point you're in sight of land all the time except for a brief stretch across Saginaw Bay. Right there you might want to rely on your equipment.

So you're following the shore mostly, keeping an eye on the fuel?

Yes. We took the shortest distance. You can take a chart and pick out the spots that stick out from land, and that are shallow--these are key points that you want to go around--and draw lines between them. That's how I went. I went as close to shore as I possibly could.

We checked the fuel near Harbor Beach. Fabio had to do the checking himself. By that time we were more than half-way through the run and staying close to maximum speed. So we slowed down to about 25, 30 miles an hour. We had a fuel gauge on board, but Fabio says, "You don't want to believe the fuel gauge, not when you're trying to set a record." We talked about it. "We're so far ahead of schedule anyway, let's make sure we finish," he says. He wouldn't even trust me to measure the fuel because he knew I wanted to go nonstop.

He always measures the fuel with a dipstick. Here we're making a go-no-go decision and he's measuring with a dipstick. Douglas Hahn, my crew chief, and I had computed the whole thing. We both figured that we'd end up with about 10 gallons. We actually came in with about 30 gallons.

The decision was go, obviously.

Fabio and I agreed that if the fuel was at or above a certain line, we'd go. Our people had landed their helicopter at Harbor Beach and were waiting there to refuel us if necessary.

Anyway, Fabio measured, and looked at the stick, and then measured again, as if he didn't believe it. It was above the line and he looked at me and said, "We go." We picked it up again. Our people were at Harbor Beach, at the gas dock, but we couldn't see them, of course. We were maybe a mile away. They saw us, so they knew what was going on. We were having trouble contacting them by radio.

56 Charters, Odysseys, Races, Gunkholes

The weather was holding?

Just great. We ran into a little chop off Saginaw Bay, but it wasn't serious. When we got close to Port Huron, though, the sky opened up. We were in a thunderstorm for about 10 minutes. Right at that point we had gotten into the St. Clair River. I'm familiar with that river; we have some close friends over near Detroit and we do a lot of boating over there. Fabio had never been on this water before. He was throttling the boat and most of the time it was a real yawner of an experience for him. He put the throttles at full speed, and he was taking pictures and everything. I was driving. Then we got over near Port Huron and the weather turned bad, and he got scared because I was running very close to the shore, on the west side of the river. Well, that's where the channel is. Then there was thunder and lightning, and he was wiping the visor of my helmet so I could see where I was going. Nobody could see anything. And lightning actually struck ground, on shore, close to where we were. It was wild for about 10 minutes, and he was yelling at me, "Get in the middle of the river, you're gonna run aground." I said I know what I'm doing, and he comes back, "You don't know what you're doing, this is your first time, now listen to me." I said, You've never been here before, now shut up, quit bothering me, let me drive. We were going about 80 miles an hour right down the St. Clair River in a driving rainstorm.

Any traffic there--there's normally some big ship traffic...

Yes, there was some. My biggest concern was that we'd be approaching just when two 1,000-foot boats were getting near each other, going in opposite directions. That never happened. There were a couple of freighters, but they were never close to each other.

The storm didn't slow you down?

It may have, just a little. And we're wearing all this gear, elbow pads, helmets, everything--you get pretty beat up on a run like that. But while it was raining it wasn't as if we were getting wet, with rain in your hair and eyes and clothes. After that the weather was clear and calm.

Down through Lake St. Clair the GPS wasn't really an issue because there you've got landmarks. When you come out of the river

The third-generation Nemschoff racer is a Fabio Buzzi-designed monohull 40 with twin turbo diesels generating 2,200 hp. Originally designated a C-41, it became a V-41 in a realignment of racing classes. Mark Nemschoff (inset) acts as driver. (Photos courtesy Mark Nemschoff Sports Ltd.)

58   Charters, Odysseys, Races, Gunkholes

into Lake St. Clair you've got the towers and the buildings as landmarks. I was familiar with that area anyway.

At the finish you're at Hart Plaza, right next to the Renaissance Center?

That's it. We had a pretty good crowd there. There was some press, and a number of people from the APBA. Their office is in Detroit. It was great. They could tell us exactly what our time was at that point. But I knew. I always keep a stopwatch on board. So our time was maybe 20 seconds off from their time. Officially it was 8:10:47

Any victory celebration?

It was very anticlimactic. I was real sad that it was over. I had been thinking, This is so great. But then I didn't want it to be over. People ask whether I'd do it again, and I have to say I have no plans to break our own record. There's no reason to do that. There are other records that I'd rather break. If someone comes along and breaks my record, I'd be tempted to do it again. Only then.

Same boat?

Probably not. We pushed it about as fast as it would go. For that run, the way we had it set up, the max speed for the boat was 81 miles an hour. And we averaged 76-point-something (76.4). You can tell from that that we ran pretty consistently. At Tampa-Miami, six months later, we made some changes in the boat and carried less fuel. That was about half the distance between Chicago and Detroit. And the top speed on the boat then, for Tampa-Miami, was 86. And we averaged about 77 for that run--but we were in six- to eight-foot seas part of the time.

And the boat took that without a complaint?

I would guess that this boat is the best for that sort of thing in the world. We were going 80 miles an hour bouncing off those waves, and I was sure that that boat was going to break in half. We were planing and flying, both. It starts planing around 25 or 30, somewhere around there.

You've got a trophy for the Chicago-Detroit run?

The official trophy, the big trophy, is at APBA in Detroit. They gave it to me, and I had it for a month or two. That's the real trophy that's in the pictures. Then they give you a facsimile trophy--I'm looking at it right here. It's a smaller version, a memento.

Your name is inscribed on it?

I believe my name is on the real trophy in the APBA office. The other members of our team aren't on it, unfortunately. We had a four-man team--my son Paul, Fabio, and Charles Plueddeman, our communications man. It was the same with the other record holders. Michael Reagan's name is on the big trophy, and Chuck Norris's. They only put down the name of the driver of record.

What are your other trophies?

I've got the trophy from the race around Italy. There were actually two races there, so I've got two trophies. Then we set the Tampa-Miami record, and there's a silver plate hanging on my wall. And I have official plaques from the APBA for those events too. Those are official world records.

This past season (1996) we ran a season of offshore circuit racing. We did quite well. Won a number of races, and we set a top speed record in Sarasota, which is a Flying Kilometer, your speed over a measured kilometer. Then you turn around and come back in the other direction, so that they can average your two speeds. We set that record in July, a new world record. And then I have trophies for every race we were in because we took first or second in every race we entered.

In November we won the world championship in C class, and I have that trophy here. We've had a pretty successful two seasons.

And a new team name.

We do have a team name: Nemschoff Sports Limited. We've gone on to other boats. I created a company to do this. And of course I'm in the furniture business, and I didn't have any other major sponsor and

60   Charters, Odysseys, Races, Gunkholes

I thought I could win a world championship, so I put Nemschoff on the side of the newest boat. I had to bring a little glory to our company.

The rumor now is that you find it difficult to cruise at 30, 40 miles an hour...

It's true. It's a problem for me. It upsets my wife, K.C., a bit because we've done so much cruising, and she really loves to do that. I just can't do it right now, I can't go that slow. Plus, and I don't want this to sound like I'm too headstrong or cocky or anything, but I had a beautiful boat, a 34-foot Sea Ray, for a number of years, and I found myself pushing that boat too hard. You can break boats, especially on the Great Lakes. The lakes can be pretty rough, pretty choppy. In fact it happens regularly. But I couldn't bring myself to slow down.

One thing the racing has done. It's becoming a family thing. My son, Paul, races with me. My daughter, Amy, regularly comes to the races. And my wife, K.C., is a great supporter of our team.

For fun, K.C. and I were in an APBA divisional race on Lake Winnebago, here in Wisconsin. During the race I happened to mention to K.C.--I had noticed out of the corner of my eye that one of the helicopters was following us--and they were filming the race as they always do. Later they play them on cable TV. So I said to her, Look over your shoulder and wave to the helicopter. This was in the middle of the race. And she turned and waved to the helicopter. I'll be darned, in the telecast of that race they show us, and she's waving at the helicopter. That's a little bit unusual, you know, these races are normally pretty intense. We had a ball and she's really into it.

You've answered the earlier question, "Who's Mark Nemschoff?"

I think so. I'm proud and happy to have had this experience.

"AN INNER VOICE"

"Yet there's something else there too. I don't know why a wild goose must fly north in the spring and I don't even know how a bird can fly. But to be true to myself, I must follow something within to do things that might not normally be rational. It doesn't always make sense.

"There is something within us, an inner voice, which if we will listen, will take us places we never dreamed of. It may do more than surprise us; it may astonish us.

"You know who I am. I'm no different from anyone else, except for that voice. A very ordinary person can do extraordinary things."

-- Verlen Kruger, 2/91

VERLEN KRUGER

(1997)

Nature and the god of chance gave him every opportunity to surrender, throw in the towel, take his canoe and go home. Out of dedication, persistence, or pure orneriness, he refused. Result: Verlen Kruger rewrote the book on long-distance canoeing in the Americas, and probably in the world. He set records, generic records and juried, timed, witnessed records. Among these, he paddled the length of the Mississippi River, upstream and downstream in different years, faster than any other human in modern times. He set a new mark for the trip upstream in the Grand Canyon of the Colorado. He has traveled an estimated total of 90,000 canoe miles, the bulk of them after he was 49 and before he reached 67.

The weekend canoe or kayak enthusiast who has bemoaned his or her sore paddling muscles on Monday morning might ponder what Kruger achieved. For starters, in 1971, with partner Clint Waddell, he journeyed some 7,000 miles over the old fur trade route that began in Montreal and ended in Canada's frozen northland. In 1983 Verlen *and partner Steve Landick began the Ultimate Canoe Challenge, a 28,000-mile paddle in, through, and around North America. That trip took three and one-half years. Nineteen eighty-nine saw Kruger and his wife Valerie completing--on March 1--a Two-Continent Canoe Expedition from the Arctic Ocean to Cape Horn.*

Kruger believes he has "carried a canoe more miles than most people have paddled one." He has also "paddled more miles in the dark of night than most people will ever do in daylight." But in 1997, at the age of 74, his memory is as functional as it was when his dreams of canoe travel were becoming realities...

* * *

You were 41 when you got into canoeing. Can you describe the circumstances?

I used to go up into Canada with some friends on fishing trips. We had a power boat, and I enjoyed that. But I get restless if I sit all day fishing. We had these maps, and you can't get the boat over there, you know? You couldn't carry that kind of boat even though I once tried to. Then it suddenly dawned on me that a canoe might be the answer. I came back and bought a 17-foot canoe. I could go almost anywhere then.

And you did...

Well, I made one trip into Canada's bush country before I even learned how to canoe. Then I read all the books and still didn't know enough. I called a canoe racing association and they said, "Come on out and train with us." I went out and learned how to move a canoe efficiently and fast. I got into marathon racing and won a few times. I beat some experienced people. That broke down some psychological barriers.

Almost like freeing your soul?

It was. For example, the concept of paddling a canoe from the top of the world to the bottom of the world would not have occurred to me--I wouldn't have allowed myself to think of it unless I had raced and done some tripping. It then became the way I lived, a way of life.

Caught in a Lake Superior snowstorm in November, 1986, a bundled-up Kruger paddles on. He was under way on the Two Continent Canoe Expedition, a journey that covered more than 21,000 miles.

Were you retired when you got into canoeing?

Not exactly. I'm still not retired. (Laughter.) From that start with my own canoe in about '63, I went eventually into experimenting with different models and styles. It took a good many years before I had a canoe that would do what I wanted it to do. It had to be comfortable, safe, and fast. And tough

Traveling was always my No. 1 interest in canoeing. I'm happiest when I'm moving. It doesn't have to be a place I've never been. For me it's almost as interesting to go to a place you haven't visited in 10 years, and see that place again. I have both kinds of dreams, and it's nice to have dreams, but they can be dangerous. You get to dreaming and next thing you know you start planning.

You were adding features as you built these traveling canoes?

Right. I added rudders, for example, on some types. I had never seen a rudder on a canoe before even though some people were putting them on kayaks. For me, the rudder saved energy. I wasn't out there

64   Charters, Odysseys, Races, Gunkholes

to master the canoe; I wanted to go somewhere. It was my vehicle, and I was its energy, its brains, the control center. I made it live; it made me alive.

I also added the partial deck on some models. That was for protection. I found that the ideal width, or beam, for me was 28 inches. That's about as wide as you want it so you can paddle efficiently without reaching over the side. I don't have to bend, I can keep my spine straight, I worked this out through years and years of racing and paddling other canoes. If you're aggravating your body in any way, by leaning out or getting out of shape in some way, you're in trouble.

These canoes I'm building are made of kevlar. They're just about indestructible. I've never had to patch one, and that's remarkable, I think. Kevlar and high-impact resin. You see, I don't practice the wet foot principle. I don't come up to a rocky shore and step out in the water. If I can't step out dry, I'll back off and slam right into it and slide up on the rocks and step out dry. My canoes are made to handle that.

Your first long trip was the voyage across North America?

Yes. It included the Great Lakes, but basically Clint Waddell and I followed the old fur trade route out of Montreal. We went in one 21-foot canoe, what I called the *Cruiser* model. After crossing the Great Lakes, we angled northwest across the continent and up into the Arctic. You go up over the Rocky Mountains, then come down the Yukon River and across Alaska and end up at the mouth of the Yukon, at the Bering Sea.

It was about 7,000 miles. We called it the Cross Continent Canoe Safari. That trip had never been done before in one season. We started out in Quebec, in ice. We hadn't gone far when we realized that if we were going to make it across Alaska before the winter freeze-up, we had to hurry. But we had problems with ice at the beginning and problems with ice at the end.

You followed the rivers all the way?

The rivers and the lakes. I look at it this way: the waterways are our highways. Whatever was the most efficient path to where I wanted to go, whether it was little lakes, the Great Lakes, upstream, downstream, the water had to be our highway.

The Great Lakes have been the highways of history, and they're still there, still highways. They aren't being given the respect due them, but they and the rivers were the highways that people used to open up this continent.

Slowly the open water lead closed in front of us. As we looked behind to see if we could turn back we saw that it was also closing there. We were trapped! Fortunately we were in a wide spot in the rift. Two huge masses of ice slowly crunched and ground against one another as they moved in opposite directions... What had been an open lead only a few minutes before had suddenly become a growing ridge of tumbling, grinding, noisy ice... We watched the unusual and spectacular display of the forces of nature until finally all became quiet... We were in the only spot of open water as far as the eye could see.

-- Verlen Kruger and Clayton Klein,
One incredible Journey, 1990 ed.

You're portaging the way the voyageurs did?

Yes, and there were a lot of portages. There must have been 200 of them on that one trip. For example, when you leave Lake Superior at Grand Portage, you head west on the border route. There are about 40 portages before you get to International Falls. There are quite a few more as you keep going.

The longest portage was way up there in the Northwest Territory. It was called the Methy Portage. Way back in 1774, I think Peter Pond went over that portage. Then Alexander Mackenzie did the same a few years later. The Methy is about 13 miles long.

Still on the fur trade route?

It's the extended route beyond Lake Athabasca. I had studied the history of the fur trade and the voyageurs, of course. In fact once I discovered the canoe I read all the books I could find. They would have stacked up higher than my canoe paddle. (Laughs.)

We planned that trip for a couple of years. Clint lived in Minnesota, about 700 miles from me, so I actually did most of it. Then

66   Charters, Odysseys, Races, Gunkholes

we completed the trip, all the way to the Bering Sea, in 176 days.

You could carry everything you needed?

Just about everything. Clothes, extra clothes, a tent, bedding. We were able to shop for food about the way we would here. Most of the time when we were traveling we would pass a town or village almost every day. That wasn't true when we got into the Northwest Territories, of course. Up there you find about as few people as anywhere on earth. There were probably more people in the jungle in South America than in the remote areas of North America.

Had anyone else done that trip in a shorter time than yours?

Not that we know of, not by manpower alone. We had done it in less than six months. I don't think anyone ever paddled a two-man canoe that distance in less than six months. It was amazing to me that we reached the Bering Sea on October 10, 1971, the exact day we had targeted in our Time and Distance Schedule.

After we got there we had a few more adventures. A blinding snowstorm hit us as we were trying to get back up the Yukon River to some kind of civilization and catch a plane back to Michigan. We had a few anxious hours before an Eskimo man in a motorboat rescued us.

Was the Safari a warmup for the Ultimate Canoe Challenge?

Looking back, I guess it was. But they don't really compare. The Challenge started in May, 1980 and ended in December, 1983. I started out with my son-in-law, Steve Landick, in Red Rock, Montana, using two canoes. These 17-foot, partially decked solo canoes I called the *Loon* model. They were built along the lines of a tandem *Cruiser*. Then half-way through I designed and built the *Monarch* model that Steve used on the rest of the trip. After the trip I redesigned the *Monarch* and built the *Sea Wind* model. I guess I was really looking for an all-terrain canoe. With the *Sea Wind*, I think I found it.

We planned that one for about five years. The route took us down the Missouri River to St. Louis, up the Mississippi and the Illinois rivers and through four of the Great Lakes. We went northeast to the Atlantic Ocean at St. John, New Brunswick, then down the east coast all the way around Florida. We followed the Mississippi, paddling upstream, to Lake Itasca, Minnesota, where the Mississippi starts, and then on up the Canadian rivers to the Arctic Ocean. The town there is Tuktoyaktuk, in the Northwest Territories. Try that name on your friends.

We came down the west coast, on salt water, after crossing over the Chilkoot Pass on the way to Skagway.* At that point we had become separated--we were using two canoes partly to have some leeway on our rate of travel, and some personal space. Steve was two days behind me and failed to make it over Chilkoot before winter so we laid over until spring and started out again in April. He dug his canoe out of the snow at Chilkoot and spent six days traveling through the pass.

On down the west coast?

Yes. All the way to the tip of the Baja Peninsula in California. Leaving Skagway, we had already covered more than 17,000 miles. I wouldn't recommend canoeing down the west coast. Most of the time you're racing from one harbor to the next. When we got down to Los Angeles Steve found out that his little daughter had died from crib death. We had to go back home to Michigan. Steve decided to quit the journey, so I continued on alone. I was hurrying to beat the approaching hurricane season.

"We came up to Blanco Reef, where the waves steepened and broke intermittently. As we crossed, the wind increased dramatically to 40, then 50 knots... Suddenly I witnessed Verlen go over as a steep wave caught him off guard. I was downwind and he came up on the far side of his canoe, out of my sight... A wave caught Verlen's canoe immediately and pushed it out of his reach... We had been only 20 yards apart but it seemed to take an eternity to reach him.

"...He latched onto my canoe. We took one long hard

* "The Chilkoot Trail involves little if any mountaineering, but the historical significance of the 'Gold Rush Trail of 1898' is worth taking a look at. The trail is 53 kms (33 miles) long...," says Michael R. Kelsey in his 1984 book, *Climbers and Hikers Guide to the World's Mountains*. Kelsey had no advice for people portaging on the trail.

68   Charters, Odysseys, Races, Gunkholes

look at his beloved Loon, his home for the past two years, then headed for shore... I had to get him out of the water, and soon... Picking up the stroke, I remembered the emergency radio device in the forward stuff sack... After an hour (Verlen) was getting pretty damn cold. An hour-fifteen and we were getting close to shore... Then I heard the Coast Guard chopper..."

-- Steve Landick, 8/82

You're chasing the seasons to some extent...

That was part of the plan. Going north from New Orleans we were traveling with the spring weather. Traveling south down the west coast we were taking advantage of the spring thaw, heading away from winter, from the 24-hour daylight of the Arctic. But actually the winter caught up with us. In the far north they have a very short summer-- maybe a week or two. Then you go quickly into winter.

By then canoeing had become a lifestyle for me. It was heavy work, but if you don't mind work, it's enjoyable. There were days, let's face it, that weren't enjoyable. But that happens wherever you are, whatever you're doing. Overall, I enjoyed it immensely.

Did you lose weight on the Challenge trip?

I'd lose weight at first, then stay steady. But a bug got to me when we were going up the Yukon. When we got to White Horse, I went to a doctor. He told me I needed tests. "How long will they take?" I said. "Oh, about two weeks." I told him, "We can't even wait two days." This was at the beginning of October and we had to be moving. I ended up taking three different treatments all at once. A huge dose of penicillin and two kinds of pills. (Laughs.)

Your next big hurdle was going upstream on the Colorado River?

Yes. I was traveling with Valerie Fons before that. Steve had changed his mind and returned to the trip about two weeks behind me. He caught up and we went up the Colorado together. Valerie and I got together later to do a 21,000-mile journey from the Arctic Ocean to Cape Horn. We decided to get married. Someone called us "Canoe-lyweds."

We had gone more than 5,000 salt water miles from Skagway to start up the Colorado. We got to Hoover Dam on April Fool's Day, '83, and started up the Grand Canyon. That was as physically hard as anything I did that whole trip. It's 240 miles up the Canyon, and there were 200-plus portages. At most of them we had no portage trails-- there wasn't even a place to walk at times. We'd have to climb and then tow the canoes on a rope. We had to empty them or the water would bury the canoes. We did a lot of poling too. At Sockdolager Rapid we spent a full day portaging and trying to walk on slippery rocks.

We made the 240 miles in 21 days. That's what the Park Service allows for the *downstream* trip.

"Getting dumped in the Pacific off Blanco Point was bad, but running into a *chubasco* storm off Baja California lasted longer. We had the whole works-- thunder, lightning, rain, hail. It lasted about a day and a half. You'd hear this rushing noise, and then there would be lightning, and in the light you'd see this huge wave with the whitecaps on top breaking down on you--the size of a house. (Laughs.) Fortunately, Valerie and I were far enough south that getting wet didn't bother us."

-- Verlen Kruger, 2/97

You're heading back north and east after leaving the Colorado...

Back toward the Great Lakes. But we had to cross the Continental Divide. You talk about long portages. From end to end, that one was 68 miles. It took me 12 days--Steve had come down with mononucleosis and had to drop out for a few weeks. At the top of South Pass you're at 8,400 feet elevation.

Anyway, I took out at the Big Sandy and put back in on the eastern side of the Rockies. This was in mid-June. Hot. When I finally got to the Popo Agie River everything that could hurt was hurting. Never again would I plan to do a portage like that. Steve followed me later. On the Popo Agie we were heading downstream for the first time since we left the Porcupine River in Alaska--and that was two years earlier.

70 Charters, Odysseys, Races, Gunkholes

Morning on the Mississippi River brings a canoe's-eye view of the City of New Orleans. Kruger was paddling upriver in February, 1981.

Dwarfed by the rugged precipices and vast → perspectives of the Grand Canyon, Verlen Kruger portages alongside the foaming Colorado River. He was traveling upriver in April, 1983.

Now you're homeward bound--smelling the Lansing roses?

We had gone about 27,000 miles and had a little more than a thousand to go when we got to Grand Portage and then Lake Superior. But we got lucky. It was November, storm season, but we had some good weather mixed in with the bad. We got to Lansing about noon on December 15, 1983. The temperature was 20 degrees and no one cared. They had a brass band there to welcome us. The governor had declared the day "Ultimate Canoe Challenge Day."

Were you already thinking of a new challenge?

Valerie and I took on a new one the next spring. Actually, we set out to break a record that was held by a British Royal Air Force canoe team. It seemed like an easy record to beat. We thought it would be interesting to have a man-woman team beat a record set by men. (Laughs.)

These are timed races down the Mississippi. It's too hard to set up a head-to-head race. They started the clock when we left Lake Itasca, and they stopped the clock when we reach mile zero, 96 miles south of New Orleans. We did carry a book for people to sign along the way-- testimony that we had passed that way. When we passed locks and dams, portaging, we collected signatures. I still have the book. The whole trip was 2,348 miles. We averaged more than 100 miles a day.

And you broke the world record for canoeing the Mississippi...

We broke the old record by 19 days. Our time was 23 days, 10 hours, and 20 minutes. Steve Landick and I already held a world

Shadows falling over Bennett Lake Yukon Territory, Canada, can't dim the majesty of the wilderness scene. Winter was approaching in October, 1981 when the photo was taken.

record for paddling upstream on the Mississippi. That was during the UCC.

You were already planning the Two Continent Canoe Expedition?

We spent about two years planning that. So yes, we were working on it. But we had a lot of things in place by then. We had a lot of experience. Valerie went with me again--as Mrs. Kruger. We started in June, 1986 at the mouth of the Mackenzie River. We were using two canoes again--17-foot *Sea Winds.*

Governor (James) Blanchard (of Michigan) had named us Citizen Ambassadors of Michigan, so we decided to come down through the Great Lakes. That meant angling southeast to reach Lake Superior. Take my advice and never travel by canoe on Lake Superior in winter. We nearly froze to death trying to cross Keweenaw Bay. We had traveled about 5,000 miles by then, after starting in June. Valerie's cap froze to her ears. I think a woman saved our lives by taking us in and giving us hot food--almond chicken and oatmeal.

"We were paddling up the Mackenzie River. This was right at the beginning, and some people had told us we couldn't do that. So that was all Valerie and I needed. The current is so powerful in the middle of that river that you have to hug the shore to make any headway. At one point we heard a big swoosh behind us. I don't know how big the chunk was, because we weren't looking in that direction. But there was this huge splash and some stones hit our canoes. We looked around and here was this big wave coming toward us. Luckily it diminished and we got out of there.

"We were concerned. Huge pieces of the cliffs were falling into the river--some as big as football fields. There are several sections of cliffs along the Mackenzie, and they run for 20 or 30 miles each. It was kind of a trapped feeling."

-- Verlen Kruger, 2/97

Did you run into other people who were willing to help you?

All over. But on the Two Continent trip we took any help we could get. On the earlier trips we wanted to do it all ourselves. Sometimes we thought we'd have to fight people who wanted to help. In one place we ran into a couple of guys and they got all excited about what we were doing. "Let us help," they said. They'd pick up our canoes and throw them in the back of their pickup truck. I grabbed my canoe and hauled it out. They threw it back, and I grabbed it again. A lot of other people would say, "We've got a spare room. And a shower." Sometimes we did accept these offers.

On the Two Continent trip our philosophy was different. We were going from the top of the world to the bottom--from the Arctic Circle to Cape Horn. And Valerie was there. So it seemed logical to accept help.

You had to leapfrog from Florida to Venezuela?

We didn't like to get out of sight of land. But in that stretch we were--often. We island-hopped all the way to Venezuela, but we had to paddle in scratches for about 50 hours to do it. We went up the Orinoco to the Negro, passing through a natural canal that joins the two rivers.

The trip through South America was one long adventure. On the Amazon we were setting up camp once when killer bees attacked us. I killed one, which was a mistake. They came after us. I ran away from our tent at first, to draw them away, then raced back and we got inside. In another case we ran into some people who wanted to take our canoes. Down there canoes are a part of everyday life; everyone has one. We bluffed them into thinking that a party was following us, then hid out until we could get away without being noticed.

There were pleasant moments too. We still have happy memories of some 40-foot whales along the coast of Argentina.

Were you on schedule when you arrived at Cape Horn?

Almost to the day. We got there on March 1, 1989. We had visited 24 foreign countries and traveled more than 21,000 miles. It's very hard to describe the feeling you have after a trip like that. You think of all you've put into it, and the intensity that you experience at times. All that blows it out of all proportion to anything really significant. We didn't do that much, really, for anyone but ourselves.

74   Charters, Odysseys, Races, Gunkholes

"We hit the upper Paraguay River, in Brazil, in the rainy season. Everything was flooded for miles. We couldn't land for 14 days. I navigated by map and compass--and by the tops of trees that stuck out of the water. After a while you could see where the river normally went because there was a gap between the treetops. At night we had to push off snakes that tried to get up on the canoes to get dry."

-- Verlen Kruger, 2/97

You've got enough records to last a lifetime...

It depends on what you call records. One is clear-cut: the most miles paddled in a lifetime--about 90,000 miles. Something like 9,000 or 10,000 of those were on the Great Lakes. Then both Steve and I have the record for the longest canoe journey--the UCC. We've more than doubled the second-place claim. You could count the upstream paddle in the Grand Canyon, and the down- and upstream records on the Mississippi. I don't think that anyone had gone the full length of both the east and west coasts.

Those last ones weren't big deals. They're records as far as that goes, and they're significant because there won't be many people who will try them. But records are made to be broken. And contrary to what some people may think, we weren't out to break records. We were out to explore a continent by canoe--to see a part of the world in a very different way. It was positively a very rare and satisfying experience.

Some records are harder to break than others...

Some of them are. These would take a lot of paddling. There's a lot of work involved. It's not like a lot of *Guinness Book* records, things like pushing a peanut with your nose farther than anyone else.

Has the rocking chair got you now?

No. I can't retire. I came back from South America broke and I've stayed that way. (Laughs.) So I'm still building canoes. Our work on the Grand River--we called that trip the Grand River Expedition '90--

has done a lot to educate people. It's still continuing in a lot of ways. We had about 110 canoeists in 55 canoes with us when we took that trip, going about 225 miles. Everyone was doing some kind of environmental or water quality study, making the Grand one of the most studied rivers in North America. For that we received an award from President Bush under the "Take Pride in America" project.

There's one other thing. It's looking good for the 14,000-mile trip around all five of the Great Lakes, the one we planned a couple of years ago. I'd like to do that one in 1998. That's the Paddle to the Sea voyage.

Would you say the Great Lakes, and living near the Great Lakes, have been inspirational?

I think so. It's more of a feeling than a cut-and-dried fact. Getting to know the Great Lakes expanded my whole feeling about canoeing, and even about reaching beyond the horizons. I knew the Lakes were there, of course, and believed they were an unusual spot on earth. But I didn't really get to know them until I got out there and tried to do something with them or on them. For me, even the smallest of the Great Lakes is awesome.

The statistics on the Lakes are almost more than a person can grasp. I've heard that if the Great Lakes were distributed over the continental United States, the water would be nine and a half feet deep. That's hard to visualize, but when you're out there week after week, heading across one of them, and you're still only half-way to your destination, you begin to get some idea of how big they really are.

Any one of them a favorite?

Lake Superior. It's my favorite of all the bodies of water I've been on. I've had some difficult times on Superior, but it wasn't ever personal. (Laughs.) I think going out on Lake Superior for the first time I was more on edge than anything else. I had done my homework and knew it would be 400 and some miles before I'd get off the lake. It certainly gave me a greater sense of competence once I had crossed Superior.

Is there something psychological or spiritual about traveling by canoe on Superior and the other Lakes?

76   Charters, Odysseys, Races, Gunkholes

Definitely. A lot of people who have been there say the same thing. They understand what you're talking about when you mention the spiritual side. You get out there, and you're paddling, developing a rhythm, and you have time to think. You start searching for answers. I found that there was a certain unfathomable depth that gets opened a little when you're on the Lakes. Your personal faith has a lot to do with this, but I do feel that the Lakes have taught me a lot. And I still haven't scratched the surface. That applies in a spiritual as well as a physical sense.

Always a new horizon?

For me--always.

II

The View from Below

When the skies grow gray
And the wind blows free,
Batten down the hatches,
Come below with me.

-- From "When the Skies
Grow Gray," Anonymous

DAVID TROTTER

(1995)

A teacher of SCUBA diving for 10 years, a deep-water "technical diver" for 20 years, an executive who retired in early 1997 after 30 years with the Ford Motor Credit Company, David Trotter has made diving into history his life's passion. His record of discoveries of virgin shipwrecks--wrecks located for the first time--ranks him at or near the lead among the Great Lakes region's underwater sleuths. He's recorded more than 60 in four of the Lakes, excluding Ontario. Probably inevitably, he believes diving can be healthy, awe-inspiring, instructive, and pure fun. The multi-media programs he develops out of his explorations include personal narration as a means of giving audiences a "virtual diving" feeling of participation as well as a historic overview of a ship's personality, record or log, and final hours. He speaks as a founder and president of Undersea Research Associates (URA), based in Canton, Michigan.

78   The View from Below

* * *

In my case this hobby or avocation just evolved, and that's an important point. It was a lot different diving 20 years ago, when I started, from what it is today. I got into it, first of all, because of the diving itself, and then pretty soon I was diving on shipwrecks. Oftentimes they are known, these ships; they've been found by accident or otherwise, and whichever they are, they're fascinating repositories of Great Lakes maritime history. By degrees I realized that not by any means had all the shipwrecks been found--some just disappeared, and there are tens of thousands of square miles in which they could rest.

We were doing research and learning things. But probably our most intense effort went into the work on the water. We will often spend days or whole weeks searching--maybe 24 straight hours if the weather's right. Sometimes we will go on Friday evening at midnight and stay out until Sunday afternoon. Sometimes you can find shipwrecks very quickly, and sometimes, like in my search for the *Minnedosa*, it can take 15 years.

You start with a pretty exact idea of where the wreck is? Was that the case with the Minnedosa?

Yes. We thought we had an idea. We had very good listings and a good data base describing the *Minnedosa* disaster--in other words, very good historical documentation. But none of that means that you have a really accurate idea of where the wreck is. In the most extreme cases I know of, there was a ship lost in Lake Michigan, according to all reports. Then it was found in Lake Huron. Searching in Lake Michigan, it would have been a long time before they found it in Lake Huron.

We knew the *Minnedosa* sank on October 20, 1905, that it was a four-master, that it was the biggest schooner ever built in Canada. The key problems were that it was about 250 feet down, not about 110, as the newspaper accounts said, and about 10 miles from where it was reported to have sunk. There are no roadmaps on the lakes, and in tremendous storms and adverse conditions a ship could obviously report that she was 15 miles from where she actually was. If it's 15 miles away, and just multiplying 15 by 15, you get a field of 225 square miles as a possible area for a search. What happened was that

we actually covered some 600 square miles of search area.
You can see what happens. You start out figuring that the 120 foot depth was correct, thinking they must have known what they were talking about. Then you say, Well, I can't go out farther in the lake, where it gets deeper; and then that means moving extensively up and down Lake Huron. We had to sit down and figure out strategy and try to guess where she was.

This time it worked.

That's really how we found her, going by all the different accounts and data, and then saying, If it didn't happen here, what else could have happened? I concluded that she had blown much farther out toward the middle of the Lake than anyone knew. This is years later. We were right at the end of a run--it was at the deepest point and we wouldn't have searched any further out. It would probably have been years before I would have gone back to extend the search.

We did solve some mysteries about the wreck. We knew that the *Minnedosa* was being towed by the steamer *Westmount*. Another barge, the *Melrose*, was behind the *Minnedosa*. The ships were crossing the mouth of Saginaw Bay when the winds really hit them and then, according to the reports, the *Minnedosa* just disappeared. The *Westmount* picked up the *Melrose* and its crew and the news accounts quoted the *Melrose's* crew, saying the towline between them and the *Minnedosa* had snapped. The *Minnedosa*, carrying 75,000 bushels of grain, must have broken the heavy, thick line when it went down.

David Trotter

None of that was true?

No. We found the ship last May (1994). I remember thinking, "Gotcha, you elusive rascal." Then we found the line, still wrapped around the stern towing bit, or post. It had been cut clean, probably with an axe. We figure the crew of the *Minnedosa* cut it, possibly to save themselves. But they may have decided it was every ship for

80   The View from Below

itself. They may have cut the line because they realized their boat was sinking and they could save the crew of the *Melrose* by freeing it. Whatever happened, an hour later the eight men on the *Minnedosa* were lost, probably because everything happened so fast. The single lifeboat still rests on the floor of Lake Huron, next to the ship.

The records aren't always as wrong as they were in the case of the *Minnedosa*. They're usually a little more accurate. We're looking through a combination of historical records in various locations--in the Detroit Public Library, the Milwaukee Public Library, the Dossin Museum (in Detroit). Historical information on Great Lakes shipwrecks is like confetti, it's all scattered all over. But you've got to do that homework, get all the information you can before starting a search.

It very, very rarely happens that you find historical records and then go out and find a wreck. That's a figment of someone's imagination. It takes searching for data, researching, then spending many hours on the lakes doing your survey work. You use the sidescan sonar in the areas of highest probability. That's really how we found the *Minnedosa*, going through all the accounts and information and then saying, If it didn't happen here, what else could have happened?

What are the working conditions on the lake bottoms? You've hunted shipwrecks on four of the Great Lakes.

It's different from lake to lake, even from one season to another. It may depend partly on the area. We need time to explore what's beneath the surface, but we have very little time down there, maybe as little as 15 or 16 minutes. And to explore you need to be able to see. Lake Superior is very clear. In the other lakes, especially Michigan and Huron, you can only see five-six-seven feet usually. Late in the year you might get some better visibility. But in October it can get very dicey out there, weather-wise, so you have to be very careful.

The surface conditions affect it. It may depend on runoff and proximity to the shore. It could depend on the algae in the water at a given time. You also need lights because it's relatively dark, and a lot of times you can't comprehend the perspective of the ship, even after many dives. If it's a big ship, it could take years to explore, and we don't have that kind of time. We find a new shipwreck--we find them every year--and it's a question of which one to dive in a given year.

We generally spend one summer on a ship, at most, and that's it. We want to document it as well as we can with photography, and understand the history--what happened to it--and then close that chapter and share that marine history with others who enjoy the Great Lakes.

The next mountain. The next ship.

That's right. And when you get to the top of a mountain you want to go on to the next one. So we leave it to others to do all the things that archaeologists like to do. We're interested in the discovery, in the documentation, in locating the wreck precisely.

I've never kept a log of my dives. One of the reasons is that I didn't want to be like people who are always tabulating all the great things they've done. Now I wish I'd kept a log for historical purposes. I'd have a chronology of what I had seen on which wrecks at given points in time.

I have to admit that each new discovery becomes a story. Some are recent, like the *Daniel J. Morrell*, a 603-foot ore carrier. She left the St. Clair River at Port Huron in late November, 1966 for her last trip of the season. She broke in half in a very violent storm on Lake Huron.

While the stern section was found the following year by the Coast Guard, it was 12 years before Larry Coplin and I located the 300-foot bow section sitting perfectly upright. In an unusual twist of fate, we relocated the stern 11 years later, and continued our search five miles further out. We had a target that turned out to be the missing half of the *Morrell*. We had relocated the stern, and then located the bow section on the same day.

Most of the wrecks are older. The *Arctic*, for example, foundered in 1893. She was carrying a load of coal. The schooner *Rocket*, a 143-foot barque, was also carrying coal when she sank in 1860--again in November. That's the month of storms and shipwrecks on the Great Lakes. We found one that we couldn't identify in Lake Huron a few years ago. A bunch of tools lay on the stern deck. Oddly, a lawyerfish watched us at work from the centerboard shield--sort of on watch for intruders.

You must have developed a system over 20 or so years.

82   The View from Below

Yes. As I said, we use sidescan sonar, a very sophisticated piece of equipment. We interpret the data from the sonar to determine if something's down there. Then we have to prepare and plan and start the diving. Over the past 20 years we've made, conservatively, over a thousand dives. That's on shipwrecks that are in shallow areas, say 50 feet down or less, and others that are down 200, 225, and more feet.

The ones that are close to shore are easier to find. But two things happen to them. First, if they can be seen, if the hull wasn't salvageable, the ship would be stripped and left. Also, the winter ice would take its toll. And a wreck naturally becomes more scattered because of wave action and currents. We've worked in Lake Erie, off Ontario, Canada, in water that's 15 to 40 feet deep. We've found about 18 shipwrecks over there, all of them in shallow water. Some of them are fairly close to shore.

That's the Point Pelee project for the SOS--Save Ontario Shipwrecks--group. We started that in about '87 or '88. We've found that the wrecks close to shore tend to be damaged due to ice. They get moved and broken up. Others in deeper water, away from the ice and strong surface conditions, may look pretty much the way they did when they sank.

You're diving into history--but some shipwrecks must be more memorable than others--because of their backgrounds, the roles they played...

The steamer *Detroit* is a real story. It's a 157-foot steamer that literally sits intact on the bottom in about 200 feet of water. The giant paddlewheels that drove the ship are still intact on each side. Even the area of the fantail, where the passengers would walk, aft--all that structure is still there. The steering pole, a small wooden pole that was on the bow and was used by the wheelsman to guide the ship, is still intact and in place.

The *Detroit* went down in May, 1854 off Pte. Aux Barques on the Thumb of Michigan. It was only eight years old, built in 1846, and was carrying some passengers and supplies for the construction of the Soo canal and locks--lumber, hay, perhaps other materials. It had left Detroit to make the voyage to the Soo, about 350 miles, when it was rammed by the sailing bark *Nucleus*.

And sank immediately?

No, it took an hour or more to sink because the collision did very little visible damage, probably just enough to loosen the caulking and hull planking. They could do a fairly orderly job of taking people off. It was a very exciting discovery for us. Historically the ship was important--it was owned by the Eber Ward family, and it was playing a major role. It had some real economic impact. It was part of Michigan's early development. Eber Ward was a nineteenth century captain of industry.

On the *Detroit* also we found something that was very unusual for us: a strongbox, maybe a couple of hundred pounds in weight and about 16 by 18 inches wide and long. That strongbox holds a lot of fascination. It's still down there, in cold storage, separate from the wreck. We've been trying to work out a project with the Dossin Museum to open it up and take a look at the contents.

The strongbox wouldn't be waterproof--it has giant metal straps or bands riveted onto it. It doesn't seem to have been opened before the loss of the *Detroit*. I think we would have been able to tell if it had been. Now, there's not going to be 55,000 dollars in there. We have to be practical about it. On the other hand, there might be some papers and coins that would have historical significance. They would of course stem from the period, which would be of tremendous interest.

How do you retrieve a 200 pound safe?

Very carefully. We're still wrestling with the problem of how to get it on board safely. We'll probably have a second boat out there with a winch device. Whatever we do, we'll want to have a photographic record of it. We'd have to coordinate all that.

The ship is probably the only intact sidewheel steamer in Lake Huron. You can see the paddles, and they're just like they were the day she sank. The upper deck had collapsed, but the ship rests solidly on the bottom, upright. The cages that covered the paddles are gone, but we found the ship's bell, and could actually "ring" it by moving the clapper. We found china with the words, "E. B. & S. Ward's Steamers" engraved on it. The smokestack had broken off, and lay to starboard of the hull.

It sounds as if the Detroit *was your most interesting find. It was a passenger ship, for one thing.*

84 The View from Below

A diver explores the unique "walking beam engine" of the steamer *Detroit*. The ship sank in 1854 in Lake Huron near Pointe Aux Barques, Michigan. (Photo courtesy Undersea Research Associates)

The crack in the hull of the *Daniel J. Morrell* widens as the Lake Huron storm of November 29, 1966 rages on. The ship's bow section (left) sank at once and was located 12 years later by David Trotter and associate Larry Coplin. The stern continued on under power, ending up on the lake bottom five miles from the bow. (Painting by Robert McGreevy)

It was also an example of how schooners were beginning to be displaced by steamers. The schooner depended on the wind to make headway. The steamer didn't, obviously, and could carry less crew. In the *Detroit's* case, she was towing a schooner. That was becoming more common in the middle and late 1800s. It was a practice that helped cause the demise of the schooner.

Certainly the *Detroit* was lucky in a way. They were able to offload the passengers and crew onto the schooner she was towing. You can contrast that with the schooner *Minnedosa*, a giant of a ship, with a 38-foot beam. She went down with all hands, including the captain and his wife and six or seven crew. That gives you a perspective on shipwrecks.

Think of it. A ship is sinking, and I would say--most people would say--Let's get off. But it may go down before people can get off, and they may be trapped somewhere down deep inside. The ship becomes a graveyard--but we visit graveyards, we visit shipwrecks. We certainly wouldn't disturb anything. The odds against finding human remains are very great. But up near Isle Royale (in Lake Superior) we had a first on the *Kamloops*, a 250-foot canaler, as they call them. It disappeared in 1927. Another diver had found it and then the next spring we were the first to get inside the engine room. The engineer was still there, still on duty. It was the only time in my 20 years of shipwreck diving that we have run across any remains.

You're doing detective work basically--researching and often rewriting the histories of some tragic stories.

No question. You get wrapped up in every case. Certainly one of the more interesting--and tragic--stories was the schooner *Hunter Savidge*. She was upbound in Lake Huron in 1899--considered a very fine craft, a fleet schooner returning from offloading coal, I think in Cleveland. This was August 20 and she got caught in what is known as a white squall, a rush of a storm that comes up very quickly and will dissipate just as quickly. Here she was, light and going under full sail. The captain and one of his sons was on deck, as crew, along with about four other men. His wife was in the cabin. The squall pushed the schooner over on her side, trapping the captain's wife and the wife and daughter of the owner in the cabin of the ship. In maybe 10 seconds the schooner capsized.

The captain was in the water, thrown overboard as the ship lay over, and his son got thrown into the water as well. The son came up, then went back under water and was never seen again. Another ship, a freighter, picked up the captain and the four crewmen. At that point the freighter's captain left the scene and continued on up north, much to the dismay of the *Hunter Savidge's* captain, whose wife was in the cabin with the owner's wife and daughter. All three could still be very much alive.

We searched for that ship for more than three years, and then didn't know that we had found her. Rudy Whitworth, one of our associates, and I went down and were going to swim off into Lake Huron. Two pieces of debris had been located off the ship, one near the bow, the other near the stern. I took responsibility for locating the debris off the stern. I was kicking up mud and silt as I moved, as my fins moved over the bottom. I got out about 40 feet and lo and behold, there's this large, 8-x-8-foot piece, and here's the name board along the port side: it said *Hunter Savidge* graphically, clearly.

It was a very sad, unique history. They couldn't go back that day because of darkness. But they went back the next day, and of course they didn't find anything. Because of the location, the fact that she spilled her anchor and chain, and other evidence we decided that she had floated for several hours and finally sunk.

Does anyone try to write up all the details of a given case--a given ship and its history? Your Undersea Research Associates, for example?

One of the fascinating parts of searching for wrecks is writing the final, accurate chapter of what actually happened. We did that with the *Minnedosa*, the *Hunter Savidge*, the *Detroit*. Each time we corrected something that had been in the public record. But no, we don't try to do an archeological study or a full history of a ship. I do prepare these programs, 20 to 30 minutes long, multi-media, and that's as close as we come.

In Undersea Research Associates we have eight or nine people who love this work and love to do it weekends and when they're free, like on vacations. There's Rob Soja, Jim and Sarah Moore. Also Jeff Moore, Rocky Arsenault and Bob McGreevy. Bob does the drawings of wrecks and wreck sites for us. There's also Danny Fader, Werner Wahl, Rudy Whitworth, and Frank Troxell.

Underwater photography is probably where my strongest interest lies. The picture is a document; it's a neat, permanent record of what you have seen, and it's happening right there, in front of you. The programs seem to hold a lot of interest for people because they feel they're right there--and you can have interaction with the audience.

We started URA about 1985. We're all volunteers. In this business you'll never make it unless you have a team together that can work as a unit and support one another. You wouldn't be able to dive effectively. You could never shoot all the film you need. Your times on the bottom are very short, as I said.

And the deeper the shipwreck, the greater the risk and the more careful you have to be.

Yes. It's an equation that varies with the depth and the time you can spend under water. You have to balance these factors--for one thing, carry enough gas or air to deal with all of the risks. It's quite complex. You pattern your time below. You've got to watch out for nitrogen narcosis, the "drunkenness" effect on your mind. It's like the nitrous oxide that a dentist uses. There's a formula that says the more nitrogen you have in your system the more it dulls your mental functioning. There's another negative--it's an inert gas. The body doesn't use it; it absorbs the gas.

Coming back up, you're on a line and have decompression to go through, waiting to let the nitrogen gas dissipate. That way, you avoid what we call the bends. You may spend an hour or more doing that.

Some ships must be more valuable as historical treasures than others.

Absolutely. I think the most historically significant ship we've found was the steamer *Goliath*. She was built in 1846 and sank in 1848. She was very unusual because she was the fifth in the line of stern-wheel propulsion vessels, and the oldest stern-propulsion vessel that could be discovered in the Great Lakes. They had had side wheels on steamers, then somebody came up with the idea that you could put the wheel in back--and of course if you had been using one on each side, you put two in back to compensate.

Well, the first of these ships was called the *Vandalia*. The fifth, the *Goliath*, was kind of a joke because they didn't think she'd work very well. And in fact she went down with a total loss of life. But it was really fascinating because we found on her stern these two very unique propellers--Ericsson screws, named afer a fellow named John

88   The View from Below

Ericsson. His claim to fame is that he designed the Civil War ironclad *Monitor*. So here we had something of Ericsson's--he patented the Ericsson screw, and it was a very unusual design.

What took her down?

She was carrying thousands of boxes of matches, and unfortunately also many kegs of blasting powder. She probably caught fire. We are guessing at that because she had a very tall stack and she got caught in a moderate storm. We think the stack worked loose. She was ablaze, according to reports, it seems, as long as a couple of hours, and then there was a tremendous explosion. That was it, except that some pieces of cargo floated all the way across Lake Huron to the area of Goderich, Ontario. But the hull of the ship, and all the mechanical components--all this stuff that is so historically fascinating sits intact down there, off Harbor Beach (Michigan).

There are supposed to be 6,000 shipwrecks in the Great Lakes. With the modern equipment that's available, will they all be found?

I don't think so. You've got millions of square miles to search. The wrecks are small and large. If they're close to shore, they've been beaten apart by wave action, by the currents, and sometimes buried mostly or completely under sand. If they're out deeper, they're lying in perpetual darkness. Also, the bottom terrain in Lake Superior is so rugged, like miniature mountains, that they easily conceal ships of 100 to 200 feet in length. On some of them, there may be no accurate report of where they went down.

You're right about the modern equipment. We're living at a time when we can take advantage of the equipment, and use it to search for wrecks. You didn't even have side-scan radar 20 or 30 years ago.

If you want to read a book on how it was a hundred and fifty years ago, there's one called *Diving with and without Armor*. It's by Johnny B. Green. This is a fellow who actually walked the walk. He did some of the earliest hardhat diving and suffered crippling injuries and illnesses because he did. But he gives what I think are very unvarnished, accurate accounts. He actually designed some of the "armor" himself. But at that time they had no idea what happens to you under pressure--the bends and so on. Really, he could and should have died, but he didn't. He says at one point, "Perhaps the reader will understand that diving is an exciting adventure. My recompense, my pay for the injuries, will be the fact that I did it." He worked in the 1850s and earlier.

Today we can dive in relative safety. We have to be very careful, but I can just imagine what he faced. He was at the front edge of our modern techniques. He tells how they used the old hand pumps to pump air down. And the air could go bad, and they actually had divers sucked up into the mask. That's fatal, of course.

We don't even dive unless we think we have something to dive on. In the spring we may use the side-scanner for a month, two months, maybe longer. The scanner goes down alone. It's a fish- or torpedo-shaped device. It's towed behind the boat--maybe one of my two boats, the *Obsession*, the 32-foot Marinette. The sonar gives you a sound-generated image; it sends out a pulse, and as the pulse impacts the bottom or objects on it, it of course reacts, it bounces back. With a lot of practice you can tell approximately what you're seeing. I've spent about 2,000 hours studying and interpreting these pictures.

There have been some terrible storms on the lakes. Do they account for most of the wrecks on the lake bottoms?

Not necessarily. Ships have been lost for a lot of other reasons. Some of them we've mentioned, like collisions or fire. Some have been lost because of incompetence--someone made a bad decision.

You mentioned storms. One of the worst was the Great Storm of 1913. We found one of its victims, the *John A. McGean*, a 432-foot freighter, loaded with coal, that was upbound in Lake Huron when she sank. The storm hit with unprecedented violence; some of the masters on the lake at the time said the waves were 35 feet high, and that the wind and the seas were sometimes running in opposite directions. That would indicate a really cyclonic storm.

The date was November 9, 1913, a Sunday. Ironically, the *McGean* sank near Port Hope, a small town above Harbor Beach. The ship's captain, Chauncey Nye, had been born and reared in Port Hope. We found the bow of the *McGean*, upside down, but what about the stern section, over 400 feet away? We dropped a grapple hook and it caught in the structure down below. We got into our equipment and went down but found the visibility poor because we were virtually under the ship, near the cabins at the stern, which was mostly upside down. I found the huge propeller. One blade was missing, another damaged. The rudder shaft had been twisted and bent, and the rudder lay at a 90-degree angle to the hull.

Our theory is that the *McGean* had foundered after losing control of her rudder, perhaps by hitting the floor of Lake Huron in the 35-foot seas. We were able to explore the outside of the partially collapsed cabin area. Near the cabins I found two emergency wooden steering wheels that were partially buried in mud. I could put my hand on the spokes while wondering about the 23 men who had died on the ship. The name, *John A. McGean*, was clearly visible in raised letters on the stern. Years later, after severe storms, coal from the *McGean* would wash up on shore at Port Hope. On the side of the ship there were intact portholes that had inside covers still in place.

A spooky feeling?

A feeling of sadness, and yes, spooky. But the history keeps us going back.

Have you any artifacts to remind you of the time you've spent on the bottoms of the lakes?

I have a ketchup bottle, unopened, from the *Philadelphia*. It's in my den at home. I may have a few other things. I know we saw bottles of vinegar, relish, and apple butter in addition to the ketchup on the *Philadelphia*, a 236-foot steel-hulled propeller ship that sank in Lake Huron in November, 1893 after a collision in fog with the steamer *Albany*. Discovered by John Steele, it's another tragic story. Twenty-four of the *Philadelphia's* crew of 47 were lost with the ship for reasons we can't explain. It was the worst ship disaster on the Great Lakes in 1893.

What's the most interesting wreck you've dived on?

I tell everyone who asks that question the same thing--the next one.

(Note: In early 1997 the safe from the *Detroit* still lay in cold storage on the bottom of Lake Huron. Stay tuned.)

"DID I DO MY BEST?"

"For those individuals who have been caught up in the commotion, it's easy to forget that while in the pursuit of such matters as ownership and archeology--that one stormy night in September of 1860 hundreds of men, women and children were awakened in the middle of a dark starless night by a terrible crash. Then, forced overboard, they hung on through a night of sheer terror and exhaustion, only to have their hopes drowned in the merciless surf along Winnetka's shoreline.

"Even though the court battle is not over, all that is left to do is hope that the authorities entrusted with the care and handling of this important resource, and the divers who visit her historic remains, will remember the example and words of the heroic Edward Spencer who pulled seventeen survivors from the churning surf, and ask themselves, as he did--'Did I do my best?'"

> -- From Conclusion, *The Lady Elgin: A Report on the 1992 Reconnaissance Survey* by the Underwater Archeological Society of Chicago, 2nd Ed., September, 1994. (Quote attributed to Don Doherty)

VALERIE OLSON-van HEEST

(1993)

Way back in 1988 Valerie Olson was, in her own words, "losing interest in diving because I wasn't understanding what I was seeing in Lake Michigan." In 1988, she joined a group of divers who were associated with the Chicago Maritime Society; she and five others formed the Underwater Archeological Society of Chicago (UASC) the next year and she became director of the three-person board. The group made archeological research its business and preservation of Great Lakes shipwrecks its primary goal. Valerie brought to the group not only her organizational and diving skills but her expertise in architectural drafting. She was also diving with renewed enthusiasm, with other UASC members researching some of the estimated 300 wrecks on Lake Michigan's floor in the Chicago area, and dedicatedly helping to protect the wrecks and their artifacts as cultural and historical treasures.

Married in 1995 to a west Michigan man, Jack van Heest, Olson-van Heest transferred her enthusiasm to Michigan. She became president of the Southwest Michigan Underwater Preserve Committee, an adjunct of the Michigan Underwater Preserve Council. The Preserve Committee launched a campaign for establishment of Michigan's 11th underwater preserve in the area off Lake Michigan's shoreline from the Indiana border to "a little north of Holland." In early 1997 Olson was hopeful that the project would succeed and that the estimated 85 shipwrecks thought to lie within the preserve would be fruitful objects of archeological exploration. Educating the public about lost ships and their artifacts remained a key goal for Olson-van Heest and her committee.

In a 1993 interview Olson recalls, first, the thrill of diving on the St. Marys, *a schooner that went to the bottom in a September, 1860 storm that also took the lives of hundreds of victims of the* Lady Elgin *disaster...*

* * *

This time I was going down with my drawing equipment, a flat board with mylar sheets attached to it. With a regular No. 2 pencil it's possible to draw under water on the plasticized sheets. We wear a pony bottle, an auxiliary air cylinder or tank, strapped to our backs. One of our UASC members owns the boat, a 21-foot Cruiser-Bonanza named *Alexandria's Locker.*

The wreck is 120 feet down, but you can get there in minutes, following a line. I've got a sealed beam flashlight that gives me just enough light to see what I'm drawing. When I finish with these sketches, and we've done the photography, we have a complete bottom survey of the wreck.

Valerie Olson-van Heest works on a drawing of a shipwreck in her Grand Rapids, Michigan office.

You already have some of the history of the St. Marys?

A lot of it. She was built in 1848 in Perrysburg, Ohio, was 114 feet in length and weighed 253 tons. She had carried cargoes of lumber and lath, and even hauled loads of corn to Buffalo, New York. She had capsized once, in 1852, in a squall on Lake Erie.

The *St. Marys* cleared Chicago's harbor on September 7. In addition to the captain, John Bennett, she carried a crew of five and several female passengers. By a strange coincidence she sank the next morning, on the same day the *Lady Elgin* went down after a collision. There were no survivors, but some of the victims of the *St. Marys* sinking were later found with the hundreds of bodies washed up on shore after the *Elgin* went down. The *St. Marys* was located in 1989.

What did you find down there?

The bow is broken, smashed. Her enrollment records indicate that she had a figurehead, but we haven't discovered it in the wreckage. Both of her masts are lying across the deck, and the ship's wheel remains in place at the stern. She's on the bottom only a few miles from the wreck of the *Elgin*.

We've had a lot of experience now with archeologists, and have learned techniques from them. We've developed our own methodology. One thing we do, and are becoming very well known for, is reconnaissance surveys. We were doing one on the *St. Marys*. That's the reason for the drawing equipment. A typical reconnaissance drawing survey shows the position of the ship, the approximate amount of damage, and other details. It's a sketch, really, but another diver looking at it could tell exactly what he or she would find.

The survey takes shape according to a set procedure?

It does. Usually we start by finding the center of the boat, often the keelson, and run a yellow tape measure down the center of the site. We then use white tape to divide the ship into a certain number of sections--typically 20 to 30 feet long.

With a lot of these wrecks, like the *St. Marys*, we'll leave a submerged buoy at the site, about 10 feet down. It's submerged so that other boats won't hit it accidentally. You can't see it from the surface. But we can locate the buoy and tie on to it. That way we don't drop an anchor on the wreck. We think it's a mistake to anchor or move anything on these sunken ships--to move or remove anything. Moving things changes the historical record. Each ship is a piece of history, a museum. You wouldn't move things in a museum exhibit.

The next stop is to assign individual divers to each section. They begin recording it using triangulation off the base line and perpendicular lines. Basically they're just recording what they see, without a lot of detail. Then we send photographers down to put together photo mosaics and video mosaics. Back on land we analyze all that and start adding in very minute details. What we end up doing is not true archeology, but the surveys can be used later to assess the importance of a site or the condition of the site. It's a management tool and an archeological tool.

How does the St. Marys *compare to other wrecks as regards integrity-- how much it had broken up?*

The *St. Marys* is deeper than most wrecks we've surveyed, and relatively intact. That often happens in deeper water; the ice and wave action don't reach that deeply. I was down there 15 minutes on that one dive. After I came up I took a couple of hours and went down again. We've got all the necessary equipment on board the boat--the "mother ship"--when we're diving. Things like LORAN, plenty of oxygen, emergency first aid supplies, anchors.

We surveyed another ship, the *Goshawk*, in Lake Huron. I think that was the largest debris field we've ever seen. We calculated that there were about 14,500 square feet of debris. The ship had broken open and the sides had fallen apart. She's in 50 feet of water and the waves have really ravaged her. The *Goshawk* was 180 feet long, and broken apart it's as much as 80 feet wide.

We're in the process of compiling a site sketch and report on the *Goshawk*. It will document the wreck and the debris field and also list the 68 artifacts that are lying loose on the wreck. The report will go to the State of Michigan as a management tool. It'll also be distributed in a drawing format for divers who might be interested in visiting the site. It'll give them an entire inventory of the wreck--to remind them of how important it is, how significant. We're trying to encourage people to leave wrecks as they find them.

How many site sketches and recon reports have you and the UASC completed?

Taking notes under water, Valerie studies the *Wells Burt* where it lies in Lake Michigan off Chicago.

96   The View from Below

We've done about 20 site drawings and three reports (in 1993). Several others are in the works. The three reports are on the *Wells Burt*, the *David Dows*, and the *Lady Elgin*. All three are in Lake Michigan, not far from Chicago.

The case of the *Wells Burt* was a sad one. She was launched in 1873 as a bulk carrier. She was 201 feet in length and could carry about 50,000 bushels of corn. A two-masted schooner, she lasted only 10 years.

We studied the *Wells Burt* in 1989, about 106 years after she went down in a really furious storm. The 11-man crew drowned. The ship had settled into the clay bottom. We took video of parts of the wreck, a database on all the artifacts, slide photos of each artifact, and a site map. We had found the hull identification number and were certain that it was the *Wells Burt*.

You had to remove things for security reasons?

We don't often have instructions to remove things for safety, but with the *Wells Burt* we did. After we completed our survey, we revisited the site six months later and found 10 deadeyes missing. They're wooden blocks with three holes in them--used to fasten ships' rigging. They aren't easily removed. There were signs that the straps holding them had been sawed through. We notified the State of Illinois and the IHPA (Illinois Historical Preservation Agency) asked us to remove the remaining artifacts as a precaution against further loss.

We removed about 30 more artifacts--blocks, chain pulls, a cable splicer, and sister hooks for lifting heavy objects. They belong to the state. We'll turn them over to the IHPA. We hope they'll one day be in a museum exhibit.

You mentioned the David Dows...

Yes. In 1988 we got a $3,500 grant to research and survey that ship. It was a fascinating case. When there's grant money--this time it was from the Illinois-Indiana Sea Grant--there has to be accountability. The project resulted in a report turned over to the Sea Grant group and a video shown on local news programs and to school groups.

The *Dows* was the first and largest five-masted schooner to sail on the Great Lakes. She was built in Toledo, Ohio and launched on April

21, 1881. Her masts were more than 130 feet high. She could carry over 100,000 bushels of grain. She was caught in a Lake Michigan gale on Thanksgiving Day, 1889, and took on so much water that she sank the next day, November 29. The water froze and really helped sink her.

Then in 1992 we received a $3,500 grant to do a photo survey of several ship sites to study zebra mussel colonization. We returned to the *Dows* to document the zebra mussels. The scientists are studying what we found. The mussels on the *Dows* practically cover the ship, much more than we found on the *Wells Burt*.

The Lady Elgin *wasn't one of the four sites that you studied for the Sea Grant people?*

No. The Preservation Agency asked us to research that one separately. They called us last September (1992). The wreck had been located in 1989, but we didn't know its exact location. The Preservation Agency has gone to court to claim ownership of the wreck. They needed site information, so they gave us the locational coordinates.

The *Lady Elgin* is one of the tragic stories of the Great Lakes. The ship was a side-wheeler, 252 feet long, and had 66 staterooms. She had come to Chicago from Milwaukee on September 6, 1860 for a political rally for Stephen Douglas, who was running against Abraham Lincoln for the presidency. The *Elgin* was carrying a number of Milwaukee's Union Guards. On the way home two things happened. A storm came up, and early the following morning, September 8, about 2:30 a.m. as far as anyone knows, a schooner loaded with lumber struck the *Elgin* near the steamer's port paddle-box. The steamer was traveling without lights.

The captain ordered his crew to use axes to chop away at the upper decks. A lot of the passengers tried to make it to shore on floating wreckage. Many died trying to get to shore, but some others made it. Some floated in on the carcasses of cows that the *Lady Elgin* was carrying in her hold. A drummer floated in on his drum. But between 300 and 400 people died. Pieces of the *Lady Elgin* are scattered over several different sites.

You've been on all three Lady Elgin *wreck sites?*

Yes. I should say there are three main sites and a lot of scattered debris. One is the forward part of the ship, including the bow section. Another is the area where the boilers went down. They just broke through the bottom of the ship and dropped down before she sank. The third site is an immense debris field of scattered objects, including Springfield rifles that we believe the Union Guards bought in Chicago to take back to Wisconsin. There were three stoves, part of the cargo, and a lot of boiler-room tools. Also handtrucks, a lot of dishes, musical instruments--everything you'd expect to find on a luxury ship.

The three sites scattered over about three miles. Everything that was on the ship and that hasn't been removed is still there. It's really unique, a real puzzle.

Can you tell what happened--more or less?

Well, the night that she went down there were strong northeasterly winds. The collision occurred just north of Highland Park. What we think happened is that starting with the moment of impact, things started spilling out. The debris field at the northernmost location is evidence of that.

The historical reports say the ship split in two and the bow floated for three days. The boilers lie about 1,000 feet south of the debris, so we suspect that's where the ship broke up. There were even reports that the bow was seen floating at anchor. When we ran across the bow site there was a whole bunch of cable paid out from a windlass. It was connected to and wrapped around a huge rock, about the size of a panel truck. Also, there are portions of the hull, with the support straps, a large bilge pump, and the bishop arch or hogging arch that supports the ship. We suspect that the rock anchored the bow when it eventually sank to the bottom.

We think there's a fourth site that we haven't yet documented. We've seen it on side-scan sonar. It's probably the main part of the keelson and the frames.

You'll be doing a report on this wreck?

Yes, we're gathering information for it. Little by little we can piece it together. When you think about it, it was September and the water wouldn't have been very cold. A lot of people floated on bits and pieces--but the waves were so high that when they got to shore, the undercurrent and the rocks and the seas killed them. Many of them had been in the water for 10 hours. Some died when they were only 100 feet from shore. What a tragedy!

You're really doing detective work...

Just as detectives out on the street, at crime scenes, are doing archeology. They're putting together pieces of evidence based on clues that are left behind.

Any diving for airplanes, submarines, other things that have been lost in the Great Lakes?

No. Airplanes fall under federal jurisdiction and not the state's, so we don't get involved in those at all. I understand, though, that there are a number of them out there. And the submarine is very deep, over 250 feet down. That's a World War I German sub, one of six that were collected as war prizes. According to the Treaty of Versailles, none of the Allies could keep any captured weapons of war, so they've all been scrapped. The U97, off the shore of northern Illinois, was the only one sunk. I've seen a videotape of the submarine, taken with a camera mounted on an ROV (remote operated vehicle).

How many shipwrecks are there in Lake Michigan in this area, by estimate?

Some say as many as 300. We are aware of about 40.

Do the shipwrecks have a future, say, in a museum?

We've been trying to figure out a way that a museum, say the Chicago Historical Society, could have an exhibit using a computer. People could be sitting at their computer screens at home and touring a shipwreck exhibit that's actually located at the Historical Society. Or they could be at the CHS looking at a video screen and seeing a wreck--the *Lady Elgin* or the *Wells Burt* or some other wreck. It would be almost like visiting the wreck in person.

We can document these wrecks and make them parts of exhibits and never have to remove them from the bottom. Both the diving and the nondiving public could enjoy and learn from the exhibits. We

100   The View from Below

think this will happen one of these days.

Do you network with other underwater archeological groups?

We do, for example with the Save Ontario Shipwrecks--or SOS--people in Canada. There's another group in British Columbia, the Underwater Archaeological Society of British Columbia, and there are groups that work in the underwater preserves in Michigan. There's really a big difference between the oceans and the Great Lakes--the lakes preserve wrecks a lot better.

Because of the difference between salt and fresh water?

And the organisms. For instance in the oceans most of the wood is gone after a few years, destroyed by wood-eating worms. And much of the structure may be covered by coral. A ship that we surveyed in Key Biscayne, Florida fooled us--the drawing shows it looking like a ship, but it was so encrusted that you couldn't tell that during the dives. We didn't know what we were looking at until we studied the video at home and found that we had captured four deadeyes and deadeye straps. The things were encrusted with coral.

That was April of this year. The ship was the *Germania*, a ship about 200 feet in length. We were there about a week. We spent two days on site. The goal of the research was to provide John Gifford, an archeologist at the University of Miami who's developing a video-mosaic imaging system, with preliminary site maps so that he could plan his future work. He plans to design a grid that's going to cover the whole 200-foot length of the ship--and then video each section of the grid.

In basically two days on site, which gave us two hours of bottom time for myself and a photographer--about four hours in the water--John got a site plan that he can now use for the balance of his project. We also, of course, had about 20 hours at the drafting table.

How deep is that wreck?

Very shallow--12 feet. It's a couple of miles out. It was on a sandbar, a German luxury yacht from Kaiser Wilhelm's fleet in the World War I era. A little different from the schooners and steamers we're used to.

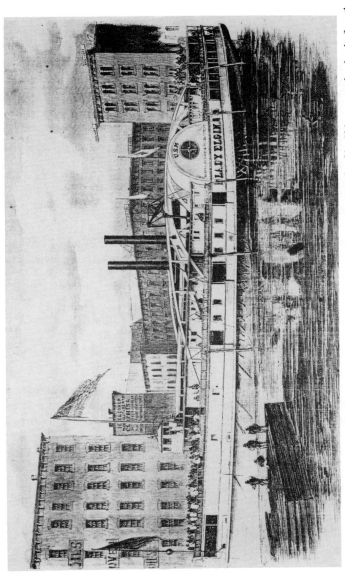

Crowds thronged the decks of the luxury steamer *Lady Elgin* while she lay at her wharf in Chicago on the day before the collision with the *Augusta*. (Sketch: Chicago Maritime Society, from a photo published in *Leslie's Illustrated* newspaper September 22, 1860)

102   The View from Below

*How much time can you spend on this--you've got a full-time job with
an architectural firm?*

I spend more time working for the UASC on land than in the
water. I average about 25 to 30 hours a week for the UASC. And
during the summer we try to get out every weekend in good weather.
That doesn't always work because even in summer the weather may
not be that good. So in a summer we may get in 30 to 40 days of
diving.

We do try it in winter, again when the weather's not too bad. The
fortunate thing about two of the wrecks we are investigating is that
they're close to shore and we don't need boats to get to them. We can
dive on them even though it's a bit more painful because of the cold.

The water must be just a little cool...

It's about 45 degrees now (November, 1993). It's not bad in a
drysuit. But that wind, when you get out. It starts forming ice in your
wet hair...

(1997)

---

*In early 1997 Valerie Olson-van Heest was still pursuing her
diving hobby, still spreading the word that every shipwreck is an
underwater museum. What is she doing as president of the Southwest
Michigan Underwater Preserve Committee?*

* * *

We're bringing these shipwreck stories to the public in every way
we can. We're interested not only in the history of this side of Lake
Michigan but of the other lakes as well. We sponsor programs on a
wide variety of subjects.

And work for establishment of Michigan's 11th underwater preserve.

That's No. 1. Our preserve boundaries would run out into Lake

Michigan to approximately a 130 foot depth. That means about three to five miles. We figure it that way because 130 feet is about the limit for a sport diver. Within the preserve there are about 20 known shipwreck sites. We hope to locate many more. Because of the terrain of southwestern Michigan, we not only have shipwreck sites but also interesting geological features--clay mounds, some pier structures. In the old days when roads and land transportation was limited, there were many more docking locations along the shore to accommodate the loading and unloading of cargo, mostly lumber and fruit. So there was a variety of pier structures.

How big is your group?

We have about 50 members. We're associated with the Michigan Maritime Museum in South Haven--that's where we hold our meetings. We're finding that a number of their members who aren't divers have gotten interested in our group. They're just interested in marine history.

The Chicago experience is behind you?

Largely. But I still remain director even though I'm not actively involved. My work resulted in site drawings and surveys on 25 shipwrecks, 19 of them in Chicago waters. Four were in Michigan, one in Canada, and one--*Germania*--in Florida. We did written reports on the *Wells Burt*, *Lady Elgin*, and *Goshawk*. To make everything publicly available, we've turned over copies of everything to the Runge Collection in the Milwaukee Public Library.

I guess I'm most proud of our report on the *Lady Elgin*. It was dedicated to the people who lost their lives in what some people consider the worst maritime disaster in the Great Lakes.

The laws now favor your ethical stance on shipwreck artifacts?

In the 1980s, they started to, with passage of the Abandoned Shipwreck Act. Now individual states are developing their own laws. That's continued. Before that, and as far back as man has found ways to breathe under water, salvaging artifacts and treasure was about the only reason people had for diving. Today, scuba instructors teach preservation and talk about laws affecting divers in every basic diver

104   The View from Below

certification course. Our influence is being felt more and more. I don't think diving for actual treasure, including gold and silver, will ever stop. But more divers are realizing that removing pieces of shipwreck that have no monetary value really destroys recreational resources.

There's a possibility that the whole mystique of removing artifacts will die out. I hope so. If it happens, our Great Lakes shipwrecks wouldn't be in anywhere near as much jeopardy as they have been.

Can you summarize the philosophy of preservation?

Sure. *Dive to enjoy, not to destroy.*

TERRY GERMAN

(1997)

To hear Terry German tell it, he's been training as a diver for about 28 years. In that stretch of time, while never ceasing to learn he's visited more than 50 shipwrecks. With his deep-water diving partner, Kim Martin, he's also in his seventh year of exploring, as time and money allow, the Leopard Frog Cave system in Tobermory, far out on Ontario's Bruce Peninsula. The Bruce is the finger of land that divides Lake Huron from the island-dotted reaches of the "sixth Great Lake," Georgian Bay.

The learning experiences that German and Martin have taken from their dives on sunken ships and into Leopard Frog have catapulted them into the status of authorities. Celluloid documentation of their dives have aired in video and film form on Canadian and French television. Their names have been associated with high-profile dives on the Empress *of Ireland in the St. Lawrence River and the* Andrea Doria *in the Atlantic Ocean. But their hearts remain firmly attached and attuned to the Great Lakes, "the world's greatest underwater museum." In 1997 they hope to finish a documentary on the Leopard Frog that will alert viewers to the exotic beauty of the water-filled, winding, sunless passage. The mind-numbing challenge of squeezing through the cave's numberless crevices and fissures may also raise a few eyebrows...*

* * *

How do you work up to the status of exploration diver and film-maker?

I was about 12 when a friend of my father's introduced me to scuba. I watched movies like "The Sea Hunt" and "The Undersea World of Jacques Cousteau." These things fueled my desire to explore the underwater environment. I grew up in Hamilton (Ontario), a steel town, and took scuba training with the Hamilton Tiger Sharks. Originally we did a junior frogman program, really snorkeling. At 16 you could enroll in the scuba course.

I got my first certification at 16. I just carried on from there, diving with whoever was available, mostly some friends that I went to school with. We went out a couple of times a summer. We had no money, were young, and I relied on my Dad to get me around. By 17 or 18 I started getting part-time jobs, I started tripping around and doing some more diving.

You joined a club?

The Pisces Underwater Club. I moved around quite a bit, and I guess it was '83 when I ended up in Toronto. Some mutual friends introduced me to this club, which was run by two progressive people, Brian and Annie Brown. They looked at decompression as not being a bad thing, whereas with other clubs you could only go to the limit on the (depth and time) tables. At 120 feet you could only have a 10-minute dive, and it was over. With Pisces, if you stayed down for 20 minutes, your decompression penalty would be minimal. So we'd practice doing it right. Decompression was not considered taboo.

You were diving on ships at that time--the '80s?

Yes. We were doing a lot of diving up in Toby (Tobermory), and

106   The View from Below

covered everything in Lake Ontario all the way down the east end to Gananoque in the St. Lawrence River. Less experienced divers usually went down with more experienced people.

That's how I got to the *Arabia*. We considered that a 120-foot dive, but it was really about 110 feet. Most of the ships I had seen until that time, in '84, were wrecks, real wrecks. Lumberyards. This was the first intact one I had seen--a double-masted schooner that was sitting upright, 131 feet long, the most beautiful thing I had ever seen. She looked like, if we could float 'er, we could sail 'er.

This was just outside of Toby. Anybody who had ever been to Toby knew about the *Arabia*. She had gone down in early morning darkness on October 5, 1884. Four days earlier she had left Chicago with 20,000 bushels of corn, bound for Midland, Ontario. One day before she sank she had sprung a leak in a Lake Huron storm. The captain, Henry Douville, ordered the crew to abandon ship just before she foundered.

This was before you started diving on caves.

That period really started when I met John Reekie, I think in '89. I had heard of John for a couple of years, then had a real happenstance meeting with him. What happened was, I had gotten myself into some serious trouble on a wreck and was talking to a dive shop owner, outside Toronto here, and John walked out of the back room. He runs Alternative Dive Products, and had been doing some business there. With no preliminaries he said, "How would you like to dive the *Empress of Ireland?*" I said, What do I need to do? Why am I getting this offer?

John said, "Well, anybody who's honest enough to tell people about a mistake he'd made, I want him on my crew." We started from there.

What was the mistake?

I was diving a ship off Kingston (Ontario), one that had been deliberately sunk and made diver-safe. It was a simple thing. I guess I was overconfident. I became disoriented due to "silt out." At some point you become convinced that you're lost, and not going to get out, and panic has an opportunity to get its talons into you. Luckily enough, for some reason--it's a big, long story, but for some reason I got a clear thought: Just stop, stop what you're doing.

When you're in a state of panic, you act instinctively rather than rationally. You try to get out by whatever means. And the human anatomy's not equipped to go through a half-inch of steel. But for some reason I managed to overcome the panic and got a clear idea. I found a way out.

On to the Empress of Ireland.

Yes. But first John wanted me to take a course in cave diving. We would be in an overhead environment on the *Empress*--inside the ship, going into areas where no one had been before. So I went to Florida and was lucky enough to learn cave diving from Lamar Hires, vice president of DiveRite Manufacturing. That's in Lake City, Florida.

Everything came together about that time, in '90. Training with Kim Martin in Florida showed that we worked well together and made a good team. Then diving with Kim and John we started to push the edge of exploration here in Canada. It was difficult for people to visualize the extraordinary geographical and historical sites we were visiting so I dredged up my nearly forgotten formal training in film, dusted off my antiquated camera gear, used my technical experience and formed Extreme Explorer Productions. I started to produce short documentaries.

One of them the Empress?

One of them the *Empress*. This was a luxury ship, about 550 feet long, owned by the Canadian Pacific Railway. She was in a collision with another ship, the *Storstad*, a collier, in fog just east of Quebec City in the Gulf of St. Lawrence. The *Empress* sank in 14 minutes. The official death count was 1,012. It was Canada's greatest peacetime ship disaster.

Mostly we were filming our work there as reconnaissance for ourselves, and to show people. We did make it available to the Musee de la Mer in Rimouski*--I gave them, I believe, 10 minutes and they ended up constructing an entire room around the video display. The room is a replica of one of the rooms in first class on the *Empress*,

---

*Actually Pointe-aux-Pere, near Rimouski. The exhibit shows the room as divers see it--on a slant.

One good turn: Kim Martin helps Terry German as the divers prepare to go down to the sunken liner *Andrea Doria*.

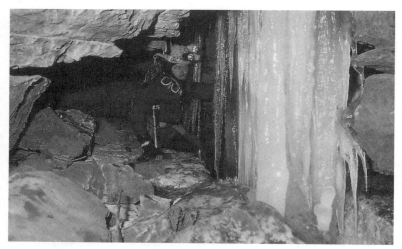

Dry entrance to a "wet cave:" Kim Martin searches for a way to carry diving gear around an ice stalactite in the Leopard Frog Cave system. (Photo: Terry German)

where we did quite a bit of work. In my wildest imagination I didn't think they'd make so much of my work that they'd construct a room around it.

You're finished with diving the Empress?

No, the *Empress* still beckons. In 1994 I filmed Kim placing a plaque on that ship. We did that as a kind of memorial service for everyone who died. We went there on the 80th anniversary of the ship's loss, May 29, 1914. We saw a lot of human remains there. One of the groups that was nearly decimated was the Salvation Army. They lost a lot of their high-ranking officers and their staff band. It had severe repercussions for the Army itself. They had something like 150 on board and I think 124 were lost.

Have you had other major shipwreck dives, like the Empress?

We've been to the *Andrea Doria*, the luxury ship that sank in the Atlantic Ocean in 1956. She was built in 1951, 679 feet long. She was launched that year and made her maiden voyage, Genoa to New York, in '53. In 1956 on July 25, the *Doria* was heading for New York, about 100 miles south of Nantucket, when she collided with the Swedish liner *Stockholm*. The *Doria* gradually heeled over and sank 12 hours after the collision. Fifty-two people died.

A lot of people have dived on the *Andrea Doria*. Kim and I went as part of an expedition organized by American diver John Moyer. This was in July, 1993, and there was a heat wave. On the open ocean there wasn't a tree in sight.

John Reekie had told me about this project in the fall of '92. No matter how hard Kim or I would pry, beg, or threaten with blackmail, John wouldn't give us a clue. This was a "top secret" project from the beginning. Moyer had requested us because of our deep penetrations, zero viz (visibility) expertise, and at the end John would own two beautiful pieces of artwork thought lost for nearly 40 years. One thing I recall as terribly humorous was that as we were loading several tons of equipment on board our ship, a 65-foot yacht, it seemed everyone had a Clive Cussler novel in hand.

In an overhead environment we usually consider that the way in is the only way out. You may go down a staircase, but you don't know what's ahead--what's collapsed, what debris there may be. You don't look for another way to exit. We followed that rule.

What was the art work?

The *Doria* was a floating art gallery, and these two pieces were the work of Guido Gambone, an Italian sculptor. They were in the first-class lounge and weighed about 700 pounds each. This took a lot of teamwork, a lot of planning, and we had teams diving in succession-- about 10 divers in all. A team would be up, and after decompression-- the *Doria* was 220 feet down--another team would go in, exchange notes quickly, and head down. So it was a series of relays, taking the panels off the walls, slinging each one, getting lift bags under them, lifting them and bringing them along the hallways.

I was doing some topside video and got pictures of these two panels, sort of abstract marine designs.   Both panels were commissioned specifically for the *Andrea Doria*. They're one of a kind, priceless.

This was '93--you were diving the Leopard Frog Cave by then?

We started at Leopard Frog about '90. While still diving as much as possible here in the Great Lakes on numerous wrecks, we had decided to concentrate on the Leopard Frog Cave project. The cave is at the northern end of the Bruce Peninsula. A friend of ours, Stan Drdla, located it, I think in 1990, and called us. Some other people started with us, but they've left the project as they had less time, or as other things took priority in their lives. This past summer (1996) it was just Kim and I.

The cave is an ancient formation?

The area is supposed to be more than 400 million years old. The cave is located at the bottom of a glacial scour. It's a series of fissure cracks that have been connected. It may have been an ancient river bed. Then the water slowly made its way down below, and with winter freeze-ups and what have you, it cracked the rock and continued to force it apart.

About 2,000 feet into the cave, it starts looking like a long, winding tunnel.

The passage is entirely under water?

Where we start our dives, yes. But we go in through a hole in the ground that's about 18-x-24 inches and leads down to an air chamber. One diver goes down, we lower the gear, then the other one goes down and we get into the gear. We kind of half-swim, half-crawl about 75 feet, go down a couple of times, and then twist to get through a vertical crack. That's where we actually start the dive. From there on it's entirely under water. We measure for distance from there.

We tell people about this, and they don't believe it. They think we're crazy. And I always say, crazy as compared to what? So we're filming. That way, it's easier to get people to understand. You're dealing with a lot of primordial fears here, in this cave diving. One of these days we'll finish our documentary on the Leopard Frog. It's named for the abundance of frogs that are down there.

Are you close to finishing the documentary?

We thought we'd finish it this past summer. We may this coming summer (1997). Last August we did all our staging in preparation for the big swim. We made eight dives in 13 days, going in farther each time. About every thousand feet we stashed air tanks and battery packs. We were going to try to find the end of the cave. We had gone in about 2,200 feet when I had a bit of bad luck. I severed a high pressure hose while passing through a tight constriction--these cracks are sometimes only 18 inches wide, horizontal or vertical. We had that auxiliary air in the cave, and there was no real safety hazard. It wasn't life-threatening, but it certainly meant I couldn't go any farther. I had lost half my air supply.

I went back and waited for Kim to finish the swim. With this dive we were setting up to go back in and complete our filming. He managed to run out reels that we had placed in there. They indicated that he had gone in 6,600 feet.

Reels of cable, wire, rope?

The line is made of braided nylon, a high-abrasion line, with a filament core and woven jacket around it. It's about the thickness of round shoelace, like on a work-boot. It's less than an eighth of an inch in diameter. That's our bread-crumb line, the trail back.

112   The View from Below

You could get lost in there without that...

Definitely. This is basically one long tunnel. But we've found a couple of smaller areas that look as if they branch off. They don't seem big enough to negotiate. As time allows, and when we know better where the cave is going, we'll be able to retrace our steps and look at some of these areas. The only reason we've been able to progress to this point is that in some places that looked like dead ends, we dug rock out of the way and found the tunnel opening up.

Right now we really don't know how far the cave goes. A lot of it will require surveying. We've been up in airplanes doing some aerial photography. That's to get the lay of the land around there, to see if it can give us some idea of a similar geological occurrence. But it doesn't tell us much. We know we're exactly 1.7 kilometers from the shore of the bay, Dave's Bay, and that's where we thought the cave was going. Then it turned somewhat more east, so we've been paralleling the shore. We thought at first the cave would go in maybe 2,500 to 3,000 feet. We've been in there double that and it could go on forever, as far as we know.

Can you photograph in there with much success?

It's difficult. There's a lot of silt that absorbs your light. It's the same with the walls. They're deep brown, stained I think by the tannic in the water, and they also kill the light. We use halogen lights that we can adjust--turn the wattage up or down--and we turn them down to make them last. But then it's tough to make pictures.

Parts of the tunnel are really beautiful. Now and then there's a chamber, maybe one or two as big as 12 feet across.

You've been to Leopard Frog a number of times--any mishaps besides the broken air line?

We've been in there maybe 35, 36 times in six or so years. We've been careful, about as conservative as you can get. We try to duplicate everything we need, like air and lights, and sometimes we triplicate and quadruplicate everything. We're trying to avoid emergencies. One of our biggest reference terms in cave diving is *becoming the swimming dead*. That's where you have an hour to travel and you've only got 55 minutes of air, and you ain't gonna make it. You've got a lot of time to think about what you're going to do with your last few minutes.

That's one thing about cave diving. Really, for us it's not that different from diving on ships, because we're going into most of the ships we dive--they're overhead environments for us. But in shipwreck diving you can usually swim around in open water and look at the wreck. You can't do that in cave diving. Also, we wear our air tanks on our sides--they call it *side-mount configuration.* That reduces your profile, and you can slide through these cracks. We joke about it. It's like swimming up an intestinal tract. Or like going up a corrugated pipe that wraps around and bends back and forth. Sometimes we have to take off the tanks and shove them through ahead of us.

We really try to pick the time for diving Leopard Frog: the season. We've found that August is the most cooperative. The cave a sump, a drain for millions of gallons of ground water. An unpredicted heavy downpour could result in a diver not being able to fight the flow of water to exit the passage. There are other ways to get in trouble in caves, and we ran into one near there.

What happened?

We were finishing up a long, really exhausting day--this was August, 1995. Kim and I were requested by the Ontario Provincial Police to assist in the location of a diver who had gone missing and was presumed drowned in another cave about two miles from Leopard Frog. As word spread, several acquaintances of ours offered their expertise. The diver was located and recovered, quite alive, after he had been gone for seven hours.

He was in a cave called Little Stream. He had managed to get up onto a ledge, out of the water. It wasn't easy to do. There was spring water coming out of this cave, and it was about 38 degrees. It was highly unlikely that he would have survived if he hadn't been able to get out of the water. His light was running out. He had gone through a small hole and hadn't run a line. He was feeling around blindly and couldn't find the hole. It was about five hours after we started looking that we were able to get a line through the hole and found him.

The governor-general of Canada, Romeo A. LeBlanc, awarded Kim the Canadian Medal of Bravery for his role in that rescue. A couple of other divers and I got Certificates of Commendation. That was one of only three successful cave rescues that I've every heard of-- and the first ever in Canada. Search and rescue usually means you bring out a body.

Do your dives have a scientific purpose as well as mapping and documentation purposes?

They do. Mapping is tough. We've mapped only about 1,500 feet of Leopard Frog. It's a very slow process, measuring and surveying. If you figure, as we do, that you need about an hour to cover 1,000 feet, going and returning, you double that for mapping.

As far as the science is concerned, the exploration is part of that. So is collecting samples of bugs or other life-forms. Last August I was going to be filming while Kim would be surveying and collecting life samples. We've just been notified that a sample isopod--a little 14-legged crustacean--that we brought out of the cave doesn't appear to belong to any known species of the group Caecidotea. It may be a new discovery, a new species.

The frogs are plentiful. We've seen them as big as your hand. There are also salamanders and minnows, but we believe they get washed in during the spring rains. There isn't much there that would be of interest to a biology department, but we think the frogs' eggs are washed in there in the spring. Then they hatch. But they don't have a good food supply. Some of them mature anyway, and we find them in various stages. We find them farther and farther back in the cave all the time. We think they're getting washed back, and surviving on air pockets that we leave on the ceiling. What happens then is, they go into stasis, lacking food and with cold water and no light--they think it's winter.

We find frogs sitting on the bottom of the cave, motionless. If you give them a poke, they'll move. If we come back a week later, or several weeks later, we find them starting to decay. Organisms begin to devour them. We can follow their degradation over a number of dives.

Do you expect to exhaust the Leopard Frog project?

We do expect to, in fact we thought we'd have it done this past summer. But it's going on and on, and again, it's Mother Nature, so who knows? If it goes on forever, that's great too. We've set a Canadian record, and would like it to go longer. That would mean we'd need a bigger team, because there would be a lot more work ahead. We might get more help, and it might be easier to get additional sponsorship.

You and Kim are doing this alone...

Mostly. But we get invaluable help. For example, the Wyonch family owns the property on which the cave entrance is located, and they are especially helpful. PRAXAIR Specialty Gases has provided our breathing gases. Other help comes from companies and individuals--Pickering Marine, Merkle Camera and Video, Haskel Booster Systems, Hercules Technical Ropes, DiveRite, Mares diving equipment, Mike and Linda McGrath of Divers' Den. Still, it's a lot of hard work, and you're using your vacations--I've worked full-time for Ontario Hydro for 15 years--and so far we haven't run into too many people who think it's fun to get up at 7:00 in the morning and work 18 hours and go to bed exhausted at 11:00 at night.

There's one thing now. Slowly, as this work has become known, we've had some biologists and geologists coming forward and saying, We'd like to get involved. And they're offering their assistance. And

At work or at rest, Terry German takes diving seriously. Working his underwater camera, he explores (left) underground waters for memorable footage. Taking a break (right), he rests near the entrance to Iceland's Silfur Hellig water-filled caverns in Thingvellir National Park. (Photos courtesy Extreme Explorer Productions)

116   The View from Below

if that continues we may be able to diversify, get a really good team together and do a lot more.

There's some public awareness too. Kim set a new Canadian cave-penetration record when he went into Leopard Frog 6,600 feet. He had earlier set a record at 4,000 feet--in 1992. And then he bettered that by 300 feet a year later. It's been a long, exhausting effort to gain recognition in the field of underwater film work, but I've provided services for CBC (Canadian Broadcasting Company) TV, CBC Radio, and a French international outlet. We give programs for all kinds of groups.

You're probably unable to stop this work now.

Right. Over the years diving has been exceptionally rewarding to me, with opportunities to fulfill my dreams. But it's also been costly. Not only in a financial sense--several friends have either been severely injured or have lost their lives. To remain optimistic--I'm bettered for having known them and am honored to have been called their friend.

I joke with John Reekie. My life changed there on that shop floor when I met him. I've thanked him for that, and say if he hadn't done that my house would have been paid for by now. I never hesitate to remind him of that.

He takes it in the spirit in which it's offered.

He does. And where I am now, I have this unexhausted desire to explore the marine environment. With the world's greatest marine museum, the Great Lakes, at my doorstep I think I'll be busy for quite some time.

III

The Creative Spirit

I gaze beyond the wilderness, and there,
    behold, the ocean —
With its deep wonders and mysterious se-
    crets, its hid treasures;
There I behold all that is upon the face of
    the raging, rushing, foaming waters,
And the spray that rises and the vapours
    that descend.

I peer far beyond the ocean and behold
    the infinity of space,
The drifting worlds, the glimmering con-
    stellations, the suns and moons, the
    fixed and the shooting stars;
And I behold the evidence of forces for-
    ever attracting and repelling, the
    wars of elements, creating, changing,
    and withal held prisoned within a law
    of no beginning and no end.

-- From "My Birthday,"
Kahlil Gibran

"THE BIGLER'S CREW"

"The word "juberju" has entered my family's vocabulary. No, juberju is not a kind of candy that sticks to your teeth. It is a slang word, fun to say and sing, that turns up in the chorus of a rousing

118   The Creative Spirit

sailing song called 'The *Bigler's* Crew.'

"That song, about the voyage of a schooner through the Great Lakes from Milwaukee to Buffalo, has hooked everybody in my house. Even the teenager and the 3-year-old have been singing (or trying to sing), "Watch her, catch her. Jump on her juberju. Give her the sheet and let her slide, the boys'll push her through." (Juberju refers to a small sail.)

"'The *Bigler's* Crew' is one of many captivating songs Lee Murdock will sing tomorrow night..."

-- "Family Fun," by Anne Taubeneck,
Chicago Sun-Times, May 8, 1992

LEE MURDOCK

(1997)

He's been called the "traveling minstrel of the Great Lakes" and the "Pied Piper of the sweetwater seas." For many, the appellations don't do justice to the reality of Lee Murdock's music and his genius for taking the listener into great lakes pilothouses, up on fly bridges, into the teeth of a November gale, across the track of a technicolor sunset. "Lee brings the motion of the water, the sound of the engines, and the broad horizon into view," wrote one critic.

His songs live, breathe, and almost re-create the marvelous phenomenon that is the Great Lakes story, the story that for the itinerant, inquisitive European began only about 400-plus years ago. Giving an average of 250-275 performances a year, he has brought his interpretations of that story to museums, historical societies, schools, theaters, folklore societies, festivals, and other venues. The ages of sail and steam, the romance and danger of water-borne commerce, the hopes and fears and loves and tragedies of Lakes people--all have become threads in the fabric of his programs. Because he believes that music is therapy and diversion as well as entertainment, he appears at

*least 75 times a year before audiences of senior citizens,
severely/profoundly handicapped children and adults, in nursing
homes, hospitals, rehabilitation centers, halfway houses, and similar
institutions. In the course of a year he'll visit not only the Great Lakes
states and Ontario but many other states east, west, north, and south.*

*He tries to explain it all in a quiet corner of the Michigan
Historical Museum in Lansing...*

* * *

*A whole bundle of influences must be at work in your life as you
compose, perform, study Great Lakes history, teach guitar, and so on...*

Really, I've been singing since I was 4 years old. As far as recent
influences are concerned, probably not a day goes by that something
doesn't nudge me, or affect me. I guess every artist needs an
awareness of his or her surroundings. You just have to be careful not
to be overly influenced.

From a musical standpoint, I listen to classical music and also
some--what would you call it?--contemporary acoustic or jazz stuff.
I'm very fascinated with the sound of the acoustic guitar. I like it
whatever the setting, whether it's a jazz trio, Django Reinhart, or
something similar. I kind of shy away from listening to other singer-
song-writers, but I've listened to some of the people who influenced
me in the past. My favorite song when I was 5 was "Hang down Your
Head, Tom Dooley."

A beautiful song.

A great song. But it's 5-year-old kid singing about a guy who
murdered his wife. And they talk about violence on TV today, you
know? (Laughs.) Maybe we have a violent streak in our nature.

There were others. The Kingston Trio, Burl Ives, who was a major
influence very early on. Bob Dylan was another, and some of the
popular groups of the early '70s, like Crosby, Sills, and Nash, and
Simon and Garfunkel, Steve Goodman later on, and another Chicago
song-writer who was actually from Cedar Rapids, Iowa--Peter Lang.
He taught me a lot. Then there was Stan Rogers, the great Canadian
song-writer.

There must have been family influences.

My father and his brother were a source of endless fascination. We'd go back to Pennsylvania every year, where my father grew up, and my father and uncle would swap stories about the old days. All of that fascinated me. My mother had some training as a concert pianist, but she gave it up. She went into nursing instead, against her mother's wishes. I never heard her play.

We had history in school, of course, and a couple of the teachers I had did something to make history very interesting. They really

Lee Murdock, "folkie" of the Great Lakes, with a laker in the background. (Photo: Chuck Aumann, courtesy Artists of Note)

opened up history in a different way than I was used to. They would discuss in extreme detail, much to other teachers' consternation, battle scenes and wars--the War of 1812, the Revolution, our other wars. Military history. That became more popular when Gettysburg was marking the 100th anniversary of the battle.

Your trend is now toward the Great Lakes, the maritime--is that deliberate?

I sang a number of Great Lakes songs in an album that I put out in '89 called "Fertile Ground." I wrote one of the songs, "The Christmas Ship," about the schooner *Rouse Simmons* that once brought Christmas trees to Chicago. That one taught me that people gravitate toward Great Lakes music--people in this region. Four albums later, I've gone in over my head.

Fundamentally I've come across this huge collection of songs and memorabilia in the Bentley Historical Library in Ann Arbor, Michigan. They have 47 hours of field recordings that were taped between 1938 and 1960. They have 13 boxes of materials. Thirteen of them. This is the Ivan Walton Collection and I've gone mostly through Professor Walton's field notes. He had had conversations with people I had written songs about. I had written one song called "The Captain and the Mystic" about the schooner *Our Son*, which sank in 1930. There were some interesting things that happened, psychic things, with the people who were rescued.

Well, Professor Walton interviewed Fred Nelson, the captain of *Our Son*, in Sturgeon Bay, Wisconsin, in 1933. And there I had another connection. That's happening to me all the time now.

You're hooked on Great Lakes history?

I think so. There's a lot of it there, and it's not as well known as some other history. That's why I feel almost compelled to get this material out.

You're finding unmined material, things that date back 50, 75, and even 100 to 150 years ago.

Yes, but most of what I find are the lyrics. Often, Professor Walton would say, "Where's the melody for this?" He was talking to

Robert "Broken Back" Collin, whom he found in a sailors' home in Chicago. Collin got his start in the 1860s or so. Sometimes he would remember the melody and at other times he would just sing whatever melody came to mind. That happened with others. So some of the songs that I've found and recorded, or am in the process of recording, almost came out of nowhere.

I'm not going to say I can put myself into the frame of mind of a late-nineteenth-century sailor, because I'm not. I'm a late-twentieth-century suburbanite. But I do have some knowledge of folk music, and sometimes, for me, a melody just happens to make sense.

Can you give us an example?

Sure. There's a song that I've just recorded called "The Stomach Robber." It was there in the Walton collection. I thought, Well, what are we going to do with this? There's no music or anything, but I started reading the words a little bit, and something sort of came into my mind. It went sort of like this... (Sings):

> You may talk about your pleasure trips
> While roaming on the Lakes,
> But the old steam barge, the *Lucy Smith*,
> She surely takes the cake.
>
> Oh the cook is a big fat jolly bum,
> In the galley all the time,
> With salt horse-sense and sowbelly lads,
> He sure keeps lookin' fine.
>
> Haul in your tow-line
> And heave in your slack,
> Take a reef in your stomach, boys,
> And the kinks out of your back.

And so on. The first part of it has the same melody as "New Bedford Whalers." The chorus is a kind of generic thing that appears in hundreds of folk songs.

How many songs have you accumulated so far?

My guess would be between 250 and 300. I may not be able to remember all the lyrics at one time, but--well, I'd say my working repertoire is close to 100 songs.

Do your programs normally have a theme?

I like spontaneity. I think that's where much of the art is. I don't really know what I'm going to say or sing on stage. I know as a rule what I'm going to start out with--if I have a new album out, I'll feature some songs out of it. It really depends on what the audience wants. Sometimes if there's a break, the whole second set will be requests. That's a lot of fun, and sometimes it's a little disconcerting.

As the songs come out, often it's like visiting with an old friend. These are just great songs, especially the traditional ones. Today (February 15, 1997), the theme is Michigan and Love--so I'll feature a few love songs. But they also said, "We want the Great Lakes music."

Did you have that kind of theme request for the ceremony at which they unveiled the Postal System's new Great Lakes Lighthouse stamp series?

I did. They had the ceremony back in 1995, and I provided some music before the ceremony started. I think I sang the National Anthem, with varying degrees of success. Then I sang "Keeper of the Light." That's about a lighthouse keeper in the Apostle Islands. It starts out with a little poem... (Sings):

> This light I've tended 40 years--
> It's now to be run by a set of gears.
> Now fair or foul, the wind may blow,
> Smooth or rough, the seas may go.
> It's all the same.
>
> The ships at night
> Will run to an automated light.
> But I wonder, will the grass stay green?
> Will the brass stay bright, and the windows clean?
> And did ever a piece of wire or gear
> A cry for help in the darkness hear?

124   The Creative Spirit

> Or did ever an automated thing
> Plant marigolds in early spring?

It goes on from there. They have marigolds all over the place. The ceremony was sponsored by the Great Lakes Lighthouse Keepers Association, I think. They really lobbied to have those stamps issued. The ceremony was held in Cheboygan, Michigan on June 17, 1995.

Do you receive requests for songs to mark specific events?

I don't have a whole lot of confidence about writing a song for a specific event. Even so, many times I'll soft-pedal it and say, Well, I'll see how it goes.

I had a request for a song about the Marblehead Light, on Sandusky Bay, Ohio. It's said to be the oldest lighthouse on the Great Lakes. It's run continuously since 1821. There was talk about taking it out of service. Well, I had written a song, "The Longing That I Feel," about a woman who took over as a lighthouse keeper after losing her husband. I showed that and another one, a hymn written about 1870, to a gentleman out there in Ohio and he said, "Boy, it would be great to have a song about the Marblehead Light."

I said I'd do what I could. And about 3:30 the next morning I was finishing the song. It's called "Deep Blue Horizon." I started it and finished it last Saturday. Want to hear the chorus?

Sure.

It goes like this... (Sings):

> I've seen the tall ships that pass by this shore,
> The sidewheel steamers, the whalebacks and more,
> The passenger packets, the self-unloaders,
> And even those noisy cigarette boaters,
> But all that I ask is, Don't let me go blind,
> Let my light continue to shine.

Your work seems to have evolved into a kind of mission...

In a way. It's very subjective. You can call it what seems appropriate. But I do want to get this Great Lakes idea out. I've been doing the Lakes studies for eight, nine years now, and for the last four or five years it's been a resonance in my life. I have the feeling that this is what I should be doing.

It'll probably stay that way, at least for a long time. I may make a little side trip into Irish music. I did a lot of Irish music before, and some ragtime. But there's a real resonance in what I do now with my life.

There's a story behind every performance. For example, the Indiana Dunes National Lakeshore performance.

Like so many others, they wanted me to do what I do. Because I'm always learning new songs and finding out new things, that creates a vibrant show that is alive, on a continual basis.

The Dunes National Lakeshore is there to protect the dunes. But the sands of Michigan City--there's something there, but for me it hasn't descended yet. There was one of the world's largest sand-dunes in Michigan City, and the sand ended up in concrete throughout the Midwest. And of course Michigan City also had one of the greatest amusement parks in the Midwest. People used to take excursion boats across the Lake from Chicago to visit the park and then go back home.

There's really so much that's gone by that could be lost, a lot that I think is valuable. But I do think people are rediscovering historical things. There's a trend there. You take the current interest in Victorian homes. There are a lot of other trends like that. My perspective is that museums talk about the flintlocks, the articles of clothing, the machines, cooking utensils, and the history that is built around those things. What I deal with is the software. The stories.

So there's a preservation aspect to your process...

Yes, there is, and people may say, "But Lee, you're just writing songs, you're just throwing a melody in with words, and you don't know what that melody is or where it came from. You don't know that it's right." My contention is this: in this country folk music and story-telling came out of a creative process. Twelve hundred years ago, 1,500 years ago, the bardic tradition--which is what much of this is based on--was in full flower. If you were a bard, you had learned at the knee of a master. You learned a way to sing a particular song. Before there was writing, that was the way history was passed on. But it had

126   The Creative Spirit

to be accurate.

With the advent of the printing press and other inventions, all that fell by the wayside. People like Alan Lomax and Ivan Walton and countless others have said, "We've got to save this stuff." This is what I'm mining right now. Child was collecting ballads in the 1850s because he thought the ballad tradition had been lost. That's a hundred and some years ago. So that's my answer to those who complain that I'm just throwing a melody in with words. With many of these songs the melodies were incidental.

Could you devise a song around an idea--take a simple kernel and embellish it after research or study?

I've actually done that. I've even adapted songs by Henry C. Work. He's the composer of "My Grandfather's Clock" and others including "Tenting Tonight on the Old Camp Ground." He wrote the song, "Lost on the *Lady Elgin*," about the ship that went down off Waukegan, Illinois in 1860. There were three verses in this song and they didn't have anything to do with the shipwreck itself.

As I was reading about it, I realized that the captain of the *Lady Elgin*, a man named Jack Wilson, was actually a heroic figure. The pilothouse came off the *Lady Elgin* as she sank. A lot of people hung onto the pilothouse because it was floating. Then even though it was pitch dark, and the pilothouse was about two feet under water, Wilson sang songs and encouraged people to continue on through the night. He drowned while trying to get to shore.

Another part of that took place on shore. A young divinity student named Edward Spencer went into the water time after time, rescuing people who were struggling in the surf. He did that 16 times, and at the end he was totally spent.* He said something to the effect, "Did I do my best?"

How could anyone leave those things out of a song? I committed the unpardonable sin and added three verses to a song that's 130 years old. I can't really take a lot of credit for this, honestly--in this medium things happen and I don't know why. This is what I refer to as tapping

---

*In another account the heroic Spencer is reported to have <u>saved</u> 17 victiims of the shipwreck. Both are apparently correct; he saved a married couple on one of his 16 trips into the pounding surf. See the Olson-van Heest interview, Chapter II.

into the collective consciousness, the collective knowledge that we have as artists.

Music like that expands on a historic event, makes it a part of our lore--would you agree?

I would. I sang this song for a couple of friends of mine, and they're very knowledgeable about English ballads and American folksongs. They couldn't tell which verses were Work's.

I had something similar happen with another song I wrote. This was about Dennis Hale, the only survivor of the *Daniel J. Morrell*, the freighter that sank in Lake Huron in 1966. I've never survived a shipwreck. I don't have the slightest idea of what I'm talking about in that area. But I tried to write it from his perspective. Then I sang it for him. As I was writing the song, there were words that came from I don't know where. I just had no idea. I included a line that suggested that one thing I remembered as a little boy was a hot summer day down at the harbor. "The big boats comin' in and the black smoke hangin' low, drifting to the horizon..." That kind of thing.

There was a supernatural aspect to Hale's story that I wanted to get in the song but didn't. I don't know how familiar you are with the story, but this old man appeared to him when he was in the lifeboat. The old man told Dennis to quit eating ice--to avoid hypothermia. Dennis also had what would be called now an after-death experience. This got around pretty early on after the wreck, and people hounded him about it. "How can you talk about this," they'd say. "It's morbid fascination."

You got that into the song?

No, I couldn't. But there is another line, "The rhythm of the engines kept the time for all the crew." That did get in. I was downbound in Lake Huron a year or so ago, as a guest on another lake freighter, the *Armco*. I had been on board for four days. We were due to hit Port Huron about 6:00 in the morning, and I wanted to get out there about 10 minutes of 6:00 to see the Blue Water Bridge and the Grosse Point Light. I had never been on a big ship before. I woke early, about 10 after 5:00, because they had checked down the engines. Here I had been on this ship only four days and already I had been tied into the rhythm of the engines.

128   The Creative Spirit

When I sang it for him in person, once when I was down near where he lives, I was pleased that Dennis didn't haul off and slug me. I would gladly have accepted that critique, you know? But he said, "That's exactly how it happened."

How many songs have you composed--can you estimate?

I'm good for maybe a couple a year. You keep busy with 250 or so performances annually. And I teach instrumental guitar on Monday nights. But there are times when I have to sit down and create the space, the spiritual, visual, temporal space and then just sit and stare at the wall and let things happen. It doesn't work every time I do that. But more often than not it does.

"The Marblehead Light" was an exception?

It just happened. I had no intention of writing that song. I couldn't sleep after 3:00 in the morning. Why, I don't know. But I was thinking, turning it over, telling myself I suppose I should write that song. An hour later I had it.

Can you give us a rundown on your albums, tapes?

Sure. I put out three, some years ago, that are on vinyl and are no longer available. Then I put out "Fertile Ground" in '89, "Cold Winds" in '91, and "Safe in the Harbor" in '93. "Freshwater Highway" came out in '95. So I've got seven albums that I've recorded, plus some educational work on the Great Lakes region that's a supplement to my school program. That involves a tape and a book together, a program of folk songs, original ballads, and stories.

As a matter of curiosity, what's the background of "The Great Lakes Song?"

It was written by a man named Pat Dailey, who lives in Cleveland, Ohio. I think he actually worked on the boats for a while. He was primarily a singer, and wrote the song with a man named Shel Silverstein. I learned it from Bob Gibson, the guy who discovered Joan Baez. Bob is quite a legend in his own right.

And the song was part of "Freshwater Highway."

It was. That was a kind of journey through time. I started with a really eerie nineteenth-century song about the schooner *Chicago Board of Trade*. There was also a musical tribute to the Irish immigrants who worked on the Illinois and Michigan Canal. Some of the other songs bring us into contemporary times--like one telling about an accident on the Canadian freighter *Cartiercliffe Hall*. Another was "Requiem for the *Mesquite*," the name of the Coast Guard cutter that went aground in Lake Michigan in 1989.

Give us a few verses of "The Great Lakes Song?"

Sure. (Sings):

> The Great Lakes are a diamond
> On the hand of North America,
> A bright shining jewel on that
> Friendship Border ring.
>
> It's a freshwater highway
> Comin' down from Canada,
> And all along the coastline,
> You can hear the people sing...

PETER RINDLISBACHER

(1996)

How do you combine a doctorate in clinical psychology with a

130   The Creative Spirit

*passion for sailing, an obsession with history and historical detail, and
a full-time dedication to painting? First, according to Peter
Rindlisbacher, you choose a father, Harold, who owns a printshop,
and a mother, Eleanor, who has pursued a part-time career as a
commercial artist. Next, you grow up with sailboats, early on
becoming a sailing aficionado with a penchant for racing and for
teaching people how to sail (for as many as 12 hours a day). Finally,
you earn your doctorate at Queen's University in Kingston, Ontario
while succumbing to the lure of paint and canvas.*

*In 1996, four years after receiving his doctorate, Peter had
established a reputation as a leading interpreter of marine history on
the Great Lakes. One of his oil paintings, "The Battle of Lake Erie,"
indicates the lengths to which the artist can go in achieving realism
and accuracy: sold in a limited edition in the late 1980s, the painting
depicts the battle as eyewitnesses described it* at 2:45 p.m. on
September 10, 1813. *Peter recalls how he migrated from clinical
psychology to painting, tells of the painstaking effort that goes into his
art-related researches, and explains how history and painting merge
to become things of beauty...*

* * *

I was doing the clinical psychology degree--trying to get a Ph.D.
at Queen's, and my research was coming very slowly, and there were
some tieups in the electronic instrumentation that I needed in order to
complete my data collection. There were gobs of time where I had to
do anything I could to ward off ulcers. I had of course always been
passionate about maritime history. I began to contact some heritage
groups--it occurred to me that they might need some visual material to
portray some of their efforts. I worked on the *Hamilton-Scourge*
Project (to raise the *Hamilton* and *Scourge* from the floor of Lake
Ontario) and did some work on the H.M.S. *Detroit* Project--they were
trying to raise funds to build a full-size replica of the *Detroit*, flagship
of the British fleet at the Battle of Lake Erie. I did a couple of
paintings for those groups and found, Gee, I like this.

In grad school anyone who tries to carry on outside activities like
that finds it very tough. So I couldn't distribute my art and I couldn't
do the show circuit, but I could turn out a painting now and then.
However, the groups were able to reproduce these paintings and were
quite happy to accept the donations. My family, who have been

tremendous supporters, produced limited prints at my dad's shop to be used as fund-raising items. The art thing got bigger and bigger as my thesis was drawing to a close, and I defended my thesis and the degree came in the mail. I just kind of threw it in a drawer and kept on painting.

I never really looked for a job in psychology. But I did do some intern work in the Psychiatric Hospital out there at Kingston, but as for getting into the psychology profession, I just never got around to it.

You wouldn't say there was a critical moment or event--the art sort of grew on you...

Well, you know I was a sailing instructor early on, in my teen years and on into university, and I was crazy about the water. Art was something I did during the wintertime, when I couldn't go sailing. Even when I went up to Alberta for a while, to finish up an honors degree from '81 to '84, I was painting, and now and then, when I had a few hours, I would nip into the historical section and get any marine book I could. Art was always there, and if I ever ignored it for very long I'd feel very uncomfortable.

In Edmonton there are few landlocked sailors, and you have to go a number of miles to get even to a shallow lake. I remember, though, coming home for Christmas--and on the day before Christmas I actually made it out on the lake--Lake St. Clair--with my Laser. And I was absolutely loving it, you know, finding that kind of mildness after an Alberta winter, and it was just like being in the tropics. I would just get it in whenever I could. My wife, Ellen, is a sailing fanatic herself. We own a boat together and sail on Lake St. Clair.

You've visited a number of Great Lakes and other ports and out of the way places, and I believe have talked of "vanishing histories..."

Yes, I went I guess in the mid-'70s. I sort of delayed my university training, took a van and traveled both along the U.S. shore on the East Coast and the Canadian Maritimes. I was absolutely staggered by how little there was up there. All the old stories about the huge mercantile fleet that the Canadians had around mid-century, the 1800s, and then I reach a town and I had read about it and knew it had a great history, and then find that there's nothing there. My God, it was unbelievable. There was probably something moving about that--

Peter Rindlisbacher works in his home studio on a shipwreck scene.

it's as if you have an inner irritation that needs addressing. And even though I was in psychology training, I got into all this stuff about vanishing history and old stories lost--old scenes that haven't been portrayed or even looked upon for so many years. To try to bring that back seemed important. There has been a movement, I think, to rediscover the water-fronts of both the East Coast and the Great Lakes. To some extent I'm feeding into that or helping it along, or whatever you want to call it.

Water-fronts were so much a part of people's history. And now with air travel and highway travel, to have just a blank water-front with just a breakwall and a bunch of high-rises. That's not what it was like--we were tied to the water back in those days.

It generates energy, that kind of experience. I guess that's what anger can do--generate energy in you and you've got to do something with it or not, I guess.

And creativity can be an answer to that challenge probably...

It is for me.

Did you study painting formally?

We had a very art-oriented high school in Essex County. The principal was very much into encouraging the art program. I had five years of high school, and during every one of those years I took art classes. They introduced us to a bunch of methods here and there. But I remember them saying in an irritated way, "Can't you do anything other than ships?" But that was good.

At the university I didn't take any history or art. I would wander into the art building now and then, and it was kind of interesting to see what was going on. There wasn't a heavy contingent of realism, in terms of doing real-life pictures. It was more sculpture and other forms as means of exploring your inner world. A lot of abstract types of training. I probably wouldn't have enjoyed it, and I might have fought with the instructors too.

I just see the abstract type of art as playtime, as fooling around, whereas this other thing, the realism, is more mission-related. It's a scientific thing with all the research, and I think I like that kind of detective work.

Re-creating history, and making it a kind of permanent re-creation?

Yes, it is permanent. But I'm often humbled by that because so often I think I've nailed a scene pretty darn good and then some new research comes out to show that the ships weren't painted quite that way, or a personal letter contradicts the official report. I usually trust the personal letter because the writers don't usually have axes to grind, or weren't covering official conduct, or whatever.

What I try to do to avoid criticism is to seek out those people that are most expert in a particular area. Their entire hobby lives, or business lives, are wrapped up in researching a certain battle, let's say. They coach me as much as possible. When a painting's almost done I'll send them snapshots of it, and say, What do you think is wrong here? Do you see anything that should be adjusted? Since it's been done in oils, I can redo it.

If I do get criticism, I sort of refer them to the experts and let the historians argue among themselves. I do have good relations with a number of historians.

On your working methods--do you go through stages? You have to do research first, presumably. And the research may be a larger percentage of your time than the painting...

It is. The painting is often the least fun and the quickest stage of the whole thing. I try to gather as much as I can about a certain scene:

134   The Creative Spirit

the time of day that it was supposed to take place, the cloud cover, the depth of the water, which changes the wave pattern. You know, what's the vantage point, how much light is there, and where is it coming from? If the event is very specific, they want to know what was going on at 2:05 in the Battle of Lake Erie. In that case, with that battle, there are many descriptions of what the ships did. So I'm on a short leash as it were.

Unfortunately there wasn't much cloud up there during that battle, so the dramatic lighting is difficult to do. Oftentimes the weather conditions don't match the dramatic things going on down on the ground. A sunny day doesn't really match the action of a savage battle, with people dying all over the place. It's better with a dramatic storm or a windy type of setting.

I can get log reports from the ships, telling their positions and what sails were up during the time the action took place, or letters home--if there's anything there. I try to go to the location that I'm portraying, as much as possible, to see what it looks like. Oftentimes it's changed beyond recognition. I take photos whenever I can. I try to get maps and put a position, let's say, on the water. That's where my viewpoint is from. I try to get the right positions for all the buildings, or headlands, or whatever.

I build models out of cardboard as well. I get, say, a draft of a ship that will be in the foreground or very carefully portrayed, and I'll cut the sections out of a body plan from the cardboard and glue that onto a profile of that same ship. Then I take balsa-wood battens and put them together so that I have sort of a quick, "two-day wonder" kind of ship model. Then I'll take a roll of film and shoot pictures of that ship from different angles. Then I take one that's suitable and that's the one I use.

I try to eliminate the guesswork from specific things, like a hull. So it's a scientific approach at least in that respect. Sails fluttering in the wind are very variable, and I try to do as much as possible to be accurate with the rigging and all of that. But in that case I don't so much revert to models. So, yeah, the whole thing is sort of designed, and the painting is the very last stage of all.

Can you estimate the percentages--preparatory time and painting time?

My guess is that 20 percent is the actual painting time. It varies, too, because sometimes the weather is the big topic. In other cases, say in the harbor scene--there was one I did of Kingston harbor, and in that case a committee from the Marine Museum guided me, showing me every building, every ship, and then the painting was a very small element. It varies, the painting time, between 20 and 40 percent.

The surface of the water is the most difficult part. You have to suggest movement in the water. If it's photographic, it looks stiff, as if it's just not moving. It has to look as if it's in movement, but not so messy or blurry that people can't tell. In addition, though, there's perspective in there, there is also what the wind should be doing to the water, there's your position, the one you are looking from in relation to the wind. If you don't get the water right, usually you get the sense that something's not right, but you don't know what it is. Very often I'll do water over and over and over again--because there's just something wrong about it. As an active sailor, which I am, you're looking at water all the time, so you know when it looks right and when it doesn't. Sure it comes from my mind, but I'm used to looking at the real thing, so there's sort of a harsh critic in there somewhere.

You do a sketch first, and then do a final draft, or a semifinal draft?

Oh yeah. I'll do a lot of three-inch by four-inch sketches in pencil, and they're very much for the tones, the light and dark, the composition.

Your work is on exhibit in a lot of places--institutions, museums, and so on.

A lot of the purchasers have been museums and heritage facilities, so there are things there for people to look at. But I don't have any official gallery that I deal with. This whole pattern has really developed out of the grad school situation, where I was able to do paintings here and there. I didn't really develop the art lifestyle, like some artists do.

A lot of times my work is anniversary related. There may be a big anniversary, and everyone knows it's coming--everyone in the marine art world is sort of cued into it. That kind of thing does occur now and then. A lot of artists are able to stock up on inventory, and then they go to the show circuit, that kind of thing. I'm in a different position. I can barely keep up with the commissions, and therefore there's not

136   The Creative Spirit

much of an inventory. People will ask if they can see some work that's for sale, and I have to tell them, There's not a lot here.

I'm busy just keeping up to commissions. Some people would say maybe that I'm not organized enough. There may come a time when there'll be a big show, or a gallery will make an offer that will be attractive enough--and when I can actually get ahead of the orders.

Are you doing Great Lakes marine history exclusively? Or is some of the work related to the East Coast or other areas?

Most of them have Great Lakes themes, but I've done some isolated ones about the East Coast, and actually I've sent a little work to the West Coast, when a sail-training association was having an art show, and I was impressed with one of their ships. Mainly I have done Great Lakes-related work, and heaven knows I could paint a picture every week, or every day, and never run out of topics or themes that need portraying. I guess the recent development has been that I'm expanding to do underwater scenes as well as others on top of the water.

With underwater scenes, we've got cameras today that can go to wrecks that are down 200 or 300 or 400 feet below the surface of some lake. You need heavy lighting even to get some small scenes. However, the artist can suggest the gloom and darkness but still allow the viewer to see the entire length of some magnificent wreck. You know, we as artists are able to go beyond the camera. However, we use the camera. I've actually made models that are based on divers' measurements--and viewed footage over and over again to capture details. Then all of that gets put together in a painting that shows you what you would see if visibility were 150 feet. This is what the wreck would look like if it were lighted up wall to wall, which of course it isn't. It's becoming very interesting--these wrecks, you know--not everybody can dive that deep, or see the stuff first-hand. So a painting can bring that kind of information to a wider public that loves it but can't see it.

Is this a new trend in your work?

Well, I'm a member of Save Ontario Shipwrecks (SOS), the Windsor Chapter. A number of the museums that I'm affiliated with also have an interest in the wrecks. They're both Canadian and

A storm brews in Peter Rindlisbacher's *"Naubinway* Ship in the Straits," 24x30 inches, oil on canvas. Marine archeologists, digging for the wreckage of this ship near the mouth of the Millecoquins River, in Michigan, found artifacts dating from the 1830's.

"Morning Salute: HMS *Ontario* at Carleton Island" is a 24x36 inch oil on canvas. The *Ontario* sank in Lake Ontario in 1780 with no survivors.

138   The Creative Spirit

American. Preservation of shipwrecks is a major trend, it seems.

The H.M.S. *Detroit* isn't a shipwreck, but it's another fascinating project. A few years after the battle (of Lake Erie), they sent that ship over Niagara Falls. So there's no wreck of that one. Just because it's headquartered in my area (Amherstburg, Ontario) I got involved with Project H.M.S. *Detroit* a few years ago. I did some visual portrayals and fund-raising prints. I was president of the group. I get into these things, heritage and underwater associations. I'm on the board of the Fort Malden Volunteer Association and do some reenactments.

I guess in terms of other underwater projects, there's a mid-nineteenth century lake schooner called the *Willis*. It went down in the Pelee Passage (in Lake Erie) after it was broadsided by another ship in the middle of the night. It's in incredible condition down there. That was one that I think is in 80 feet of water or so. And I did a painting so you could see the entire ship, from end to end, where she lies on the bottom with her spars lying over her.

Videos of these wrecks are tough sometimes because there may be distortion from the lens. You can see what the ship looks like, but you've got to take into account this sort of fisheye effect from the lens. But there's no substitute for actual visual footage, whether it's from a camera above the surface or below.

Will you do any more on the Fitzgerald?

Yes. The picture I've done so far (showing removal of the bell) isn't really a final painting--it's more like a study, an initial portrayal. It's a small version of the actual painting, which I believe will be three feet by four feet. So a lot more detail is going to be necessary. I guess I don't now have any further plans to paint the *Edmund Fitzgerald*. A lot of artists have painted her, with all the public interest.

I think though that there are an awful lot of other wrecks that need portraying. There are so many others where just a handful of divers have seen what's down there. It seems that the public would be interested in seeing some of them.

There's also a cooperative project with SOS for the Pelee Passage wrecks. They want to establish a dive park in that area. This is what you might be able to see down there if you come this way--and both divers and the general public might be interested in that.

Could you talk about the Hamilton-Scourge *Project?*

These ships weren't British warships, they were American. One was British-built. Apparently the ships prior to the War of 1812 used to sail in company together, and exchange crews and everything else even though they were of different nationalities. In the prewar era, they barely recognized the border, and I think the border was just kind of an irritation in those days.

The American side, just prior to the war, seized the British schooner *Scourge*. She was called the *Lord Nelson* at the time, and they seized her for smuggling. Then when war was declared, she was taken into the American squadron. The two ships sailed as part of that squadron for the first half of the war, so in August of 1813, I think, they were doing some squadron maneuvers when this squall came through. And they went down. They're beautifully preserved down there, and the *Hamilton-Scourge* Project is trying to raise the funds to bring up one or both of them and establish a waterfront park. That would allow the public to see these ships.

Are they close to succeeding?

It's been difficult. They've been trying to get the massive amounts of money that you need for such a project. There's a contingent of people who are telling everybody not to move them until the technology is up to the task. It wouldn't do to raise them part-way up to the surface and then run out of money.

There have been rumblings that perhaps one of the ships might be moved away from that area, or that in other cases they might leave these originals down at the bottom, but then take such careful measurements that two lifesize replicas could be built of them. Some purists are convinced that the moment you move them to the top they are going to start deteriorating rapidly. And until we know a lot more about preservation in the long term, we might be destroying an irreplaceable heritage.

They were visited, it seems, by robots some years ago.

Oh yes, Jacques Cousteau was down there, and they took umpteen photos with their robot cameras. It's been very carefully documented, and that's an interesting angle for an artist--when you're dealing with something that old but yet we have pictures of it. You're constantly humbled, mostly because there's an accurate reality to reflect.

One is never done with things, but I painted a picture of the *Hamilton* and *Scourge* back about '87. I also painted one of the two ships coming out of Sackets Harbor. That's about all I've done on those ships. They had a high profile a few years ago when the word got around that I was in this work.

What's been your most interesting project--is that identifiable?

I guess for me anything having to do with the War of 1812 has tremendous appeal. I do this reenactment stuff too, so that sort of feeds into it. But I get interested in just about any project. There are some turn-of-the-century steamers that are very sought-after in this particular area. Those were gorgeous ships, you know, sort of crystal floating palaces. And it's not hard to see esthetic appeal in them, even if they are stink-potters.

If it floats, I can be convinced that there's something very attractive about it, and it's worth putting it into some different lighting conditions, or weather conditions, or in some neat position. It's not hard, really, to generate enough motivation to get a painting done and make it as good as I can.

Have you worked on scenes or ships from or on all five lakes?

Superior...Michigan... Yeah, I guess I have. There was one that I did in Lake Michigan--they don't even know what the name of the ship is, but they know that it washed up on the shore of the Upper Peninsula. They suspect that it dates back to the 1830s or a little earlier. It was sort of sailing along--sort of an early fishing schooner. In the main, though, the bulk of my paintings have dealt with Lake Erie and Lake Ontario, mainly because I've lived on the shores of both of them. Since I moved from Kingston, left there and moved to Amherstburg, I've had increasing contact with the western end of the Great Lakes scene, partly with the Association for Great Lakes Maritime History. An awful lot of good people are based out your way (southwestern Michigan).

The Association is actually an association of museums and other institutions preserving Great Lakes history. The secretary is in Bowling Green, Ohio.

I've seen a name very similar to yours--Peter Rindisbacher. A

Canadian artist of the 1800's. Is that a relative?

A woman went to Switzerland and I guess did some research. She'd have to do an awful lot more research to substantiate it, but she feels that there's this little village that the Rindlisbachers or any variation of that name came from. But that particular artist--his father spelt his name the way I spell mine--the artist, it appears, lost an *l*, so it's Rindisbacher.

These poor Swiss folk of the early 1800s were conned, it seems, by a land agent. They thought they were going to Louisiana, and then they were brought down through Hudson Bay and dropped off in the Manitoba area. They darn near starved to death through the winter. Finally the colony just fell apart and they drifted down to St. Louis. From the time that this artist arrived, as a 15-year-old, to the time when he died, I think at age 27, he was doing apparently eyewitness pictures of Indians, their canoes, the settlers, and later on portraits of people in St. Louis. He developed tremendous skill and accuracy--the poor guy just died too early. But his pictures are virtually the only records we have today of the early attempts at colonizing the Canadian West. His pictures are in all our history books.

At times my parents have gotten calls from people saying, "Congratulations, I heard your son sold a painting for $40,000," and it was this poor dead fellow's painting being re-sold. I don't command those prices yet. (Laughs.)

His paintings are on exhibit in a number of Canadian museums and galleries?

Oh yes. Nobody else took the time to paint what they saw. This fellow was extremely accurate. I was well along in my marine paintings before I ever knew much about him, so it's not like I learned about an ancestor and decided to emulate him.

I've seen a mention of a painting of yours, "Harbour at Niagara." Where is it now?

It's a pre-war scene, pre-1812. The *Lord Nelson* and the *Diana*, which are the pre-war names of the *Hamilton* and *Scourge*, are sailing out of the harbor at Niagara River. They were sailing down to Oswego or Kingston. The painting is in Hamilton City Hall, I believe. It's

142   The Creative Spirit

owned by the *Hamilton-Scourge* Society, and there were fund-raising prints made from that. It was a limited edition of 950, I believe, and that's now sold out. That's one that I brag about--it's very difficult to get a print of that now because every one has been purchased.

Do you have a favorite painting--one you've done?

Not really. I guess I've got some that I can look at and say, Yeah, I'm pretty satisfied with my attempt at that one. But I don't think I have one particular favorite--very often it's the one I did last year or something like that. And then I'll have another one that displaces it.

There's one I did of Louisbourg, which is a fortress town from the 1740s, out on Cape Breton Island in Nova Scotia. It's a harbor scene, and it was done in poster form, but it seemed to come together pretty well. That was done for a tall ship circuit that occurred in '95. But now, I don't think I have one that I can say--Yeah, that's my premier work. Or I can say I haven't painted it quite yet.

DAVID IRVINE

(1996)

Seen in retrospect, most things in life seem inevitable. For David Irvine of Shelbyville, Michigan, inevitability came in the form of wooden boats. They have been part of his life since his father, the late Keith Irvine, moved to Algonac, Michigan when David was 9. David not only caught the "woodie" bug; like his father he went into publishing. But books haven't been his thing. Video production has. He's got three woodie-related videos on the market as of late 1996 and has others in mind for the future. He's been past president (1995-96) of the Mid-Michigan International Television Association and a board member for five of his years as a member.

* * *

My start in video production was about as basic as you can get. Early on I found work as a videographer, particularly for weddings. I had about 180 weddings behind me by the time I had completed my B.A. (Bachelor of Arts) in Communications at Oakland University in Rochester, Michigan. While at Oakland, I also worked in the Instructional Technology Center. I worked as a producer-director for Parke Davis Pharmaceutical, a division of Warner Lambert, making instructional video programs. At Michigan State University, I worked as a graduate assistant in video and audio production. While finishing my thesis, I assisted with video, print, and press conferences for the State of Michigan Department of Management and Budget in the Corporate Communication Department.

For the past six years, I have worked as Chief of the Medical Media Production Service department at the VA Medical Center in Battle Creek, Michigan. I oversee the production of a variety of media, including video, print, computer graphics, photography, and satellite/audio education activities. This job has been very challenging. There is hardly a day that I don't look forward to being there. It is a media producer's dream. Management is supportive and works with us to maintain the department in a cost-effective manner.

You've got your own company, run out of your home. What's involved there?

Video-Craft, Inc. was established in May of 1990. Physically, the company consists of a small office. Production facilities include ¾" U-matic portable recorder, off-line video editing system with time-code reference for use in an on-line production facility. With her production background, my wife Joyce, whom I met in graduate school in the Department of Telecommunication, has helped in many areas, from conceptualization of the programs to generating interview questions, production planning and shooting, and marketing/advertising.

Can you tell us about "Runabout Renaissance," *your first production for the "woodie" or wooden boat-enthusiast market?*

The idea came about between 1988 and 1989 when I began researching topics for my master's thesis. The first idea was to design a video production department for a corporate environment. After much reading and no idea of a "niche" to research, my thesis advisor, Gary Reid, at Michigan State, suggested I go out in my father's wooden boat for the weekend to "think" about other topics.

My parents lived and used their wooden boat in Algonac, Michigan, the original home of Chris-Craft Corporation, a place that produced more wooden boats than any other in the world--a quarter of a million wooden boats from the 1920s through the early 1970s. Little did he know what I would return with. He was very supportive of the whole idea, as was my family.

It does seem as if my interest in woodies was foreordained. I had grown up with the family runabout, *Big Dipper*, a 23-foot Cuthbertson Craft, on the St. Clair River.

But the renaissance of interest in woodies was real?

Certainly. Up through the 1980s and into the '90s buyers were putting down money for wooden boats out of love--they wanted to maintain and use them. There was an article in a national magazine called, "Wild about Woodies." That was '88. The article contrasted the motives of today's owners of wooden boats with those of the owners of yesteryear. Relative newcomers to wooden boats have become involved for reasons of nostalgia. Others have purchased them for purposes of investment or status. A $60,000 restored runabout in pristine condition in 1990 could rise in value by at least 10 percent a year.

By the late 1980s wooden boats of the '20s and '30s were being restored by skilled craftsmen. There weren't too many classic models available for restoration, so they started to build replicas of famous name boats. From the outside these boats looked identical to the antique classics. But in the construction they used wood and polyester resins.

The year 1980 saw a major event in the woodie field. That year Steve Northuis, his father, and his grandfather produced a 1930 24-foot Chris-Craft triple cockpit runabout in their workshop in Holland (Michigan). Their company, Grand Craft, had help from the grandson of Chris Smith, "father" of the old, famous Chris-Craft. Grand Craft was still building these early mahogany boats into the '90s under their

David Irvine, woodie buff, on the St. Clair River.

new owner, Dick Sligh. They built them for Chris-Craft because that company was making only fiberglass boats.

What approach, what working methods did you adopt for "Renaissance?"

It was a documentary, so a lot of research went into finding out about the methods used by John Grierson, founder of the British documentary movement, and Robert Flaherty. Flaherty in 1921 made the cultural film "Nanook of the North," which mastered the "grammar" of film using production techniques to view an episode from many angles and accept the presentation as "natural." As no documentary had been done on people who made wooden pleasure boats, it was necessary to research the few books that were available. More importantly, I had to find out through interviews who was working on boats now and what techniques they used.

It was very hard to prepare more than a working outline before shooting the interviews and "b-roll", which is cutaway footage to illustrate key points. Over a nine-month period, a total of 50 or so 20-minute tapes were shot. Of that, almost 20 hours were interviews. To get the best quotes, each interview had to be typed word for word to find not only the best quotes, but the thoughts or points that were articulated the best. Eight rough edits were performed. The first one was a 60-minute program. The final was cut down to 30 minutes. My final thesis was both a 120-page written document, including a 60-page script of the program, and also a finished television program. This program has aired numerous times on all of the Michigan Public Television stations and has sold over 1,500 copies worldwide which I consider to be a success, considering the limited audience appeal and the part-time nature of one person marketing the video by himself.

You had to be all over the lot while working on this first video.

Was I ever. I contacted about 100 people. I think there were about 20 in the video itself. I traveled what I estimated to be 5,000 miles, including trips to the Upper Peninsula of Michigan; to Manistee and Algonac, Michigan; to Holland and then to Clayton and Watervliet, New York. I also went to Lake George, New York. I couldn't afford to go to the Lake Tahoe (Nevada) Boat Show, but we did visit the site of the show and the Sierra Boat Works.

I spent about 14 months on that first video. That included six months of shooting. We went to the Algonac Boat Show, "Where It All Began." Other boat shows were in the Les Cheneaux Islands, in the town of Hessel; the Clayton, New York Boat Show--that's in the Thousand Islands region of the St. Lawrence River--and the Century Boat Show in Manistee, where the Century Boat Company got its start. I remember that we camped for 10 days in New York to visit multiple sites in a short period of time.

You were talking to people along the way.

I had to. For that first video I had to contact not only people who were involved in the content, such as book authors and wooden boat specialists, but also people involved in production. Thanks to my professor, Gary Reid, contacts with high end video and audio production companies in the Detroit area were made to allow the transfer of 24 track audio and ¾-inch video synchronized and rerecorded to 1-inch broadcast videotape. Also, J.P. McCarthy, a nationally known radio talk-show host, was contacted and agreed to do the narration. McCarthy, of Detroit's WJR, has since died.

The technical stuff that goes into video production is mind-boggling. You're not only working out a kind of story and including what they call the experiential and the testimonial types of material. You're trying to make sure that you're adhering to your informational and explanatory functions while managing a huge array of data, interviews, and so on.

Then you get into script formats. I decided to use the Corporate

Teleplay Format that puts scene descriptions in single-space, upper- and-lower-case type and the narration in caps. You get into background music. It seemed that period sound from the 1930s would be most appropriate, meaning a lot of '20s and '30s jazz. That stuff, believe it or not, is still copyrighted, and royalties have to be paid. You get into on-camera and off-camera narration, natural sound, and allocation of the various sound elements. We had more than 100 natural sound elements in the half-hour production. They included boats running, sea gulls crying, water lapping.

One problem was just getting people to visit, share their ideas--and allow us to enter their "culture." But keeping a camera steady while videotaping from a boat may have been a bigger headache. We had to keep the camera dry while taking footage. We finally solved it by using a tripod mounted on a foam base covered with plywood. There was some other hocus-pocus in there. We had the camera mostly covered with plastic.

Your second video, now on the market, was "Runabout Renaissance II: Restoring Your Wooden Pleasure Craft.*" It should have been easier after No. 1.*

On the contrary, it was more detailed and expansive. It was designed for those who are interested in buying a woodie or who have one and would like to know what is involved in restoration.

It took four years. When my wife became pregnant, it made me want to finish the project. All of the interviews were conducted in 1993 and 1994 in Michigan, Virginia, and various places in New England. Transcription and scripting took place in 1995. I was only able to complete a rough edit by the time my daughter was born in September, 1995. On Friday, March 6, 1996, with the help of my good

David Irvine's camera has been his almost constant companion while he's researching a video.

148   The Creative Spirit

friend David Haggadone from graduate school, we sat down in an edit suite at 6 p.m. By midnight, we had finished the first minute of the hour-long program.

Our deadline was Tuesday. We edited straight through with only a few hours of sleep each night and completed the program at 2:40 a.m. the following Wednesday morning after 59.5 hours of editing time, or approximately one hour per finished minute. I had taken Monday and Tuesday off from work. I made it to work in Battle Creek a few minutes late at 8:00 a.m. The program was tested and surveyed by various content experts and was released on May 15, 1996 with 1,000 copies duplicated and ready to go.   Several hundred have been distributed to date (six months later).   A half hour version was purchased by a West Michigan Public TV station for broadcast over the next three years.

Where are you with new projects?

I'm only in the conceptualization phase. I've been talking to people about a documentary on speedboat racing in the 1920s and 1930s. We'd have to include some of the leading lights of that period. I do have another program that needs editing. It's on the routering technique for plank replacement in woodies. It'll be a 40-minute instructional film. We're currently distributing a new production, "*The Roll and Brush Method of Varnishing.*"

Aside from that, I'm trying to spend some time with my little daughter. Some of the time we'll be in our boat--a woodie of course.

What's your take on the renaissance half a dozen years later? Continuing?

One interviewee from my first video says interest is tapering off somewhat, or at least leveling off. It doesn't have quite the interest it had in the 1980s, or the high prices charged for some of the rare boats. One of the craftsmen in the second video could not handle the hours and labor required to do his show-quality work on boats. He now does it as a sideline and works outside the wooden boat industry to be able to have regular hours for his family and not be so consumed by his business.

I figure that wooden pleasure boats will continue to be an interest. Whatever happens, I've really enjoyed working on woodies, mostly with Great Lakes people who want or are willing to present important information. I'm working to keep up with all the exploding technologies, and of course running into the age-old problems--how to do it fast, cheap, and with good quality. You can usually achieve only two of those. The easiest part is working with people who enjoy what they're doing.

Any long-term ambitions?

I'd like to do documentaries full-time, but for now will keep it as a sideline. Eventually I'd like to produce a small multi-media program using CD-ROM to integrate text, video, sound, and photos.

CHARLES VICKERY

(1997)

Sometime in the 1950s, Charles Vickery experienced a kind of epiphany. One of his early seascapes was on exhibit in an in-town gallery display window. A big-city art critic saw the painting, found herself entranced, and wrote of what she had seen. Vickery became part of the "talk around town," and decided to concentrate more heavily on water scenes--oceans and the Great Lakes, purling brooks in bucolic winter settings, clippers and ships of war. Great Lakes schooners appeared on his canvases with some frequency.

Forty-some years later Vickery has gained fame as one of the foremost painters of seascapes in the United States. His exhibits have attracted audiences over the years to galleries from Rockport, Massachusetts to London, England, and back to the Union League Club in Chicago. Some of his works, like "The Christmas Tree Ship," have become perennial favorites among collectors and dilettantes alike. In fact, all three of his paintings of the ill-fated Christmas tree schooner--showing the Rouse Simmons *at dock in Chicago, in*

Chicago's Harbor, and on the open lake (Michigan)--have remained top sellers for Vickery's gallery outlets, The Clipper Ship Galleries in La Grange, Illinois, and New Buffalo, Michigan. Who's Who in American Art *describes his way with water as "realistic."* He would add to that description...

* * *

It's not quite as simple as that, then?

No. I'd call this style *realistic with a dash of romance.* For me, it takes a lot of study. It just seems that all the colors of the water come from the sky--and every color of the sky is reflected in the water. From night to day I see a pretty complete range of colors.

But whatever the colors I try to add a little bit of excitement. I call it romance.

That applies to any water, rough or calm, stormy or lightly rippled?

Having always lived inland, Charles Vickery is nonetheless considered a leading seascape artist. At work in his studio, surrounded by ship models, canvases, books, and other paraphernalia, he can look back on an illustrious career.

It applies to all of it. There's a big difference, though, between wind-blown water and inert water. With wind-blown water you get sort of dusty foam crests. Things may go wild. The waves may reject the color of the sky. Then the wind turning or driving a wave can change the color of the water.

It's hard to explain. I work a lot on the shores of Lake Michigan, in Indiana. The Dunes area. For me, the lake is never exactly the same twice. Movement is always there. A gust of wind can create drama in the time it takes to blink an eye. The rougher the water gets, the more independent it becomes--of the sky, of sources of light.

You've done a lot of seascapes in oil with nothing in them but water. Pure seascapes. Does that tell us something?

I believe it does. I do love the water. If you really work with it, you draw out a sense of the life in it. You have to greet the sea, or the Lakes, on their own terms, with respect. The water will give respect back.

I should add that I also like to do ships. I do a lot of work on commission, and it seems a lot of people want tall ships. There's an endless call for them because they're so dramatic. But you have to be careful. Putting a ship, or ships, into a scene takes you into dangerous waters, if I can use that phrase. The test then is how you work the ship--whether it's a tall ship or a schooner or a ship of war, or whatever--and the sea together. They have to live together. You have to see the ship moving and the water reacting. You have to gauge the wind and pay attention to the light.

In 1968, fresh from a trip to the Oregon Coast, Vickery painted several seascapes that became best-selling prints: "Sun and Surf," "Sea Witch," and "Ocean Drama." "All have sold out," says Bert Jacobs (owner of The Clipper Ship Gallery). "Those that are around (in owners' hands) have gone up 10 times in price." Frost and Reed, top printmakers in London, England, printed the set, and they were best sellers there.

-- *Chicago Tribune*, July 20, 1986

In an earlier stage of your career, did you have models, or were there people who influenced you?

152   The Creative Spirit

I used to haunt the galleries. This started right after I completed high school. I got hooked on seascapes but had to work on them for years before they started to catch on--before I really had a technique for doing them, I guess. I remember seeing marine paintings by Frederick Waugh, an American from Nantucket, Massachusetts. There were also prints by Montague Dawson, an Englishman, that I really admired. With people like that, I'd study their techniques and their use of color.

In the early years I studied at the Art Institute and the American Academy of Art, both in Chicago. But then like a lot of people I went through a period of indecision. Some of the mechanics of painting seemed kind of useless. You try to figure things out for yourself in cases like that. So I was doing different things--even doing portraits and church art. I worked in a factory, punching a time-clock, and for a while I was a surveyor's assistant.

The church art was pot-boiler art? A way to keep eating?

It was. I was doing murals, Biblical scenes. I'd sit on a scaffold like Michelangelo to work on sanctuary ceilings. Sometimes I was pretty high up, pretty close to heaven. But there was some decorative art in the churches too.

In one church in Waterloo, Iowa, I tried a portrait of the Deity. The monsignor wasn't impressed with that, so I painted the God figure out and replaced it with some doves and other symbolic things. All that seemed like adventurous stuff. I was experimenting and being a little irreverent, I guess.

You did one later of Christ walking on the water.

Yes, that's "Jesus Walking on the Sea." There's a story behind that one. I did it after my twin sister, Florence, died of cancer. That was in 1973. I painted "Jesus Walking on the Sea" in her memory, kind of a tribute, I guess. I gave the original to the ministry of a nursing home in La Grange, Illinois, where I live.

Copies of that painting have been consistent best-sellers. So has another religious painting that I titled, "No Greater Love," which shows the empty cross in the rain.

Quite a contrast to the sea-battle scenes you've done.

Visited by history: In "Farewell Chicago," a 22 x 30-inch oil on canvas, Vickery recalls the 1976 visit to the Windy City by the Norwegian "tall ship" *Christian Radich*. The ship was on the way back to Norway after hosting thousands of visitors.

"Come, be not afraid, it is I." In "Jesus Walking on the Sea," Vickery captures a solumn moment in the biblical account of the Lord's life on earth. The painting has been sold in sizes as large as 28 x 38 inches.

Against a background of gauzy clouds and a rocky Great Lakes bluff, lake waves crash on rocks and gulls provide an appreciative audience. "Song of the Sea" is considered by many the finest of Vickery's seascapes.

154   The Creative Spirit

I've got to move around even though I'm pretty much committed to seascapes. I've even done some flowers in recent years. But I get really involved in historic scenes. It's been fascinating to work on the *Victory*, the ship that Admiral Horatio Nelson commanded in the Battle of Trafalgar in 1805. One that I did of the *Victory* was called "Peace before the Storm." A second one was "Storm of Battle." I had an ancestor who was a midshipman at Trafalgar, so that comes pretty close to home.

Where do you do most of your work?

I have a studio in La Grange. I work there a lot. But I also like to go out to Indiana to work. I can get close to nature there. Lake Michigan is a short distance away. I've seen it in all its moods.

One thing I've always avoided. I never use a camera. I don't even own one. I work from models of ships, especially tall ships, and reference paintings. There seems to me to be much more truth in what the eye sees than what the camera sees. Critically, for me, the camera takes the air out of shadows. Everything in shadow goes dead black. I think it can mislead someone who's trying to do a painting. A lot of beginning painters rely too heavily on the camera and it sometimes ruins their work. But granted, used right it can record a lot of detail.

Not having a camera, I make a lot of notes. Sketches. If the weather's too wild, I may make pencil drawings.

Worthy marine artists have been scarce... In the 19th Century, "There were a number, but they were stiff. There wasn't a sense of water. They'd taken a boat and stuck it on the water. The waves are up and down. I don't know what caused the beginning of realism. Winslow Homer began breaking the tyranny of the brown gravy school."

-- Chicago Tribune, July 20, 1986

You've visited both the east and west coasts, studying the oceans?

I've been to both coasts a number of times. I've seen the Atlantic Ocean so rough it looked like the waves were 20 and 30 feet high. I've seen the streets running with salt water in some eastern towns. A storm threw boats way up on the shore in Gloucester, Massachusetts. We

"After a lazy hot summer the sun moves southward. The breezes change into winds, the temperatures fall." So reads the description of "Joy of Winter," a Charles Vickery oil that shows the artist in a different, winter-landscape mood.

have bad storms on the Great Lakes, but they don't often hurl trees or branches into motel windows.

I took a trip on a Turkish freighter once and made endless notes and sketches. It was really amazing the way the ocean provided different seas all the time.

Can you put a number to the paintings you've done? Your numbered prints total more than 100, don't they?

I've done about 100 limited edition prints. Paintings in all? I'd have to guess. Maybe 3,000 to 4,000 .

And still going strong?

I can't stop now.

Does it bother you that people refer to you as "the seascape artist from a land-locked suburb?"

Not at all. I don't have to go far to find water.

156   The Creative Spirit

That painting in a gallery display window in the '50s--did it keep you from missing your calling?

I guess in a way it did. After the newspaper items came out, I came back here and started working more seriously on water scenes. That painting that was in the show-window was a seascape, open water with the light of the sun glinting off the crests of the waves.

The critic mentioned me in that item as a budding Winslow Homer. I really appreciated that. I hoped she was right.

IV

Asleep in the Deep:
The Edmund Fitzgerald

I shall go back again to the bleak shore
And build a little shanty on the sand,
In such a way that the extremest band
Of brittle seaweed will escape my door
But by a yard or two; and nevermore
Shall I return to take you by the hand...

> -- From "I Shall Go Back Again
> to the Bleak Shore," Edna
> St. Vincent Millay

BEYOND THE CALL OF DUTY

"Presented to the officers and men of the Ford Motor Company vessel *William Clay Ford*, by the Great Lakes Maritime Institute, in appreciative recognition of their heroism.

"On the night of November 10-11, 1975, these men voluntarily left a safe harbor to face the dangers of gale-force winds and vicious seas, in the blackness of a storm which had already claimed as a victim the steamer *Edmund Fitzgerald*, to search for possible survivors of that disaster, exemplifying the finest traditions of the maritime profession."

158   Asleep in the Deep

Officers
Captain Donald Erickson, Master

Taylor Larson   Elmer Dunn   Dale Lindstrom

Roy Bottrell, Chief Engineer
Reed Clark   Charles Holcomb   Paul Hanket   Warren Benson

Crew

Ahmed B. Ali	Mosaed Ali	Robert Bellmore
Robert Byl	Fred Carroll	Antonio Eguizabal
Patrick Field	Shirley Fralbion	Larry Israel
Rowland Kennett	Jerrold McCart	Robert McClain
Mason Nasser	Walfrid Popp	Ahmed Saleh
Kenneth Scott	John Szaflarski	James Trevor

Charles Vaselopulis   Michael Zielinski

Presented to this ship at Detroit, Michigan, January 27, 1978

-- Plaque on display in the Dossin Great Lakes
Museum, Belle Isle, Detroit

DONALD E. ERICKSON

(1996)

If there are defining moments in our lives--moments in which we project our images sharply against the horizon of time--Capt. Donald E. Erickson experienced his on November 10, 1975. As master of the bulk carrier William Clay Ford, *property of the Ford Motor Company, Captain Erickson had anchored that afternoon in Whitefish Bay, not far from the old Coast Guard Station at Whitefish Point. In that relatively sheltered spot Captain Erickson and his 28-man crew were riding out one of the fiercest storms ever to hit Lake Superior. It promised to be a night for cards and sea-talk. But somewhere around 9:00 p.m. the* Ford *received a call from the Coast Guard station at Sault Ste. Marie. Could the* Ford *head out into Lake Superior to search for the crew members of another "laker" that had disappeared in the howling winds and 30-foot waves on the open lake?*

The Ford *could. Ponderously, as befitted her 647-foot length, the ship made a long turn and started out. The search went on all night without result: no survivors, no debris, nothing. Twenty-one years later Captain Erickson's memories are fresh...*

* * *

Capt. Donald E. Erickson. (Photo: David C. Coates, *Detroit News)*

We were comin' up and we were heading for Duluth, Minnesota. We generally went to Duluth to pick up pellets (taconite) and take them back to the Rouge. We were up on the River (St. Marys) that day. It was really windy, and was getting worse. We got up through the locks, and when you make it through the locks you figure it's pretty good, you know, especially when it's windy like that, and you're light (not loaded). We got up in Whitefish Bay, and the weather was really bad. So we went over to anchor under the Point--under Whitefish Point. We were pretty close to the Point. This would have been around 4:00 o'clock.

And you were getting the weather reports, of course.

Yeah, I always watched the weather. So we're anchored up there, and we're sitting around in the pilothouse. We figured we didn't have to go to bed right away because we were there for the night; we'd have

160   Asleep in the Deep

all night to sleep. So we're listening to the radio there in the pilothouse, talking, and we're pickin' up these conversations. There were people out on the lake, and we wanted to see how the weather was, to see if we could proceed on up.

We heard the *Fitzgerald* and the *(Arthur M.) Anderson* talking. I knew both of the skippers, McSorley and Cooper. I knew the mates too--in fact, they had a wiper named McClellan. His father, Gordon McClellan, was my first mate at one time. Anyway, we're sitting there, listening to them talking. This would have been right after we anchored. We had been listening earlier, but maybe not to them. Anyway, we went back to eat--the dining room was back in the after-end--and after that I went back to the pilothouse and heard them talking. We heard the *Anderson* out there trying to get hold of the Coast Guard. He was saying there's something wrong with the *Fitzgerald.*

This was about 8:30?

No, it was before that, I think. It happened about 7:10 in the evening--that's when the *Fitz* went down. We listened to Bernie (Cooper) trying to get hold of the Coast Guard down in the Sault. Actually the Coast Guard was more interested in a 16-foot aluminum boat that was overdue. They didn't think about the *Fitzgerald* too much. They kept this conversation going for awhile, then Bernie called me and asked if I had seen any boats coming around the Point. I told him no, we had been sittin' there and there was nothing comin' down downbound.

You know, you keep track of all the friends of yours that you've got out there. So after a while, the Coast Guard started figuring that something wasn't right out there. They started askin' a lot of the boats that were in the Bay that night if they would go out and look. So, everybody said no. They said the weather was too bad out there. I said no, and also that I had anchored there in the first place because I thought the weather was too bad.

Bernie's still comin' down, and he gets down to the Point. The Coast Guard is asking him at this time to go out and look. He wasn't too happy about that. He said he didn't want to go out there alone--he had just come out of that. There's bad seas out there. I went down to my room and started figuring: somebody's got to go out there. You've really got to go out there. What happened is, all these guys are friends, you know, back and forth. They're ship masters, they belong to the (International) Ship Master's Association. Then I figured, If my son was out there, wouldn't I be ticked off if nobody came out there to look for him? There's all these friends, and they don't go out to look for him.

By this time you knew about the topside damage on the Fitz *obviously.*

Oh sure. By this time we were sure that the *Fitzgerald* had sunk. So I figured, we've got to go out there. So we picked up the anchor. This would be close to 9:30, 10:00 o'clock. So we picked up the anchor, and it's a little tricky getting around the Point--when the wind's blowing you get a big backset on the water. You've got to head back down into Whitefish Bay and then head back up. You roll really bad--you can't get close to that Point because you get a confused sea. The sea is comin' down from the northwest, and then it hits that Point and bounces back off it. No matter what you do, you're gonna really roll.

About this time, when I decided to get under way, the guy in the *Hilda Marjanne* decided he's going to come out too. We went down and around, so we could head back up and go over that spot where Bernie said it probably happened. We got over there after rollin' pretty bad, and headed that way, and at the Point the ship handled pretty good. It didn't roll anymore; we were pitching into it. And the *Hilda Marjanne*, he came around--actually he came around too close to the Point. And he got a real bangin' out of it. He got into that confused sea, I think, and he decided he couldn't make it. He turned around and went back and anchored again.

That went on all night 'til dawn, around 5:00 a.m.?

No, not at that time of year. It's close to 7:00. We weren't able to really criss-cross over the place where she went down, not very much. So after the wind started to go down the Coast Guard calls and says we did as much as we could, and they released us. They said the other guys would take over for us. Then Bernie turned around and went back down into Whitefish. He was downbound anyway.

Did you find any debris--anything at all?

162   Asleep in the Deep

No, we didn't see *anything*--nothin'. We were right over the spot where the *Fitzgerald* went down too. Bernie was maybe half a mile to the north of me. Then they had the Coast Guard helicopters and a C-130 out there. They were flying back and forth, and I called the Coast Guard and said, "Well, okay, we're out here, what happens if we find something?" (Chuckles.) The seas are runnin' 30 feet out there. "What do we do if we find something?" Well, the Coast Guard says, the helicopters can hover over it and maybe do something to help. It would have been pretty near impossible--we could find the spot where the *Fitz* went down, but to maneuver around and pick up somebody would have been pretty tough, you know.

About November 10th, had you had clear warnings about a storm brewing?

Oh absolutely. That's why we went in to anchor. But at that time of year, you have storms movin' across all the time. Then comin' up Huron, and the Soo, you watch what's comin' across Lake Superior. Then lots of times there's a storm comin' from the north, you just go around the north shore and stay in the lee. If it's from the south, you go down the south shore. In the lee you can get a good run, you know --five miles off the beach.

Then later we could hear the talk between the *Fitzgerald* and Cooper. And between Cooper and the Coast Guard. That's all on tape. A lot of people think this tape is all that was said out there that night. But you have a whole bunch of different channels out there. I think that was Channel 12 that was taped. That's the Coast Guard channel. All the conversations on 6, and 8, and different channels like that are not on that tape. So you can't go by that tape because there was a lot said that wasn't on it. The only thing on that tape is when they were talking to the Sault controller.

About 4:00 or 4:10 in the afternoon, there was a report from McSorley that he had lost his radar. That would cripple him?

Absolutely. The thing about radars, and this other stuff, they are aids to navigation. They are not the whole thing. So you better know at any time where you are--and could do without 'em. When your radars are out, it makes it that much tougher, but you'd better be able to navigate without them. It wasn't too many years ago that they didn't have radars.

And they still got there--navigated.

Not all of them got there, but it makes it easier, that's all.

There was a question from the Fitzgerald *about 5:00--"Will I clear the target?"*

Yeah, well there were two other ships comin' up at that time --the *Nanfri* and the *Benfri*. They were comin' up around the Point just before the *Fitzgerald* sank. They had to be clear of the Point by some distance. Like I said, you get a confused sea around there. I think they were smart enough to know that they can't go that close to it. So that's why, when they're upbound they're usually a mile and a half off that Point, which is pretty close. And that's upbound. When you have bad weather, you might be six miles off it. Maybe more than that even. The same thing--these confused seas--happens anywhere. You get a northwest wind off of Copper Harbor, you have the same problem up there.

Another problem that night was that the radio beacon at Whitefish Point was out. The light was workin', but the radio beacon was out.

Did you have any rest during the night of the 10th to the 11th of November, or was it all work through the night?

When we got around Keweenaw, the Point there, I got a little sleep. Before that, no, there was no sleepin', you're just out there. In fact everybody on our ship was out there lookin'. Everybody! There was nobody that wasn't lookin'. We were in the portholes, or they were lookin' out the portholes, whatever. They were tryin' to find somebody, to do some good out there.

We were travelin' empty, with ballast of course. You've got to have ballast. We couldn't carry as much cargo as the *Fitzgerald*, she could take about 5,000 tons more. She was a little longer and a little wider. She carried about 25,000, someplace in that area. We could take about 20,000.

Was there a point at which there was no hope of finding survivors-- there had to be at some point.

164   Asleep in the Deep

Yeah, we passed over that area, but we really didn't know it exactly at the time--the *Anderson* had just guessed where it would be. We did pass over the spot, but toward morning we figured that it would be just a miracle if anybody had gotten off. We were havin' snow squalls during the night. When you weren't in a snow squall you could see 20 miles. Then you'd get a squall through there and you couldn't see the other end of the ship at times. That went on most of the night, until close to the morning. We didn't take any damage though. I wouldn't have damaged that ship, any ship, not if I could help it..

We did locate the spot from what the *Anderson* told us. We went right over it. We didn't know it then, but later when they located the *Fitz*, they marked the spot and we had gone right over it. We didn't travel a great distance. Like I said, we were checked down. We had all the radars going, and the searchlights, everything. We were really checked down as low as we could when we got into that area, so that we could do the most good looking for people.

When the Coast Guard released us, we went on to Duluth. The sea was abating at that time. We went on, but when we went around the (Keweenaw) Point, Copper Harbor and Eagle Harbor, it was pretty near calm. By the time we got up there, you know, it's about 12, 14 hours later. Then when we got up to Duluth, the wind was blowin' so bad that we couldn't get into Duluth. And there's only maybe two other times in all the time I've sailed that I couldn't get into Duluth. We had run into another storm, a different one.

That's a relatively protected harbor, isn't it?

Oh yeah, you can go in there full speed. In fact I used to do that all the time. You have to, in fact, because it's a narrow, long opening and you've got to get through there before you set down.

I talked to Cooper, I think the next trip. We met in Duluth. We sat up there in a guard shack at the dock and we talked for a long time. He's dead now, you know.

He died two, maybe three years ago at the most.

He was in the NTSB (National Transportation Safety Board) and Coast Guard hearings, wasn't he?

Yeah, he was. I was too. In fact the NTSB took a trip a year later down the lake with us. And we had pretty near the same storm conditions. In fact, (chuckles), we went north of Isle Royale instead of south, and this guy from the Transportation Board says, "Let's not make it exactly like they did it last November." Yeah, he said that, Let's not go down to the bottom, let's stay up on top. (Laughter.) That was about a year after the *Fitzgerald* sank.

Did you follow the later investigations?

Oh yeah, they came down and interviewed us. Then--have you ever seen a 3-D picture? (Yes.) These were in three dimensions, and you had to wear the glasses to see 'em, you know? We had to look at them, I think it was in Ann Arbor or one of the universities. They had all kinds of experts there, from the NTSB. Then they had this guy from Michigan Tech, and a few others who knew about boats to go over these pictures. Actually, some of these people didn't know about boats and I think that's why they had me there. I was to tell 'em what they were looking at when they'd flash a picture up on the screen. They showed the top of the pilothouse and the windows inside the pilothouse.

Cooper maintained later that McSorley had gone too close to the reefs off Caribou Island. Would you agree with that?

When I talked to Bernie, he said that at 4:00 o'clock in the afternoon, when he was up in the *(Anderson's)* pilothouse, following the *Fitzgerald* down, he said to his mate, "Look, he's too close in to the island. We're not going in that close," and he said to the mate, "You keep 'er further out." So he gave the mate a certain distance--I forget what it was. He thought that shoal sticks out too far to be safe. This was about 4:00 o'clock in the afternoon, and the watch changes, you know? Especially in bad weather like that, a good skipper is up there when they change watches. Then you've got the continuity goin' from what one's doin' to the next one.

There was also a contention that they couldn't have lost a fence railing if they hadn't hit a reef--that that caused a buckling or something like that. That possible?

Yeah, it is.

Also, the government report says that the Fitzgerald *had no sounding tube or other device that would show flooding in the hold. Is that normal?*

That's right, she didn't have one. But there wouldn't be any sounding device in the hold. See, they're all double-hulled. So if you holed your outside hull, it would indicate on your gauges that you were taking on water. But if it got into the cargo hold itself, you have no gauges there. You could only tell if it was leaking into the tanks-- inside the double hull. Maybe he had nine tanks on each side. They're divided in the middle. They go the whole length of the ship. Theoretically, if you don't have iron ore, if you're not loaded, you'd have no problem staying afloat if your inner cargo tanks held. That's where you put your ballast water.

So the Fitzgerald *had to be losing buoyancy.*

Yeah. But I have no doubt that McSorley thought--he was a good skipper--he could get down into Whitefish Bay and get up close to the beach there. But when you're out there, and you see the seas runnin' like that, you can't really tell how deep you're gettin' in the water. At

The ore carrier *William Clay Ford* had an overall length of 647 feet and a carrying capacity of 20,300 tons. The Ford Motor Company ship was built in 1953.

night-time especially. You can't judge, there's nothin' to see.

McSorley was using old charts apparently. Was there a chance that they were really out of date as far as the shoals were concerned?

The Canadians had charted it. But that shoal was on American charts too. It's very possible he had American charts. And I don't think the charts have changed any, in that area, since the *Fitzgerald* was lost. Six-fathom shoal is still shown there. You could get a new chart today, and the shoal would still be listed. It was charted there, that shoal, but it may be that he got in too close. It might be that the shoal went out farther than the chart said, but I don't think so. He could have gone too close--it's awful easy to happen, you know.

Do you think the Fitzgerald *had any structural problems?*

No. What I would say, knowing the ships and how they were built and that, I'd say that the sea itself didn't sink that ship. It had something wrong with it--like he hit bottom. But it could have been something else; I have no idea what it could have been. I have to figure the way that Bernie Cooper figured--that he got in too close to the shore. And the shoaling would have caused the flooding.

According to one theory, they hit a wave, and everything shifted toward the front, the bow.

No, that couldn't happen. He may have hit at the forward end (on the reef), and water kept comin' in. That would put the forward end down. Then it would have gone deeper and deeper. With a hole in the hull, water could have kept on comin' in. And when the sea is runnin' like that, if you've got a breach in it, you've got a week spot. It could open up more. In fact, that National Transportation Safety Board, when they put it on a scale, with their ship models and tanks, and stuff like that, they found that it was going 41 miles an hour when it hit the bottom. And that's why it was buried 22 feet into the mud. If you've seen pictures of the bow, you can see it's buried up to the draft marks at 22 feet, so it had to hit pretty hard.

There was an earlier theory--I think it's been discredited now--that it broke up on the surface.

Well, I don't think that's the way it happened. But funny things happen out there. It could have broken up some way or other. Like the *Daniel J. Morrell*, when it sank, they found the stern about five miles away from the bow. She broke up on top.

There was an NTSB report on that loss. They figured that the water in the cargo hold was sloshing. Those old boats didn't have ballast tanks that were very big. When they had bad weather, and had to put ballast in, they just put it in the cargo hold. Then you've got free water in the cargo hold. A big area of free water. That water rolls from side to side. The water's goin' one way and the boat's goin' another way.

There had been a load line change not long before November 10, 1975. Would the Fitzgerald *possibly have been overloaded in light of that change--that change in the winter load line requirement?*

I don't think so. No. Those boats are built in such a way--the load line is higher than you go down the Soo River anyway. These 1,000-footers, that's why they get their real good cargoes out of Escanaba to South Chicago. They don't have to go through the locks. And they don't have to go through the Soo River. The controlling factor there, really, is the Vidal Shoals, which is just above the Soo Locks. You wouldn't have been able to load the boats down to the marks anyway. No, I don't think she was overloaded.

Can you give us some details on the William Clay Ford?

We had a crew of 29. I was part of the 29. You know, one thing about it is, the *William Clay Ford* was Hull No. 300 out of Great Lakes Engineering Works. That's on the Rouge River. The *Fitzgerald* was Hull No. 301. The *Fitz* was the next ship built by the Engineering Works.

The *William Clay Ford* was 647 feet, at that time. I think the ships built at the time followed the same pattern. The *Anderson*, the *Clark*, the *Calloway*. The *Green*, the *William Clay Ford*. The *Fitzgerald*, the *Arthur B. Homer*, I think all those ships were basically the same and that the *Fitzgerald* and the *Homer* and I think one other that came out-- I think they just lengthened them a little bit. They made them five feet wider too. They were 75 (foot beam) and we were 70. The *Anderson* was an exact replica of the *William Clay Ford*.

The *William Clay Ford* was completed in '53. There were four years between her and the *Fitzgerald*. Now, see, I was the first one to go and live on the *Ford*. I was second mate when it was built. I came out with it. I took it out of the shipyard. She was built in '52 and came out in August of '53. She's been scrapped now. They lengthened it in--oh, '79 I think it was. They didn't put an unloading boom on it. And there are only one or two ships on the American side now that haven't got booms on board. For carrying iron ore, there's no rigs to unload them any more. They're all self-unloaders. At that time Ford bought the *Edward B. Green* and the *Walter A. Sterling* for less money than it would have cost them to put a boom on the *William Clay Ford*. They got two ships--the *Sterling* was bigger, they could put more cargo in the *Sterling*; the *Green* was the same class as the *William Clay Ford*.

We used to come in the Rouge River, and they had their own docks, and they had unloading rigs and stuff like that. They figured they would keep them that way, but then all the ships got their own booms. Then they lengthened the *Ford* in '79. They added 120 feet. I think it was '79--you'd have to check that in the books. Then they stopped runnin' her in '84. Then she sat there in the Rouge for a year or two, and they took her down to Canada and scrapped her

I was in the maritime service 45 years--25 years as a captain. I was captain on the *William Clay Ford* from '64 to '84. I had the *Henry Ford II* from '62 to '64.

Did you carry different cargoes in the William Clay Ford*?*

Yeah, we were up on the St. Lawrence Seaway, and the Gulf of St. Lawrence, carrying coal and limestone. Then taconite, but years ago it was red ore. Our home port was listed as Dearborn, Michigan. See, the Rouge plant (of the Ford Motor Company) is in Dearborn.

There was one other question about the afternoon of the tenth of November. Captain Woodard was on the Avafors, *and he heard Captain McSorley say no one should go out on deck. Would that be normal?*

Yes. That's Sid Woodard. He's dead now, but he was a good friend of mine too. He was a pilot. But any time you have seas runnin' over the deck, you pass the word and let everybody know--see, you can go any place on that ship on the inside. You don't have to go outside.

170   Asleep in the Deep

Any time you've got a sea runnin' over, even if it's not a bad sea, it could knock you down. Even if it didn't wash you over, it could knock you down and break an arm or something. So that would be a normal procedure--you tell them that nobody's to go out on deck. We had boarding seas while we were searching for survivors. But we were light, see; we were a lot higher than they were. But we still had sea comin' up there.

Changing the subject, you've been to the services at Mariners' Church for some years?

Yes, ever since I retired--since 1986. I don't think I missed one since I retired. Father Ingalls and I are good friends.

Do you have future plans, or are you taking it easy now?

Well, I'm active in the Propeller Club and the Ship Masters, and different things like that. My wife, Joyce, and I have a place on the Upper Peninsula, on Lake Superior. I have a cabin up there. And I've got a boat. I take my boat up there. It's a 27-foot Rinker. I take it out on Lake Superior. The cabin is half-way between Houghton and Marquette. That's about 200 miles west of Whitefish Point, just north of L'Anse on Huron Bay. The Huron Islands are there, just east of the Keweenaw Peninsula.

It's a great place.

JIMMIE H. HOBAUGH

(1996)

The 60,000-plus visitors who pass through the museum ship S.S. Valley Camp *each year don't see the ghosts that wander the gangways. But Capt. Jimmie H. Hobaugh does. They're the ghosts of his memories from a long and distinguished career with the U.S. Coast Guard. As executive director of Le Sault de Ste. Marie Historic Sites, Inc., Hobaugh finds reminders on the ship of his 37 years with the Coast Guard in almost every exhibit. Less reminiscent is the other historic site overseen by Le Sault: the Tower of History, a 210-foot column with a bird's-eye view of Sault Ste. Marie, the St. Marys River, and Canada across the way.*

The memories emerge from display items like lighthouse lenses, old buoy lanterns, bells, and gongs. "We've also got a 36-foot motor lifeboat exactly like the one I ran off the coast of Maine in the '50s," recalls Hobaugh. But the most poignant exhibits of all are the two lifeboats from the S.S. Edmund Fitzgerald, *the laker that sank in a Lake Superior storm in November, 1975. Jimmie Hobaugh was commanding officer of the Coast Guard buoy tender* Woodrush *that day. Docked with his ship in Duluth, Minnesota, he received a call to make haste over the 200-plus miles to the disaster scene to look for survivors...*

* * *

You were in Duluth in the 1970s.

I was. I became Coast Guard Group Commander in Duluth in 1972. Also captain of the Port of Duluth. The group title included service as captain or the port. The group area ran from Baraga (Michigan) to the North Dakota border, and from an east-west line at Minneapolis all the way to the Canadian border. So it included about half of Lake Superior and most of the land mass in that area. I was in that assignment three years. In '75 I got transferred to the tender *Woodrush*.

Pure coincidence in view of what happened?

Yes. I commanded the *Woodrush* from July of '75 to August of '77. A two-year tour. Our home port was Duluth. We didn't have many emergencies until November. Then we did the search for the *Edmund Fitzgerald*. That was the most traumatic and dramatic of my career. It was futile. But it was probably the fastest scramble we ever made.

I think we got the call around 10:00 p.m. (November 10, 1975). We sailed in an hour and 14 minutes, when normally we were on six-hour standby. We didn't really have to sail for six hours, but we got out fast. We got all hands on board except one cook. As we went past the Duluth piers, he was standing there, waving, wanting us to pick him up. But you couldn't do that. That's probably the most critical, or urgent, thing that happened to us.

You're traveling how far?

It's about 265 miles, somewhere in there. We sailed fast even though we were going to have to sail for 24 hours--and actually it took us 22 hours to get to the site where the *Fitzgerald* went down. It's clear across Lake Superior to Whitefish Point, really. Let me do some quick figuring here. Twelve knots times 22 hours. That was about the speed and the time.

Capt. Jimmie H. Hobaugh.

The weather was worse than I had ever seen it, even in a North Atlantic or Pacific storm. You know what happens in the Great Lakes. You get a chop instead of a rolling sea, like you'd get on the ocean. The things that I remember were the chop, the 25 to 30-foot seas. We were out there getting beat to death--the *Woodrush* is 180 feet long-- but still we had to be out there, trying.

You stayed there for a while?

We were out there for five days. By then we knew it was futile.

And then we went back in April and May, the next year, and took actual photographs. That was from the lst day of April to the 10th of May, '76.

That second trip we had a cable-controlled underwater recovery vehicle--C-CURV. You may remember the hydrogen bomb that was lost off Spain, in the Mediterranean. They used this same piece of gear to find that bomb. It had video cameras and we could take pictures. It had an arm that we could use--but it was controlled from inside our ship. You could swim that thing around anywhere you wanted it to go. It wasn't like the equipment that they use now. It was a primitive version of the new stuff.

There have been numbers of theories on the cause of the loss. Do you have one?

I really don't. I believe it was a combination of things. I think it plunged, bow first. That seems obvious. Keep in mind that it was a 729-foot ship, and was in 530 feet of water, so when the bow was on the bottom, the stern would still be on the surface. It dove to the bottom, and broke up the way it did, and part of it is upside down--and no one knows when the propeller stopped turning. And if you dive your finger into a table top, let's say at a 35-degree angle, you'll see what happens to your finger. That's basically what she did.

You were on the scene for a while?

The storm went on for three or four days. That's my memory of it, and it brought snow, and those high waves. We went out later on-- we came into Sault Ste. Marie and loaded up a side-scan sonar and went back out and pinpointed the actual location.

Within days after the loss?

Yes. It was lost on the 10th. We searched I think until the 15th. And then we went back, I believe, on the 18th with the sonar. A little late we went back again and picked up a different crew--a Navy supervisor of salvage crew. Then we went out and did it again, this time with the more advanced gear. It wasn't really photographed until the next May.

We spent part of the winter preparing to go back and take pictures. We had a lot of planning. We continued operating--we broke ice all that winter. I did make a couple of trips to Cleveland and a couple of trips to San Diego to look at the gear and talk to the people who were actually going to do the photography.

The Woodrush *was an ice-breaker?*

She had an ice-breaker hull. A 180-foot buoy tender is a multi-mission vessel.

You must have had other memorable experiences in your Coast Guard career.

It's funny. Things happen in bunches. The *Fitz* seemed to precipitate some other emergencies. Not long after she went down the *Pontiac* thought she had a split in her seam. They were off Devils Island (in the Apostle Islands), and we got a call. That time we sailed in about an hour and 20 minutes. We weren't sure whether she was going to go down or not.

The *Pontiac* was a freighter, 611 feet long, with a 70-foot beam. She made it back to Duluth,

The Coast Guard Cutter *Woodrush* under power in the harbor at Duluth, Minnesota. Inset: Captain Hobaugh.

and they kind of patched her up, and she sailed down to the shipyard. There was no loss of life. There was just the fright of the crew, thinking she was going to split. Of course we're not talking about the same kind of severe weather, but it was winter. And then icing up is always frightening.

That would have been early '76?

I think so. Maybe March or early April.

You've got mementos of a lot of experiences on the Valley Camp.

I have. Some of them bring back memories of my early years as an enlisted man in the Coast Guard. Not only the lighthouse lenses, old buoy lanterns--a lot more than that. We've got a 36-foot motor lifeboat. I ran one exactly like that, up off the coast of Maine in North Atlantic storms and on searches for lobster fishermen who were lost. People would say these boats rolled over and I didn't believe it. Then it did and now I do (believe).

When you're in your 20's, remember how invincible we felt? Immortal? The idea that that boat would ever roll over on me was never a part of my thought processes. Then it happened to me in a storm. Thirty seconds feel like 100 years when you're under water and that thing's rolling. But it was one of those boats that right themselves. I wasn't in the water more than a few seconds, and I was strapped in, so I came out all right.

The Coast Guard background must help you in this job, running the Valley Camp, *the Tower of History, all that.*

I think so. We have a great crew here, about 20 people. We get into local history in all kinds of ways. The Soo Locks are three, four blocks from us. And the old Fort Brady is near there. You begin the Walk of History right there. As you walk east you pass Fort Brady, what's left of it, and off to the right is the River of History Museum. That's the old courthouse, then you continue on east and pass the Coast Guard base. There are three old houses there, or four, and we're building a marina behind those. Then the *Valley Camp* is right there.

She had to be rebuilt to become a museum ship?

176   Asleep in the Deep

What we did--we cut a hole in the side so you walk right into the ship. They built a 'tween-deck, in two of the holds so far. And that 'tween-deck allows us to use the tank tops as display areas. Then the lower deck is open--we've got the 36-foot lifeboat down there. We've got a 40-foot model of the tug *Belle River*, some other things.

The *Valley Camp* could, if necessary, be turned back into a freighter. It would just be a matter of ripping out those 'tween decks, and everything else is intact, and we even retained the pieces that we cut out of the hull. All that remodeling took about a year.

Would you have a thumbnail history of the ship?

Sure. She was built in Lorain, Ohio for the Producers Steamship Company in 1917. Her original name was *Louis W. Hill*. In 1936 she was sold to the National Steel Corporation. The Wilson Marine Transit Company bought her and re-named her *Valley Camp* in 1955. Republic Steel took her over in 1957 and she sailed with their fleet until she was de-commissioned in 1966.

We have some stats on her. She's 550 feet long, with a beam of 58 feet and regularly carried a crew of 32. Empty, she weighs 11,500 tons. People coming here to visit are amazed at her size.

Bought by the Historic Sites when?

In 1968. We have here more than 100 maritime displays and artifacts connected to the area and the Great Lakes. Some of these are models and paintings. The *Edmund Fitzgerald* exhibit is one of our highlights. So are the four 1,200 gallon aquariums containing a variety of Great Lakes fish.

One other thing is that marina. We're starting construction. It'll be a 61-slip facility operated by us. It'll take boats up to 60 feet long. In the future we'll also be restoring those buildings, the historic homes. We call them Baraga, Schoolcraft, and Johnston, for their original occupants.

The homes are open to the public?

The Johnston house is. The other two aren't. Johnston was one of the original settlers here. Except for the Baraga home, the buildings are owned by the city. The Johnston house is operated by the

The museum ship SS *Valley Camp*, originally the *Louis W. Hill*, was built in 1917 for the Producers Steamship Co. The Sault de Ste. Marie Historic Sites purchased the 550-foot *Valley Camp* in 1968.

Chippewa County Historical Society. In that house you'll see some early French-style construction. It's the oldest house in town. Next to it is the Schoolcraft House, where the first Indian agent lived --Henry Rowe Schoolcraft.

You must have lived a lot of history before you got here.

That's part of Coast Guard life. In 1980 I went as commanding officer of the Coast Guard cutter *Taney*, based in Portsmouth, Virginia. I participated in the Mariel Boat Lift.

In '82 I went as chief of the Readiness and Reserve Division in Cleveland. They do all the war plans, and armament and law enforcement training. I was there for six years. We wrote the plans for what became the Coast Guard participation in Desert Storm/Desert Shield.

Speaking of Desert Storm, my son was a fighter pilot during that little war. He's now working to be an astronaut. He's in astronaut training, just beginning (in June, 1996).

178 Asleep in the Deep

You retired in '91?

Yes. We were living here in Sault Ste. Marie. The kids--three daughters and our son--were grown and gone. I actually retired, and it was the most miserable time of my life, I think. Didn't do a thing. Sat at home and felt like an old man. The best thing that happened to me was when they offered me this job.

Now we're adding exhibits, rearranging them, making them more complete. We've got all these things going on. We're even working on improvements on the *Fitzgerald* exhibit. We have those two lifeboats that were ripped off the ship. One of them was ripped right in half. We've also got a video on the wreck.

The lifeboats washed ashore on the Canadian side. The Canadians brought them back and they became part of our collection. But we're looking at possibly building a model that would show the ship on the bottom. If we do that, we'll enclose it somehow. And that takes money.

Did you ever think about the Great Lakes before you joined the Coast Guard?

Never. Never even thought about them. I was raised in Oklahoma. Now I couldn't leave the Lakes.

PROCESSIONAL HYMN 338

Eternal Father! Strong to save,
Whose arm hath bound the restless wave,
Who bidst the mighty ocean deep
Its own appointed limits keep:
O hear us when we cry to thee
For those in peril on the sea.

*--Hymn verses sung as part of
Memorial Service, Pilgrim Lutheran
Church, Superior, Wisconsin, on
November 14, 1975*

CHERYL ROZMAN

(1996)

*For 19 years Cheryl Rozman coped with her grief in dignified
privacy, mourning the father she had lost when the* Edmund Fitzgerald
*sank in Lake Superior. A veteran of some 30 years in the Great Lakes
maritime service, Ransom "Ray" Cundy had died at 53. He was a
watchman on the* Fitzgerald.

*An event occurring in 1994 roused Cheryl to a new, determined
vigilance, to a desire to be heard on the subject of the shipwreck in
which rested her father and 28 others: divers came up with photos of
a body. It became clear to Cheryl and relatives of other crew members
that unless they acted, their loved ones might never be allowed the
repose and respect that a grave is commonly accorded in civilized
communities.*

*In 1996, 21 years after her father died, Cheryl was engaged in a
campaign to restore, by legal means, the sanctity of the* Fitzgerald
gravesite. She recalls how she first learned that her father had died...

* * *

How did I hear about it? I was living with my children. I heard on
the 11:00 o'clock news, on November 10, that there was a ship missing
in Lake Superior. And they didn't give the name of the ship. Right
away I thought of my Dad, you know, and went to bed praying that it
wasn't him, that he was okay. The next morning I got my kids off to

school, and had the younger ones at home. I turned the TV on and they said on the news that the *Edmund Fitzgerald* was believed to have sunk.

My son still remembers me screaming. He was about 6 at the time. I couldn't believe it. I guess I went into like a zombie state. I remember going through the day and making some phone calls to relatives, and calling my stepmother in Superior, Wisconsin. She had heard it the night before, but hadn't wanted to worry me. And then I made plans with an aunt of mine to go down to a memorial service in--I believe it was Superior. I think it was the fourteenth.

Three or four days after the loss.

I remember being at that ceremony and shaking so bad that a man that I didn't even know slid over to me in the pew and held me, to comfort me, because my emotions were so overwhelming that...

I didn't even know whether he was there for the same reason I was, to mourn a relative. I know that the church was full of people, and they took the flowers afterward, to take on a ship out to the site (of the ship's loss). I don't remember it all--my memory was--I was really in a zombie state.

I started a scrapbook right at the time the boat went down, adding to it throughout the years, and whenever there was a mention of the *Fitzgerald* I'd cut it out and paste it in. We did get some coverage up here.

Your aunt went with you to the service?

Yes, just my Aunt Eleanor, an aunt on my mother's side, went with me. I didn't take the kids with me. I had five kids and three were in school. My baby was, well, only about 2.

There was only that memorial service at that church?

I think it was just the one service. Later I found out that Reverend Ingalls had rung the bell of his church (Mariners' Church, Detroit) 29 times when he heard of the loss of the *Fitzgerald* and her crew.

You've been to those services over the years?

I've only gone to a couple. And just in the past couple of years. It's 400 and some miles from here, I believe.

Did you have other close relatives in Gwinn?

No. At the time I was living in Copper Country. In Hubbell, in the Lake Linden area (of the Michigan Upper Peninsula). I grew up there as a child. I had some relatives there on my mother's side, but my Dad came from a small family. There was just my grandma and grampa and my Aunt Carmen and him. That's the aunt that I was telling you about, my Dad's sister; she was living in Minnesota at the time. Since then they've retired and taken on my grandfather's home, in Hubbell. She came with me to go to the service, with my Aunt Eleanor. Both aunts are deceased now.

At the time, it was such a loss... I had a hard time handling it, accepting it, for a while. I was mad at the Lord, for taking my Dad. I was mad at the lake for swallowing up the ship. I had a lot of mixed feelings for a while, for quite a while.

Your father wasn't that old when he died...

No, he was 53 years old. Relatively young. He had sailed for many years. I think it was close to 30 years. Dad joined the U.S. Marine Corps shortly after his high school graduation. He had gone in the war, and was overseas, and fought at Iwo Jima. He came back and started on the boats. He started through a friend of my grandfather's. Grandpa Cundy had a friend on a ship that used to come into Hubbell, and he had told my Dad, "When you grow up, I'll get you a job on the boats." Later on he did.

He had started with the Hanna Company as a deckhand and later went over to Oglebay-Norton.

Where are your efforts to have the Edmund Fitzgerald *established as a heritage shipwreck site? As a legal gravesite?*

We've been trying to deal with the Canadian government for a couple of years now, and we're still trying to, but we keep bumping into walls. There's been a Shipping Act, and a Heritage Act, and for a lay person it's really hard to understand.

Is it the complexity of the whole thing?

I think it's a combination of things. I don't think they've ever had anyone ask to have a shipwreck declared a gravesite--a legal gravesite-- and then to have it declared off limits. And that's what we're asking.

Ruth Hudson has been making a lot of phone calls. She's been working with the provincial government (in Toronto). But now we're told that it's a matter for the Department of Transportation, or the Coast Guard. We were just told that recently, just in the last week or so (November, 1996). We were told that one particular person would be responsible for making the decision, but now we find out different, so... We went through this before, with the removal of the bell (from the

Cheryl Rozman's personal monument to her father occupies a quiet corner of the beach at Whitefish Point, Michigan.

Edmund Fitzgerald in 1995). We finally found out how to do it. It just takes time, and we're willing to spend the time.

It's not a matter of our distance from them. Ruth spends really a good deal of time in phone calls and communicating. I try to do my part, but Ruth does much more. She's got a way with talking to people, and getting her points across. Both of us are willing to travel to Canada or anywhere else to speak to officials.

There was a precedent in Lake Superior, and an article on it...

I was quite taken, because I didn't know the Canadian government had banned diving on that ship (the *Gulinda*). If they can do it for that ship, there's no reason why they can't do it for the *Fitzgerald*. As far as the body issue, I guess there was one man lost, on that ship. And it was a diver that went down on it. It doesn't say in this article if his body was ever recovered or if it was left. I was kind of wondering about that. It doesn't really matter whether it's one body or 29. I just feel that they're gravesites, and they shouldn't be intruded upon for photos of bodies--to exploit the pictures.

I've gone to Lansing (Michigan) for hearings on legislation in Michigan, prohibiting pictures of bodies on shipwrecks. I told them down there that *Webster's Dictionary* defines a grave as a pit for a dead body. Unfortunately, the grave for my father and those 28 men with him is 530 feet deep. But it is still their grave. There are laws to protect graves and cemeteries and people in graves, and there should be laws to protect those that are in the water.

Is there a question about policing the site out there in Lake Superior?

I really don't know. It could be the cost of policing it, and then the distance (out in the lake)--there's various reasons, we've been told. I'm sure something could be worked out. There's been things worked out for others. Other ships. Ruth could probably tell you more about that. But I would certainly like to talk to the Canadian government about this other ship. We just got this (information), and we didn't know about the salvage rights, for this other ship, and we didn't know that they had forbidden diving on it. So there are a few things that we should really be asking about.

I really don't know how to take it yet. But we do intend to continue to pursue it. It's taken a couple of years, but we're going to keep on. I think we'll eventually have it declared a gravesite.

There are other articles indicating that some people have had to approach a number of Canadian government offices or agencies...

We've had that experience with the recovery of the bell. The Ministry of Culture, Recreation and Tourism was one. All that was part of the work of the (Great Lakes) Shipwreck Historical Society Expedition '95 and being able to go to the *Fitzgerald*--obtaining a license or permit. My understanding is that as part of their conditions for obtaining a license, they have a rule that no photographing of bodies is allowed.

Would you say there has been bonding among the families (of victims of the Edmund Fitzgerald *loss)?*

With Ruth and me it's been a little different. Ruth has been in touch with some of the families, whereas I had never met any until I met Ruth Hudson two years ago. I had gone to Whitefish Point. I had called Whitefish Point because my husband and I had gone there previously, on our own, on the shore. That's the nearest to where the *Fitzgerald* would be. And we had decided that we would like to go to the Canadian side, to the closest point. We went one summer day. I had called the Historical Society to find where the closest point would be. In that conversation I was told that Ruth Hudson felt the same way I did, and believed that there should be no diving on the site--and no photos taken of bodies. It should be left alone.

We did start looking up other family members. And that's when my bonding with other families started. I met so many wonderful people who share that common bond of losing a loved one.

Ransom "Ray" Cundy.

Did you visit Canada--the nearest point to the Fitzgerald *site?*

I did. It was a remote area. I remember going there, and it was real rocky and desolate. I spoke to a couple of people who had cottages and property around that area. They talked to us--one man in particular talked to (me and my husband). He mentioned something that was found a day or two after the ship was lost.

My husband and I went to Whitefish Point a few years after the *Fitzgerald* went down--my family and friends couldn't understand why I would want to go to Whitefish Point. "Why do you want to go there?" But it was just something I had to do. I felt that it was the closest point that I could go to, to feel close to my Dad. I've been drawn back there. This was before the (Shipwreck) Museum or anything was built. It's a comfort, or something that comes over you when you just sit there and think of Dad and years past.

It gives you time to think a little differently...

Yes. We can't go to a gravesite in a cemetery, and kneel, and pray, and talk to my Dad. So Whitefish Point was the place to go.

Having recovered the bell means so much. And my father and the others are sort of alive, with that bell being at the Whitefish Point Shipwreck Museum. When it's rung, it's like... they're alive. I was there at the recovery last year (in '95). That was July Fourth, that was when the bell was recovered. Then there was a ceremony in Sault Ste. Marie on the seventh. Both were experiences that one can never forget. And then there was the bonding between the family members there. We were able to have different families out there. Out on the lake first, and we were there to see the bell brought up. That was really something. It was like bringing part of them back.

The families hope the diving that's been going on, at the Fitzgerald *site, can be prevented?*

I think the majority of the relatives want diving to the *Fitzgerald* and photographing of bodies stopped. There's a small number of people who feel that they have to go down to it. But I really do think the large majority of people do respect our wishes.

Have you found other sources of comfort, or solace, that would help others--books and reading, or prayer, anything at all?

That's covering a lot. Like I said, I feel more of a bonding the last couple of years, with different families. And I've accepted my Dad's death now, throughout the years, and I'm not upset with God any more, like I was years ago. I've accepted it. I'm remarried now, for about three years.

Marriage itself would be a source of consolation, and comfort.

Yes. I met my husband maybe a year or two after Dad died. And he helped me a lot. Like I said, I hated the lake, and we lived right on

Lake Superior. Up in the Copper Country. I didn't want to go near the lake, and then we'd take rides, and my husband would edge closer and closer to the shore. I'd get very quiet, and I'd sit there and I'd be crying. He brought me more and more (in contact with the lake), and I was finally able to deal with it. I have to give him a lot of credit for helping me get through that. But it took place over a period of years...

Do you keep a journal?

Not really. Just with my scrapbooks, and my letters that I've received. For a while there, we were doing so much correspondence. I had tried starting a journal, but it just fell to the side. I was making so many calls per day, and receiving so many calls that it was really hard to do. When we were just starting this up, and then with the bell recovery, and contacting the families, and politicians, and the Canadian government and everyone, I just had no time.

The negotiations for the bell recovery took close to two years?

Well, maybe it wasn't really two years. It's just been in the last two years that all of this has taken place. It was in August that I did my first interview on any of this. That would have been '94. I've got pictures of the first time that I had gone up to Whitefish Point. But I had never spoken out on any of the dives, or anything. And I know that there had been four or five dives, where they had wanted to try to find out what had happened. When the pictures (of a body) were brought out, that's when I started speaking out. It was September 4th of '94, the first interview that I had. That was in a local paper. The *Marquette Mining Journal.*

I had called them and told them that I was very upset with what had taken place. I felt that I should speak out, and that's when Ruth and I started doing what we've been doing.

Do you feel that establishment of the shipwreck site as a legal gravesite would put closure to the long journey of the past 21 years?

To me it would be a final closure. Then my Dad could rest in peace, knowing that he'd be safe from desecration or any disturbance. That would end it all for me. But final closure--every year, in the winter, you have a sense of (the site's) being safe, not having to hear that another diver had gone down there. And looking around and digging around and taking pictures of bodies.

Then spring comes and you've got to go through that wondering. I don't think the family members should have to worry about the *Fitzgerald* and their losses. There are laws here, that if someone would go to a cemetery and disturb a tombstone, or disturb the grave itself, they could be prosecuted. That's how I feel about the grave that is the *Fitzgerald*.

With the museum as a kind of shrine, it would almost be complete...

We have the memorial at the museum now, and that's a great comfort. I can't get over the amount of people that have gone up there to show respect for the men (of the *Fitzgerald*). My husband and I put a little marker on the beach. This was last Memorial Day. It's made out of wood, with a picture of the *Fitzgerald*. It's from the cover of a magazine. I put that picture there plus the last picture taken of my father. I have the date there, with the name of the ship--the date that it went down.

We put the marker in the sand, and we dug it down deep enough so that it should hold. I put a little bouquet of flowers, artificial flowers, by it. And I took rocks, just a couple of rocks, to put in front of it. I guess that was for a little design, or whatever. And I was told by people at the museum that I should really see the memorial and the rocks that people have put in front of it. They put them there as a sign of respect. I went up there on the anniversary, on the 10th of November, and I walked down to the beach, and it just blew me away. To see the mound of rocks--it has gotten *huge*. It's just from people that go there and see that little marker. They take a rock or a stone and put it there.

My husband and I happened to be standing there, and a couple came up and asked if he would take a picture of them. They had no idea it was for my father. They saw it, and they went and got stones to put there... I think it's just great.

188   Asleep in the Deep

DEVOTION XII

No man is an iland, intire of it selfe; every man is a peece of the Continent, a part of the maine;...any mans death diminishes me, because I am involved in Mankinde; And therefore never send to know for whom the bell tolls; It tolls for thee.

-- John Donne, 1623

RICHARD W. INGALLS

(1994)

In his sacerdotal robes he looks regal, almost ethereal. The altar is his bailiwick, his country. He shares it at appropriate moments with his assistants; with the honor guard of more than 40 fully uniformed members of the International Ship Masters Association, the United States Coast Guard, and other U.S. military units; and representatives of Canadian military and police organizations. It's the 19th anniversary of the sinking of the Great Lakes freighter SS Edmund Fitzgerald, *lost with all hands on November 10, 1975. Rev. Richard W. Ingalls, rector of the Mariners' Church of Detroit, is officiating at the annual memorial service.*

A day before the service he remembers how he came to the church in 1965, how he rang the church's Brotherhood Bell 29 times on the morning of November 11, 1975, and much more...

* * *

I was called to Mariners' Church--the official day was January

14, 1965. But I had met with the trustees about four or five weeks before that, of course. The official call came in '65.

In fact I turned the call down, very definitely; and then four of the trustees waited on me, and I said I would come if there's a contract. And there was a tripartite contract, signed in Mr. (Donald) Sweeney's law offices. He had his own law firm. The three parties signed, and now the trustees have kept their word with me and with the diocese, and I have kept my word with the diocese and with the trustees. But the diocese, in what I call retrogression in church law, canon law, became more and more centralized, until today their corporate sole--which was unheard of for two hundred years in the Anglican church in this country--they thought they could just move in and take over. But the trustees never violated their sacred trust, and never amended the act of incorporation, which enabled them to fulfill the will of Julia Anderson. The will established Mariners' Church in 1842.

There were a few clergymen who would have contracts in those days. I was walking on eggshells if not land mines. So that's what I had. It was completely above-board.

Earlier, I served at St. John's Howell. And I had been on the staff at Christ Church, Dearborn, and associate at St. John's, Royal Oak (Michigan), as well. So I knew the diocese. There was no belligerency about it; I just wanted to protect myself, and protect my family, and I wanted to protect the trustees.

For seven years, '47 to '54, I was lay reader in charge of two little missions in Illinois. For seven years, while I completed my education, I also taught high school English and biology because they

Father Richard with a scale model of the *Edmund Fitzgerald*.

190   Asleep in the Deep

were very short of teachers there in 1950.

The missions were on Route 66, which has now been replaced by the new one, Route 80, going through. I took an A.B. degree at Olivet in Kankakee. Later I went to Garrett Seminary. I became a deacon in '55 and was ordained in '56. Then I had grad work at the University of the South, St. Luke's Seminary post-grad, Union Theological in New York City. These were mostly as summer courses, or seminars.

I wanted ecumenical outreach, and I've found it. The reputation of Mariners' Church has of course gone across the United States.

How do you get from infantry basic to the priesthood?

There was a handful of us in his school that had belonged to the V-5, V-12 program. They closed down that program. That was why our assistant principal, Duke Williams, and an official of the Draft Board, called us in one day, and said, "Fellas, I've got to throw you to the winds." And that's why we were taken immediately. Anyway, it was infantry basic. Then ten thousand of us 18-year-olds took advanced training at Fort Meade, Maryland, with tanks--and all of a sudden we were shipped back across the country; of course they knew then that the Battle of the Bulge was over, and we went to the 13th Replacement Depot, right outside Honolulu, near Schofield Barracks. And again a handful of us and I ended up in Fort Shafter, which was Mid-Pac headquarters. I was in the headquarters detachment under the Army Port and Service Command. Back into the Navy!

Not long ago an old buddy of mine and his wife, and my wife and I went back. And saw some of the places of 50 years ago. To Fort Shafter. And the Royal Palm Circle, where all the generals had homes. Hawaii's all different now. But there was a new building-- Richardson Hall--which was built to honor the memory of Lieutenant General Richardson, and it was magnificent.

Richardson was pilloried because he and General MacArthur didn't want to demobilize the troops. They both felt that if that were to happen, there would be a vacuum in Korea. And they hit it right on the head. I know some of my friends went back in for Korea. I talked with one of them --Kimo McVay, son of Admiral McVay, who was then Captain McVay of the cruiser *Indianapolis*. Although I refused a commission, Kimo, a fellow teenage sergeant, accepted a commission and was called back to serve in Korea in 1950.

Mariners' Church in Detroit, established under the will of Julia Ann Anderson, 1842.

A sidelight on history. The *Indianapolis* was torpedoed by a Japanese submarine on July 30, 1945 on its way to the Philippines. Three hundred and sixteen of the 1,196 crew members survived, but had to endure five days in shark-infested waters before they were rescued. A lot of people believe that Captain McVay became the Navy's scapegoat--covering the Navy's embarrassment for failing to report the ship's overdue arrival. Captain McVay survived, but was court-martialed for failing to maintain a zigzag course. That, even though there were standing orders that this tactic was not mandatory and would not have prevented the torpedo hit. Kimo has been fighting to clear his father's name. I hear from him now and then.

Can we talk a little about the Brotherhood Bell? Has it been rung for other lost ships besides the Edmund Fitzgerald?

The *Bradley*, for example (the SS *Carl Bradley*, lost in Lake Michigan in 1958). We remembered the anniversaries. You remember the *Bradley*; she was out of Port Huron, or off Port Huron. What I have done, privately, is just ring the bell and have my own prayers at the altar. And in wintertime, so what if the church isn't heated, just as it wasn't on that November morning (November 11,

192   Asleep in the Deep

1975)? I would go up for just a few minutes and have what I always considered a private prayer--I don't think the trustees even knew what I was doing, it was just part of my ministry. And that morning, when I did that on November 11, when I finished there were the media.

The sinking had been confirmed.

On November 10 we didn't have confirmation. But then it was confirmed and I rang the bell. It may have been around five-thirty or six o'clock in the morning, November 11--I don't remember. They might not have wanted to disturb me. It was really a shock. Lost with all hands, that was the thing. And by the time I got down to the church and rang the bell, it was somewhat later, maybe 9:30 or 10:00. The media descended like a flock of geese.

This is what I often refer to in the New Testament--your closet prayers become known. And that's what it amounted to. And Gordon Lightfoot read an account or two somewhere, and holed himself up and wrote that ballad, "The Wreck of the *Edmund Fitzgerald.*"

There were rumors around here the night of the 10th. It was bruited about. I remember talking with Captain (Donald E.) Erickson later--he was the skipper of the *William Clay Ford*--and he had asked his crew if they were willing to go with him on a mission, and they did. They left the safety of Whitefish Bay and went out. And I remember that later, Bob Lee, who was the curator of the Dossin (Great Lakes) Museum (Detroit) and I collaborated on the text of a plaque for Captain Erickson. When we've talked, we've always mentioned finding out that night or the next morning--I have never identified in my mind the exact time.

I call tomorrow's service the *Edmund Fitzgerald* Memorial Service No. 20. There was the first one and then 19 more is 20. Somebody corrected me and said, It's not the 20th anniversary--and I haven't called it the 20th. It's the 20th *service.*

Is there a pattern to the service? Can you describe it briefly?

Yes. It's within the context of a regular parish Eucharist, within the Octave of All Saints. And then we will have an honor guard around the model ship at the altar--the honor guard consisting of ship masters and military, mostly Coast Guard. The bell ringers are from the community at large. For the first five years we didn't want to go public here--didn't want to exploit--we always had it, we always rang the bell and mentioned the names, again within the context of the parish Eucharist. Then people from the Great Lakes community weighed on me, so I said yes, let's do it then, as long as the bell ringers are from the community at large. So we do have bell ringers.

How many?

This year there will be 58. Two for each victim of the sinking. There have been so many requests to be part of it. We can't have everyone, of course, but if there's some connection with a family, or the maritime industry, admiralty lawyers, the head of the Seaman's Union, for example. Labor and management come together. Right after that we go into the rest of the liturgy. And we do administer the sacrament of Holy Communion. The bagpipers will play--one of our choir members will sing the Lightfoot ballad, and this year there will be several members of the families present. They want to be known this year--that is, they will be seated in a reserved section of the church for the first time. I don't know how many--not for sure--I've heard from here and there, and I've said, well, come and identify yourself.

Our Brotherhood Bell is in the tower. But we will have the *Fitzgerald* Bell itself, the one that we had made, right at the bell altar. The bell ringers will ring that, and then the echo from the Brotherhood Bell in the tower. The latter is a solid parish church bell. There will be a double sound--once in the church and once in the tower.

The *Fitzgerald* Bell is portable. It's in the Julia Anderson room now, and before the memorial ceremony we will take it upstairs and put it on the altar, with the bell-pull rope on it. It has a support structure, on a base of about four inches, and there's a brass plate for each victim of the sinking underneath. It also has a suitable identifying brass plate, an ecumenical gift.

The bell ceremony falls in about the middle of the service. After the remarks, after the readings from Holy Scripture, the Epistle, the Gospel.

Who made the Edmund Fitzgerald *Bell?*

We don't know. Two of our bell ringers owned it. And they wanted me to look at it. I did, and said, Well, that should be the right size for within the church. And so they had it refurbished--and we carry something in the bulletin about it every year. Every year we have this to refresh the minds of the people who attend.

There's been some talk of a monument to the victims--actually at Whitefish Point, near the Shipwreck Museum.

I hope they do it. You remember the *Arizona* (sunk at Pearl Harbor, December, 1941). When I was there, it was submerged, but the military, even with its needs, did not bother the *Arizona*--they had a sense of decency. It's a monument now. And it's the same way with Punch Bowl theater--that was just a horrible thing when I was in Hawaii. But they've made it into a very fine cemetery now. The Punch Bowl is right in Honolulu. So this is what I hope they would do--I don't know if it's feasible, but they might put a buoy or something over the wreck to mark it. We need something, I think, to make it mindful for all of us--that here's a total loss. We could make it paradigmatic. That's what we've attempted to do here.

Members of the victims' families may make their own wishes known this weekend.

I hope so. Some years ago the owners of the Rooster Tail, somewhat of a nightclub on the river front--they have dinner groups that meet there--they were going to have a *Fitzgerald* memorial, with a man in one of those old-fashioned diving suits, and eerie sounds. A columnist for the *Detroit News* called and asked me if I was going, and I said, You must be kidding. I had never really met this man before. And I said, That would be grisly. Then he wrote a column that I've used with the families. There has always been this crass commercial approach, and that's why we didn't do it for five years here at Mariners'. To me it's a kind of grave robbing. We don't go and dig up a grave just to get publicity.

There's a Barnum and Baily hunger for things like this. We shouldn't cater to it. It's a hunger that we should let starve.

Have you gotten more interested in ships, and shipping, and things like that since coming here nearly 30 years ago?

Well, yes and no. I've grown from a basic appreciation--I was there in Honolulu, and the Army Port and Service Command, and with my work there I had an open door to naval air stations, and Pearl Harbor, and Ford Island, and all of that. In fact my immediate commanding officer, who didn't know exactly what I was doing, said once, Where have you been? Actually, it was a kind of undercover assignment.

Here I was, a punk kid, 18. I graduated from East Des Moines High School (Iowa) in June of '44 and my Army service began soon after that. I came home in August of '46. It was not quite two years. I was going to go back to Drake (University, Des Moines). I had a scholarship. But my brother was going to Olivet and I followed him there. My degree was in English and biological sciences.

You have a March service annually--the Blessing of the Fleet?

The first year I was here, when I realized that there was nothing done in the way of recognizing shipping and sailors, that's when we began our Great Lakes Memorial Service. That was '65. And that first year that we had it, we had just a handful of people. Now we have more organizations involved than we had people that first year.

That service has been filmed, publicized by *National Geographic*. We never reached for publicity, but they heard about it, and they came. It takes place here, in the church, on the second Sunday of March every year. The first time we had it, I got a parade permit, and closed off some streets. That was before the Renaissance (Center) was built. We went down, and jumped on Frank Becker's yacht, and dropped wreaths into the (Detroit) River. But it wasn't fair to anybody, as the Sunday traffic grew. The tunnel traffic has just multiplied hugely over the years. Now the service takes place in church and it's open to the public.

That Great Lakes Memorial is more what we call a morning prayer service, as opposed to Holy Communion services. The film of it has been shown on Arts and Entertainment. And public television.

The fleet of course, the one we honor, is the maritime fleet on the Great Lakes.

Did you ever see the Fitzgerald?

Yes. Before it was finished. I was in Dearborn, and I had no

196 Asleep in the Deep

Annual services commemorating the loss of the *Edmund Fitzgerald* include participation by an honor guard composed of members of a number of organizations and associations, among them the International Ship Masters Association (ISMA). Father Ingalls (in white) officiates on the altar at Mariners' Church.

idea that I'd ever come to a place like this. I knew the marine architect, Howard Varian, who was working on the *Fitzgerald*. He called me one day, and said, Would you and your sons like to come on board? We went on the *Fitzgerald* while it was being built. He pointed out some of the things that were new. That was '57, I think. It was under construction on the River Rouge. That shipyard is closed, I hear. We could see the wiring, the pumping system. The ship was massive, 729 feet, and very impressive. We could look into that great mass of space. A strange coincidence for me.

Does it seem to you, as it does to some other people, that the Fitzgerald *was born under some unlucky star?*

I look beyond to the God of Nature, of course. And there are so many coincidences. But who knows? Some say that someone died of a heart attack when the Fitzgerald was launched. But you can find something that will relate to almost anything if you're superstitious.

So I don't look on it that way. One year I think I mentioned something about that, saying that Holy Scripture says, *They were taken from us, and they seemed to die*. It's grievous to us, but they could be better off, so it could be a star-blessed ship if we have the faith that there is a better life. And those waves, cruel to us, could have been a welcome home to them.

I've mentioned that to others--that Death is the world from which no one has ever returned. But we know one has, and He's told us not to worry. And that's my faith.

You've just won a legal struggle?

Well, I knew the hierarchy was trying to prevent the revitalization of Mariners' Church. They were able to control it with benign neglect over the years, as a pigeon roost. I've lived in plaster dust every year since I've been here. And they did their best to drive us out. It seems that other churches do not want Mariners' to be reborn.

When I came here I said it wouldn't be at the whim or the desire of anyone that I'd serve here. I believed that I would serve a vision to which Julia Anderson responded--not with mere words, but with her own money. She wanted a Mariners' Church. And I'm hoping that we can be faithful to her will, we and the trustees. I said then, We

198   Asleep in the Deep

will be blessed, and we have been. Now that sounds pious, but I'm talking like a hard-bitten...(Laughter.) I'm practical too. It's been just unbelievable. I came for three years...

And stayed for 10 times that.

Yes. And I have no inclination toward retirement. I'm blessed with health. As long as the trustees want me, and feel that I'm not being a detriment to the parish life, I'll stay, *Deo volente.*

RUTH HUDSON

(1996)

She was driving to work when she heard on her car radio that an oreboat had gone down in Lake Superior. Maddeningly, the announcer broke off to read a commercial before he gave the name of the ship. When he came back on and said the ship was the Edmund Fitzgerald, *Ruth Hudson turned around and went back home, dazed, agonizing.*

Twenty-one years have passed since that nightmare Tuesday, November 11, 1975, the day Ruth learned that her only child, Bruce, 22, had perished in the cold waters off Whitefish Point, Michigan. Time has eased the anguish--to an extent. But in many ways Bruce is still there, touching her life, whispering behind the voices of his friends who even today come to visit. The friends are "40-something" now, but they can't forget any more than Ruth and her husband, Oddis, can. She remembers that the friends grew up with Bruce, went to Sunday School with him at the United Methodist Church in the family's Ohio hometown, attended classes with him at Ohio State University in

Wooster.

Her faith has been her salvation. Ruth has found the strength to become a leader of the movement to have the Fitzgerald's *last destination declared a legal gravesite. Only with that, she believes, will Bruce and his 28 shipmates be able to rest in peace, reasonably safe from looting, depredation, desecration. Only that will complete the circle of grieving, of taking farewell almost as a funeral and interment would. But not even that will close the log of her mother's sorrow, her memories...*

* * *

Do you remember how you found out about the loss of the ship?

Yes, I do. And you probably won't believe, if you haven't heard, how the families found out. I was on the way to work in my car at 7:00 o'clock on November 11th. And I heard it on my car radio.

The news came on, and they said that an ore ship sinks in Lake Superior. And naturally I thought of the *Fitzgerald*, but then I thought it couldn't be the *Fitzgerald* because it was too big of a ship, and that it was probably one of the smaller ships. And then a commercial came on. So I had to wait until they came back with the news. When they came back they said it was the *Edmund Fitzgerald* and there were no survivors.

There was nothing on the night of the 10th.

No. Of course, it went down at 7:10 in the evening. But none of the families were notified. They did say later that the news came out earlier in the Upper Peninsula. But you know as a rule they don't put things out when the families haven't been notified. But they sure did put this out without notification.

I couldn't go on to work. I turned around, and it was very difficult getting back home. I was about five miles from home.

The reports were very definite about no survivors?

Yes, they were. I can't remember everything that they said, whether there was anything about a search or that kind of thing. I kind of lost it after that, after they said no survivors. My husband was at home when I got back. I didn't know what to say when I walked in the house. Finally I just said it. We turned the radio on, and I called an engineer that we knew at the company, and he said they had been up all night. And they hoped that the antenna hadn't blown away. That was just to console me, I know.

Did you have relatives nearby, in Ohio?

Yes, my sister lives nearby, and I was able to call her, and I had brothers. My husband had relatives not far from here.

Was there a memorial service?

Yes, the ship went down on a Monday evening, and the following Sunday they started with the memorial services. We had one service at our church, United Methodist in North Olmsted. Bruce grew up in the church. That service was for Bruce only.

My husband and I were members of the congregation. Bruce had gone to that church all his teenage years. He was active in the church until he went away--until he went away to college.

What college?

He went to Ohio State in Wooster. He went one year there, and wanted to take some time off to sail. He was on the *Ashland* at the beginning. He was going to be laid off from the *Ashland*. He was painting on the *Fitzgerald*, this was in the springtime, before they fitted out. He heard them talking about there being an opening, and thought that would be great. He got the job on the *Fitzgerald*.

That was in March of 1975, and of course the *Fitzgerald* went down in November. He was on the *Fitzgerald* from March until November. That was to be their last trip (of the season).

Did you go to other memorial services or ceremonies in subsequent years?

At that time there were other families, other relatives of *Fitzgerald* victims in the area of Cleveland. And they all had memorial services. There was a service for John McCarthy; he was from Bay Village. There were actually several memorials around the country. I'm sure

Ruth Hudson and Cheryl Rozman with Canadian balladeer Gordon Lightfoot, author of "The Wreck of The *Edmund Fitzgerald*." Mr. Lightfoot took part in the July, 1995 bell ceremonies.

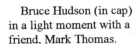

Bruce Hudson (in cap) in a light moment with a friend, Mark Thomas.

most of the families did have services for the ones they lost.

Did you hear of services at Mariner's Church early on?

When the ship went down I didn't, but I'd say within a year I did. I never could attend every year. I went to the fifth year and the 10th year. Also the 15th year. Then I attended in '94, and '95. The religious context was very helpful. It was my faith that got me through. That's really what got my husband and me through. It helped us at the time (of the sinking) and it has helped us all through the years. I believe that's the only thing that has saved us.

Could you address the question of where your effort now is--to have the site of the sinking made into a legal gravesite and placed off limits for future dives?

We are still working with Canada. We've had support letters from our congressman, and from some of our senators. There are going to be some laws passed--it's an ongoing thing for two years, that they are going to come up in Canada's House of Commons. They're coming up either this month (December, 1996) or next spring. Course, this has been going on for two years. They are trying to get this law passed, and it'll be some protection. It would not make the ship a gravesite, but it'll be some protection.

But we are working to have it made a legal gravesite, with no dives to the *Fitzgerald*. We are hoping for success, but right now we are writing letters and talking to the different departments in the Canadian government. Right now this is about where we're at--writing letters and getting support from our congressmen.

Would it be Parliament that would have the final say, or some other agency of government?

There are so many different government branches, I can't tell yet which one it will be, or if it will be federal or provincial.

The article on the *Gunilda* might be helpful. Because if they can ban the dives to a ship that that has no bodies on it, I don't know why they can't do it for the *Fitzgerald*. I just think this may be a good thing to know about. I will be bringing that up to the people that I talk to.

Are you receiving help on this?

Yes, I'm working with Cheryl Rozman. We worked with a lot of people--a lot of the families--when the bell was retrieved. There was also Janice Armagost. We try to contact and work with all the families that we can. Cheryl and I won't give up until we do find some answers.

The other families have worked with you recently...

Yes, we've been in contact with most of the families. We first started when the body (of one of the victims) was discovered--that's what made everything different. We had been quiet for 20 years.

None of the families would talk to the media. I had never talked to the media. For 20 years we had no reason to, and we just wanted to be private. But after that happened, we had to do something. We had to reach the public--it was time to speak out. That's when we started looking for the other families.

When this happened in '94, I knew two of the families, or family members. I knew Mrs. Bentsen in St. Joseph (Michigan) and Mrs. Peckol in Ashtabula, Ohio. And those were the only two that I had ever contacted through the years. We had no addresses, nothing, for anyone else. That year we found Cheryl and Janice Armagost and most of the other families. We were able to contact all the families but five.

And some lived some distance away?

Yes, they did. But everyone felt that taking pictures, and coming back, and announcing it publicly, and then selling the video with the picture in it, and selling the book with the picture--we felt that was desecrating. Everyone that we spoke to agreed that that wasn't right. That's when I started writing letters. We just felt that the ship was a gravesite, and that no one should desecrate it.

Do you think some of the families felt left out--the ones living far away?

No. David Weiss's family lives in California, and they came to the bell ceremonies (in 1995). They were there last year. They've been very supportive. And Beth McCarthy the same. Beth McCarthy has come to the ceremonies. She helped us a lot in the retrieval of the bell.

Did you have a chance to see the bell up close not long after that?

We saw it when they brought it to dockside at the Sault. We didn't get to see it close up until then.

I think we all believe that the bell is the soul of the ship. And the recovery meant so much to the families. For the bell of that ship to come back again, it was just unbelievable.

And then there was a ceremony on November 10, last year, at Whitefish Point?

204   Asleep in the Deep

That was the 20th anniversary. And last month (November, 1996) was the 21st year. I was there, and Cheryl was there--there were quite a few other family members there too. Gordon Lightfoot was there, and he doesn't appear in public very often. So that was a tribute to the families too. He has been most kind to all of us.

You know, back in the '70s there wasn't any support group. Back then we had to rely on, I'd say first our religion--our faith in God and then our family and friends.

I never really looked for help outside my friends and family. We just relied on God and my family and friends. And on Bruce's friends. His friends still come to visit. They still stay in contact.

This is 21 years later.

Yes. They were friends from school, and kids he grew up with, and being so young, he just had a lot of friends. He did plan on going back to college. The job on the ship was kind of an interim job for him.

Bruce had friends on board the Fitzgerald?

Yes. He wrote about David Weiss. In fact, that was to be their last trip of the season and they were going to drive to David's home in California. David's family lived there. He was the cadet from the Great Lakes Maritime Academy.

The two of them were going to come back through Traverse City. Bruce was going to drop David at the Academy and then come on home. We thought he would be back for Christmas, and maybe Thanksgiving. Bruce talked about John McCarthy, the first mate. I met Mr. McCarthy, in Toledo. We went there to pick Bruce up in that summer of 1975.

When did you hear the Lightfoot ballad first?

The summer of 1976. A couple of Bruce's friends came over and said, "There's something we think you should hear." And they played it. It was--well, painful and marvelous.

Have you been to Canada to talk to government officials about your efforts to create a legal gravesite?

No, not really. Cheryl and I did go to Toronto this past summer for a diving show. We talked to some people there, and they seemed as if they might be able to help. Other than that we haven't been there. We've done it all by mail and telephone. We really have to do it that way because we're not sure yet who can make a decision.

Establishment of a legal gravesite would be a kind of final act...

It would certainly help to know that our loved ones would have a grave. Knowing that no one would be going down (to the ship)--that would certainly put my mind at ease. It would just be great to know there wouldn't be any more of these intrusions on their gravesite.

Then there's the museum exhibit at Whitefish Point. It's a great comfort to us to have a place to go, a place where we can remember our loved ones, which we never had before.

Will you be going back to Whitefish Point next year?

Well, I hope to. I didn't get to go this year, but I do hope to go back next year.

Does accepting get easier with time?

I guess somewhat--it does get a little easier. But it's still just as lonely. It's just lonely without Bruce. He was the only child we had. And that makes it more difficult, On holidays it makes it very hard for us. The services have helped. They're all very appropriate and tasteful--like those at Mariners' Church.

(Note: Mrs. Hudson's husband, Oddis, passed away in January, 1997.)

THE CHANCE CONNECTION

206   Asleep in the Deep

Great Lakes Engineering Works
cordially invites you to witness
the launching of the
S.S. Edmund Fitzgerald
on Saturday, June 7ᵗʰ, 1958
at twelve o'clock noon, Eastern Standard Time
at its River Rouge, Michigan, shipyard
under construction for
The Northwestern Mutual Life Insurance Company-Owner
and
Oglebay Norton Company -
Columbia Transportation Division-Charterer

Sponsor:
Mrs. Edmund Fitzgerald

— ***Engraved invitation to the S.S Edmund Fitzgerald***
christening and launch

FRED D. LEETE III

(1996)

_____

_____

Of all the ways in which individuals and families found themselves
connected to the ore carrier S.S. Edmund Fitzgerald, *that of Capt. Fred*
D. Leete III may be the strangest.   By invitation, Captain Leete
attended the ship's christening, and the reception that followed, on
June 7, 1958.   At the time he was not only in the United States Coast
Guard; he was a seven-year veteran of the sales force of the
Northwestern Mutual Life Insurance Company, the vessel's owner.
The rest of the story spans some 38 years.   In 1959, the Edmund
Fitzgerald *took advantage of a labor strike to leave the Great Lakes*
shipping lanes and visit the Northwestern Mutual headquarters city,

Milwaukee. Fred Leete toured the ship with an estimated 26,000 others. In November, 1975 Captain Leete was in Sault Ste. Marie, Michigan taking the Coast Guard's ship master's exam when he heard the news that the Fitzgerald *had foundered in a Lake Superior gale. Twenty years later, in 1995, the diving and under-water-rescue instructor, insurance agent, maritime service captain, sometime writer, and widely honored civic activist visited the* Fitzgerald *in its submarine grave. He was one of the organizers of the Memorial Dive '95 that brought up the* Fitzgerald's *bell, the same bell he had seen, shiny and full of hope, on that long-ago June 7...*

* * *

Memorial Dive '95 must be fresh in your memory.

It is. We--Capt. Janet Provost Cummings and I--went to Whitefish Point. The first night I was up there, there's a white building beyond the gift shop; with a large room that we call the bunkroom. It's for divers--groups of divers. And since communication is bad up there, the Coast Guard has put a van there. I pulled up behind the van and got out, and introduced myself to the Coast Guard man: Where's the bunkroom around here? He says, "What did you say your name was?" I told him, and he said, "The Captain of the *Cormorant* wants you on board immediately. He's sending a launch for you." That's how they were.

This would have been about June 26 last year (1995).

Yes. You have to climb a Jacob's ladder (on the Canadian ship *Cormorant*, the dive platform for the expedition). It's high. You know, when you go aboard ship in uniform you make two salutes. You salute the colors and you salute inboard. And that's where, in ancient sailors' days, the crucifix was tied to the mast. You'd make the Sign of the Cross and then you'd salute the national colors. Anyway, you climb up that Jacob's ladder, and you're really climbing a ladder, and then you end up on your knees. A bunch of these reporters were coming aboard, and Janet and I were giving two salutes. I thought the officer of the watch would return my salute. And when Janet gave her salute 14 people returned it. That says "This gal knows where she is!" And from that point on we were treated with great deference. One man

208   Asleep in the Deep

broke loose from the gang and said, Have you eaten? We said no.
And he just started leading us to the wardroom and then down to the
galley, and he said, Do you want ham, or do you want beef, or this or
that? And he had trays, and he gave a signal to someone...

The whole experience was like that?

Yes. One of the great fortunate things that happened was that at
the last moment we got to take out Mr. (Al) Kamuda, the photographer
for the *Detroit Free Press*. His car had broken down. He had missed
the press boat. He knows Janet and me and he called to us by name as
we were going out on the Coast Guard boat. So he was able to make
that picture (of the *Edmund Fitzgerald's* bell emerging from the water).
This is the bell coming out of the water--the very moment.

We got to escort the bell to Sault Ste. Marie. The *Cormorant*
engineers fabricated a cradle to carry it. It was aboard the *Cormorant*,
then they transported the bell to the ceremony, where they transferred
it to the United States. Later the bell was polished brightly. The
archeologists were furious at us for doing that.

They took off all the encrustations.

Yes. I saw the proposal that Michigan State made out before they
worked on the bell. Their physical plant wanted to do the cleaning.
They proposed, after it had been under water for 20 years, that they
immerse it for several months in a bath of fresh water. Well, we
weren't going to let it spend several months anywhere. They cleaned
it up, and they wrote a nice article about themselves. They were on
television, scrubbing it with a toothbrush. I was up at the museum,
and I told them, Listen, I was at the launching (of the *Edmund
Fitzgerald* in 1958), and the bell was brightly polished. You can't hurt
it by polishing it brightly.

Naturally, the bell appeared in a crusty condition at the ceremony.
It wasn't touched until after it came into U.S. possession. Then it was
shipped to East Lansing. It weighs 195 pounds. I don't know what the
frame weighs. The bell is now inside the Shipwreck Museum (at
Whitefish Point). The only thing we have done is put it inside a clear
plastic case so people won't be poking at it.

When you walk into the museum it's right there. Part of the
Edmund Fitzgerald exhibit. They have the big light from Gray's Reef

Capt. Janet Provost Cummings and Capt. Fred D. Leete III provide an escort for the bell of the SS *Edmund Fitzgerald* after the recovery from Lake Superior on July 4, 1995. The bell, on the deck of the Canadian ship HMCS *Cormorant*, was on its way to a formal transfer ceremony in Sault Ste. Marie, Michigan.

(in Lake Michigan), so the bell is right there, the first thing you see when you come in. There are plans to extend, to add a *Fitzgerald* wing on the museum. They have put out some details on a new painting that's being produced by a Canadian artist, showing the two submersibles that helped recover the bell.

The bell recovery, as you know, was an all-Canadian operation. The Newtsuit came from British Columbia, the *Cormorant* came from Newfoundland. The Canadian tug *Anglian Lady* came from Soo Canada. They were thinking of something smaller, and I didn't think something smaller would be able to handle it, so I recommended Jack Purvis' vessel.

210   Asleep in the Deep

You saw the Fitzgerald *on the bottom.*

I was asked to go down in one of the submersibles for five hours. I went down in the *Pisces II*, the smaller one. This must have been in late June. Normally, the dives were three hours. But they wanted to use the one ship for lighting, and there was a slight current, and the ship was drifting away, and things were getting away. It wasn't working out right, so pilot Emory Kristof asked for an extension of time. And this has to be granted by the ship's diving officer. So we measured our oxygen, and checked the batteries, and everything was in order so we were given permission to stay for five hours. Two pilots and me.

For me it was extraordinary, naturally, because I had seen the ship *Fitzgerald* launched and then to see it on the bottom... I had seen pictures of it down below, and then to actually be there... I took some snapshots while we were in the submersible. A propeller blade. One of the crewmen. Once down there, we could see that the radars (on the *Fitzgerald*) had been made inoperative. On top of this should be the whole antenna. The rotor box had been swept away. And this is on top of the foremast, in the front of the ship. We were attempting, with a robotic arm, to hook to the crow's nest, and then pay a line out to the surface so the Newtsuit man would have a line to follow right straight down.

Did you bring back mementoes of Dive '95?

Pictures. And Captain (John) Creber presented me with a drawing that one of the crew had made of the *Cormorant*--a limited edition of the ship. We were given every privilege of the ship. Creber is called captain because he was the master of the ship even though he's a lieutenant commander in the Canadian Navy.

Have you met Bucko Teeple? He's the spiritual leader of the tribe, the Chippewa. And in a case that he had there was a 100-year-old peace pipe, a ceremonial pipe. He did the ceremony for the dead common among Native Americans. He's a grand man; he lives at the Sault in the Chippewa community there. It was a marvelous thing. I'm glad he was able to do it.

For about a year Janet and I had written literally hundreds of letters--and summing it up, we got permission from the Northwestern

211

Mutual Life Insurance Company, as owners of the ship when it sank, to remove the bell. We got Canadian government permission in the last days before the recovery, and got the Columbia Transportation Division's and the Oglebay Norton Company's approvals, as the operating arm. We went all the way to England to get an approval from Lloyd's of London. A judge studied all the letters in court. He consulted the Michigan laws, the Michigan bottomland laws and the Aboriginal Laws before approving the bell recovery.

Your work had paid off.

Yes. I've been an agent of the Northwestern Mutual Life Insurance Company since 1951--and that is what got me into the position where I could get permission from the Northwestern. Some total stranger could not have walked into the marble halls and said, "I want that bell."

Even then it was only because it was for the families. Removing the bell wasn't for any individual. We knew it was going to be difficult to get people to a spot 17 miles out, and the press from Germany, from Sweden, and other countries wanted to be there. They had to have the cameras and other gear that they carried. The (Shipwreck) Museum has only a small boat.

In that remote location there aren't a lot of boats you can go downtown and rent. So I was trying to arrange for Janet and me to get out onto the ship (*Cormorant*). I was told to call Mr. X. And I phoned Mr. X. I was told, "Fred, we can only take the important people." So, before I melted the phone lines--we were on a speaker phone--we sat there and thought for a minute: How else can we get there? Various possibilities were going through my mind. At the last moment, then, we decided to call Capt. Thomas Trosvig. He's the commander at the Sault. I called Tom, and told him I wanted a Coast Guard boat. He didn't ask me what for, when, how--he just said yes. He offered me a Bay Class cutter. To make a long story short, we went to his office, and we looked at the boats available; we decided that if we were carrying people who might slip and fall, a cushioning boat would be better than a hard boat.

Captain Trosvig was responsible for making possible the U.S. Coast Guard presence at the bell-raising. He had the foresight to see that this was a historic event. He's the one who called in the commanding officer of the lifeboat station at the Sault and said, These

212   Asleep in the Deep

people want a boat up at Whitefish Point. When do you want it? Well, we had to say July Fourth. And we're thinking, That'll be out of the question. But no, "That's fine." What time? "About 6:00 o'clock in the morning." Anyhow, the boat was launched and ready for us when we got to Whitefish at 6:00 o'clock in the morning. We were leaving the harbor with this boat when Al Kamuda hailed us. He had missed the press boat.

One thing about this Coast Guard boat: that day it must have carried 400 people. It brought out the minister who was going to do the homily. It brought out family members who wanted to come closer and touch the bell. The one museum boat broke down. These people had no other way to get there. We brought in engineers from the *Cormorant* to fix the museum boat.

What's your overall impression of the operation out there--the bell recovery operation?

It was splendid.

They needed all the dry runs, all the practices...

Absolutely. You saw the pictures of those two submersibles going down--they had to survey to find out what the possible entanglements might be. They were snaking in and out here and there--those things have skids on them, and you could snag. You're old enough to remember Ed Link--the Link Trainer. Well, after the war he went into oceanography, using these submersibles, and his own son was killed in one. The craft got tangled. There were two compartments in the submarine, and one of them was heated and one wasn't heated. And then we've talked about the rest--there is a limited time with batteries, with the air.

The Newtsuit also has limited time on the bottom at 500 feet?

There are different Newtsuits, all named after their inventor, Phil Nuytten. He has different models. He can go down 500, 1,000 or more depending on which model of Newtsuit is used. As long as he is being served by the umbilical, he would have unlimited time. On his own air I think he has 54 hours.

He did have a 100-meter suit, a 1,200-foot suit. He has a

manufacturing company, and is always making improvements and changes. The diver has what they call onboard life support for 54 hours. In other words, if he had to cut his umbilical, which he can do, then he has 54 hours. He could drop his extensive weight system, and go up to the surface. And he wouldn't be hurt, because he would not have been under pressure. He's in this one-man submarine. And he also has communication--he has single-band radio even if his umbilical isn't connected.

The account that I read did not mention any side-scan sonar as means of locating the wreck.

They did use sonar. Every fisherman who thinks he's a fisherman has one of these little hummingbird things. It's a fishfinder. The pulse goes along here, and it's showing bottom-bottom-bottom, and then boink! It shows the outline of a ship. You criss-cross the area a couple of times and throw an anchor over and you're there. It doesn't show that much shape--but of course if you happen to go along the length of a ship you'd get the main deck. To that extent you might get an outline. You have to be lucky enough to be going in that particular direction.

Another thing we did: put a transponder down so when you're on the wreck--we planted this little thing about as big as a beer can. And it sends out a signal, and you can home in on that.

You were there when they launched the Fitzgerald...

This historical note may be of interest. I was invited to the launching of the *Fitzgerald* in 1958. The invitation was signed by Mrs. Edmund Fitzgerald, Sponsor. I was also invited to the reception that followed the launching.

The reception banquet was at the Sheraton-Cadillac Hotel, Detroit. There was an interesting seating diagram. On one side it's by tables, so you know who you're sitting with, and on the other side it's alphabetically, so you know which table you're going to. So Mr. and Mrs. F. D. Leete the Third, we were at the last table, No. 60. But still we were there.

I am very unhappy with some of the television narration that says at the launching the ship broke loose. It did no such thing. It was difficult to make it go. They originally had to just keep on working

214   Asleep in the Deep

because it was married to the land. Then when it went the engineers knew how big it was and how much water it was going to displace. Then they say it went BANG into the far side--but there was a water cushion there.   And any time you get 50,000 people together, somebody's going to die of a heart attack. That had nothing to do with it. And they splice that into one of the films, and they've hardly said that when they go on--the *Fitzgerald* is the greatest ship, everybody wants to sail on it. The food was the best and so forth.

Northwestern Mutual owned it. But only once did it ever come to Milwaukee. Northwestern has an annual meeting--they don't call it a convention. The national agents, maybe 4,000--about 80 percent come and bring their wives. There was a steel strike, and Northwestern ordered the ship to Milwaukee so that all the agents can see their ship. Other companies like Metropolitan had owned ships but they'd never built them. So when they launched the *Fitzgerald*, they said, Is this a good thing?

As the ship hit the water, the *W. E. Fitzgerald*, named for Ed's father, was the first ship to give it a salute--in its 57th year of active service on the Great Lakes. Some of the accounts said Mrs. Fitzgerald had trouble breaking the champagne bottle. Well, a lot of people do. Later the *Fitzgerald* had several captains. I think the first one was Captain Larsen. Later it was (Ernest M.) McSorley in 1975.

The Fitzgerald's *visit to Milwaukee was in July, 1959?*

Yes. I don't know how many people were there to see it exactly, but 26,000 persons toured the ship.   Fifteen hundred home office employees and retirees, and the rest were members of the public. It was open to everybody. There were pictures of Ed Fitzgerald and his wife.

Ed Fitzgerald was a shy--well, I shouldn't say shy, but he was. And we got to be such great friends, and he's the president of a big company, and who am I, you know?   He was a member of the Wisconsin Marine Historical Society, and then he invited me to address it.

He didn't want the ship to be named after him. He wanted it to be known as the *Seaway*. But they finagled a board meeting when he wasn't present... There's a book you may have seen: *Five Fitzgerald Brothers--Ship Captains All*. It tells about his relatives, and of course this was back in the days of wooden ships--and what ties Janet and me

June 7, 1958: The bow of the *Edmund Fitzgerald* looms over the crowd and the ceremonial platform in the Great Lakes Engineering Works in River Rouge, Michigan. Mrs. Edmund Fitzgerald (inset) holds the champagne bottle that will make the christening ceremony official. The launch took place shortly afterward.

to the old ships is that we dive on them when we've had the good fortune to find a couple.

Did you see the ship while it was under construction?

No. Only during the last day, when they were putting up the flags and bunting and decorations.

Did you have anything to do with the Fitz *in the years in which it was riding the lakes?*

No, except to do what anybody would do with the company--to try to keep track in a way. I was much like other agents would be, and when she would set her records, and beat her records, I'd notice that. And I spend half a year at Mackinaw (City), so I'm frequently at Sault Ste. Marie, and might see her when she went through the locks--things like that.

You have your own company--Underwater Diving Technology...

Yes. We do assignments now and then. But shipwreck diving is a real hobby. One ship we found has been down since 1827. It's great to see those ships, and to think of the days of wooden ships and iron men. I don't even know how they could have built them. The planks are so wide and thick. And the great iron fittings that they used--man! Those trees grew that big, did they? You can't get your arms around the masts. It's just fascinating to dive on those ships...

One of the ships we found is the *Sandusky*. It's so old that the tiller is up on deck. But lines have been run through blocks to a standing wheel on deck. Just last week this gentleman from Detroit, a General Motors engineer, found his fourth shipwreck. In pictures you can see the spokes of the wheel--and the wheel has a drum behind it. And the rope went around that drum, and out to both sides of the ship. Both blocks are there. So that makes this just a little bit more modern than the one they found last week that just has the tiller and no wheel.

Have they identified the new discovery?

No, we don't know the name of the new ship. The location of the

Sandusky is known because when it sank the masts stood above the water and seven of the crew were clinging to the rigging. There was a big gale, and a paddlewheel ship that was in at Mackinaw City tried to save them. But a paddlewheeler in a gale is nothing to steer. And one by one they saw the seven men die.

So this is a big problem now too, because the *Fitzgerald* families want the ship designated as a grave site. No more intrusions. Then the other side will say, That's not the only ship that took lives. Well, we're trying to say, It was an American ship--can we make it a symbolic ship?

We are working for the *Fitzgerald* to be designated as a gravesite. People from the Canadian government say to us, "We can't keep you people from walking through the cemetery. And even making rubbings of headstones--that's allowed." I've got every sympathy, working with these who lost loved ones--so I don't know. We were very unhappy with one of the movies that were made. They went downtown in Toronto, to the ships that were moored there, and leased one. It never left the dock, but they leased it. And since you can't make the ship rock, you turn the camera. They did get a man who looked amazingly like McSorley. And somebody else who looked like the first mate-- maybe you've seen the film--and they threw buckets of water on the windshields. They have the men *staggering* about the bridge. I've been there--I've been in hurricanes in the North Atlantic and a ship doesn't move so rapidly (motions with hands). But they had it going that way in the movie.

Your Coast Guard experience would help you spot those things.

I was privileged to train under square canvas, and the Coast Guard has a training ship, the *Eagle*, which was built in 1936 by Hitler, in Hamburg, Germany, and named for a friend of his who was a martyr for the Nazi Party whose name was Horst Wessel. In German it was the *Segelschulschiff Horst Wessel*. We took it as a prize of war, and it's the Coast Guard Cutter *Eagle*.

You have to train a mariner to know what the wind is doing to your ship. And what the currents are doing. And they say, If you can run the Queen Mary, you can run anything smaller. That's not true. And that's why the Coast Guard Academy and the United States Naval Academy start you out sailing in 16-foot dinghies. And rowing. When I started my Coast Guard career I had two chief petty officers--a chief bo'sun's mate lifeboat man, and they don't have that rating any more. He came from the days when they rowed to the rescue. He entered the service at the age of 14 as a second-class boy. My machinist-mate-chief was a machinist mate lifeboat man in the early days when they put the first motors in the lifeboats. He was the one who told Eisenhower what boats were able to go in the invasion (of Normandy, 1944). He put a screwdriver to his ear and against the side of the engine and said, That cylinder is not gonna work tomorrow. And heartbreaking as it was for the skippers of those boats, they were not allowed to go.

Those men brought me up. The chief was always good to relieve the watch; he'd come on about 10 minutes early, And he'd smell. (Sniffs.) And he'd come into the chartroom and he'd put his finger exactly where we were. It's a different breed. We got so low on supplies one day that we pulled alongside another cutter and they threw us some food. We were on a mission and they had more food than we did, so they tossed us a dozen loaves of bread!

When did you start with the Coast Guard?

My Coast Guard career started at boot camp in Cape May, New Jersey. This gave me an opportunity to play on the Coast Guard Bears football team. I was proud to advance to the rating of Seaman. Then I became a "Mustang," an officer who has come up from the enlisted

Belatedly, two crewmen in Captain Leete's command receive medals for service and heroism in World War II. Captain Leete (center) makes the presentations.

The man and the ship: Edmund Fitzgerald leaves the ship that bore his name. A friend of Captain Leete, as chairman of the Northwestern Mutual Life Insurance Co. Mr. Fitzgerald initially resisted the proposal that the SS *Edmund Fitzgerald* receive his name.

ranks--and my Academy ring is dated 1951.

I'm staying active because I started my licensing process and became a Merchant Marine captain. The Coast Guard can name you the captain of the *Mackinaw*, or any ship. But as far as they know, you have no Merchant Marine documents. When you come out of the Coast Guard service and you want to run a ship, you need radar school--prove you can do the plotting, and they put you through an examination. And then you need firefighting school plus service time.

We've done all that, and qualified for 1,600 tons now, which is pretty darn big. You see, naval architects can do all sorts of things with a ship. And passenger compartments don't count toward tonnage. Only the cargo--and there are different kinds of tonnage. There's deadweight tonnage, and you've got gross weight tonnage, documented tonnage.

People ask me, Do I keep a log. No, I'm too busy to keep a log. Ship masters are so modest and self-effacing--they'll say, "I aimed the ship that way and it went that way." They're mindful, as I was, of the guys in the engine room. I'll give you a clue. I was in the Coast Guard so long ago that we had messmen, and steward's mates, and others who were supposed to shine my shoes and serve my soup and all this stuff.

220 Asleep in the Deep

Two of them--one was Hughes and one was Baker, and they were Mutt 'n Jeff. One was tall and one was short. Shortly afer I got aboard I went through all the service records of the crew--interviewed everybody. Then we had a dress parade, and Hughie and Baker weren't wearing any medals. Afterward I called them into the wardroom and said, You boys weren't wearing your medals.

"They didn't give us no medals," they said. They had manned the machineguns and got credit for a Japanese Zero. I got on the phone, right from the wardroom, called Washington, and I said, "What's with these men?" They told me, the former captain resented the blacks, and wouldn't give them medals.

Well, I got the medals. They wanted the presentation on the ship so we had it on the ship. We mustered on the bow and I pinned the medals on, and we got a picture of my executive officer holding the boxes, you know. But that's the way I figure about the crew; the captain is just a figurehead. In the words of the old song,

> The captain he rides in a giggy-boat,
> The admiral he rides in a barge.
> It don't go a damn bit faster,
> But it makes the old bastard feel large. (Laughter.)

You've been the recipient of a number of awards and commendations-- written about diving in the Great Lakes--what else?

I've gotten some kind words from the Indiana State Police. We've trained their underwater rescue teams. In 1973 I wrote about diving in the Lakes for a book put out in England--*The World Under Water Book*. But the thing I'm proudest of--Gov. Bob Orr of Indiana gave me a "Sagamore of the Wabash" Award. The sagamore is the wisest of chiefs, the one that the other chiefs go to for advice. The honor is akin to being named a Kentucky Colonel.

The bell recovery has to be the most memorable of your contacts with the Fitzgerald.

It was. The whole process was. Bringing up the bell. Turning it over to the United States in a ceremony at Sault Ste. Marie on July 7. We felt we had accomplished something important. It was all at the request of the families--the 29 families. They're brothers and sisters, mothers and fathers, nieces and nephews who want to have something they can touch, a place where they can come to honor and remember their loved ones.

A kind of shrine.

Yes. A seaman's shrine. We're a different breed, mariners. We depend on each other. It's a different culture. There's an old saying, "One hand's for yourself and one's for the ship." Of course, that came from the old sailing days, when you're up in the icy rigging and you're climbing in a gale.

It's hard to hold back tears when I think of all that's happened.

DWIGHT "BUCKO" TEEPLE

(1997)

The modern history of the Sault Ste. Marie Tribe of Chippewa Indians grew out of the record of a much more extensive period in which the Chippewa lived in the region now known as Northern Michigan. In the 1940's, tribal records show, a group of Sugar Island residents "gathered to talk about their common history." The residents were descendants of the Anishnabek, *or Chippewa, who "for hundreds of years had made their homes near the rapids of the St. Marys River, which they called* Bahwating--the Gathering Place." *Now the City of Sault Ste. Marie, Bahwating provided the setting in which the Chippewa in 1665 first met French fur traders. French sovereignty ended in 1763 as the British gained control of the region, and by 1820 Americans had replaced the British.*

The residents who had gathered on Sugar Island became the Sugar Island Group of Chippewa Indians *in December, 1953. Nearly 20*

222   Asleep in the Deep

years later, gaining U.S. government recognition of their treaty rights and community status, the Group became the Sault Ste. Marie Tribe of Chippewa Indians, with a membership descended from six historical bands: the Grand Island, Point Iroquois, Sault Ste. Marie, Garden River, Sugar Island, and Drummond River bands of Chippewas. The Constitution and Bylaws of the Sault Ste. Marie Tribe went into effect in the fall of 1975.

Against that background, aware of the Tribe's centuries-long history of interaction with the Sault region and the Great Lakes, Mr. Bucko Teeple took part in the July, 1995 recovery of the bell from the SS Edmund Fitzgerald. A pipe carrier according to Indian tradition, Mr. Teeple began a ceremony commemorating the 29 crew members while observing the hulk of the lost ship from a Canadian Navy submersible. He completed the prayer for the crew and their families on the Lake Superior shore.

* * *

Can you tell us about the prayer observance?

Basically it took place in two parts, one under water in the area of the *Fitzgerald* pilothouse and the other on shore at Whitefish Point. It's what we call a pipe ceremony, with a pipe much like one that a person would use for smoking. People call it a peace pipe, but for us it's a prayer or ceremonial pipe. I had also brought an eagle-bone whistle for use during the prayer ritual.

I went down to the *Fitzgerald* in late June for the prayer ceremony. We had a Canadian pilot and copilot, of course, since the recovery was a Canadian operation. We found the pilothouse area, a strange feeling, because the ship has been on the bottom since November, 1975. The SDL-1, the sub, has a big bubble window, a kind of observation window. So we could see very clearly.

How long were you on the bottom?

We stayed down nearly five hours. I had brought the pipe and the eagle-bone whistle. The pipe was in a bag made especially for that purpose. It also contained tobacco, which is important to the ceremony.

I explained to the crew members, Phil Frazier and Chuck Hulsizer,

Conferring on his participation in a dive to the wreck of the *Edmund Fitzgerald,* Bucko Teeple talks with Lt. Cmdr. Robert Gwalchmai, senior diving officer on the HMCS *Cormorant,* and Lt. Cmdr. John Creber. The *Cormorant* served as the mother ship for the submersible SDL-1. (Photo: Jene Quirin)

Relatives of the victims of the *Edmund Fitzgerald* sinking gather for the tent ceremony marking the transfer of the ship's bell from Canadian jurisdiction to American. Among those taking part were Bucko Teeple (second from right) and Candice Miller, Michigan Secretary of State (seated, right). (Photo: Frederick D. Leete III) ↓

what I wanted to do. It was a ceremony for the dead. The ship's bell would be a symbol for those who died and their families, and the recovery would hopefully help to end the dives on the wreck. We all hoped the bell would also help in the effort to designate the wreck as a permanent grave-site.

It wasn't my plan to light the pipe, and I mentioned that. But I did want to fill the pipe. Then I was going to finish the ceremony on shore after we got back to the surface.

It went according to your plan?

Yes. The pipe was in two parts, the bowl and the stem. I simply put the two together. The stem is about 18 inches long, and the bowl

224   Asleep in the Deep

nearly eight. So together the pipe is more than two feet long. I did fill the bowl with tobacco, and I did blow the whistle.

There is religious meaning in these parts of the ceremony?

Absolutely. The tobacco comes from the earth, and represents the earth. Some of it is green, what we call Indian tobacco. But part is also a mixture of some commercial tobaccos. The whistle is made from the wing-bone of an eagle, a bird that represents strength and the power to fly. The whistle, in our way of believing, calls on the thunders, the thunderbirds, the thunder and lightning to hear our prayer. It is a call to those elements to assist us in what it is that we are doing, or seeking. We ask the thunder to have our ancestors hear the prayer that we are offering. The thunders are also asked to take our prayers to those ancestors.

The ceremony doesn't really take very long, probably five to eight minutes. I had to fill the bowl with tobacco and make offerings to the four directions and to the earth and the sky, the earth beneath us and the sky above.

All part of the prayer?

Yes. Each part is essential. The ceremony may vary, depending on who is making the offerings, but there is a general recognition of what each phase is about--what it means. The first offering is to the East, in an easterly direction. The East represents daybreak, or springtime, or that time in our lives when we are little babies. Everything, even life, begins in the East.

The second offering is directed toward the South. The South is similar in meaning to the East. We look upon it as a grandfather would. It represents noontime, the noon of life, or our summertime, when we become young men and young women. The South is represented by the color red. Where the East is yellow, meaning birth and first growth, red represents to us fire and earth and all the negative things in creation. We speak of those things when we offer the tobacco.

The third offering is to the West. The third direction stands for the autumn, the evening-time, the time of middle age. West is represented by the color black, signifying things that are unknown as well as the great changes in our lives--even changes from light to darkness, or dusk, or the change from fall or autumn to winter. It even represents the change from life to death.

North, finally, is represented by white, the last of the four colors of man. The northern direction is the grandfather, that represents the wintertime. Part of it is also night-time, and the unpredictability of our dreams, and the hardships that winter can bring. It's that time in our lives when we are elders, or old people, who are completing the cycle of life. We make an offering of tobacco in each case and then place it in the pipe.

There were offerings to the earth and the sky?

Besides the four directions, we offer the tobacco to the earth, which is the mother who provides us with everything that we need to live. That includes our food, our clothing, our shelter, our medicines. When we die, our mother takes us back. That's all part of the offering to the earth, and the water that flows over the earth is seen as part of it. At the site of the *Fitzgerald* I mentioned that in my prayer, with the hope that those who died there will rest there.

A burial in water is also a return to the mother, which is earth?

Yes. Then there is a final direction, toward the sky. We offer tobacco in that direction. Our attention to that direction means that we acknowledge the Creator, the Great Spirit, God, Kitchi-Manitou-- however we want to recognize that great creative force.

At that time we also ask that the Great Father look down on us and give us His blessing for what we are doing, and to forgive us if we have offended anyone. We were there for the families, and trying to carry out the wishes of the families. So I offered tobacco toward the sky, even though it was not visible--even though it could not be seen unless we went up about 530 feet.

We make an offering of tobacco to acknowledge the Creator, but we also make that offering for the higher direction in each of us: the direction that allows us to think, and feel, and reason. It's that direction that helps us to decide what we are going to do as human beings as we walk the path of life. We offered the tobacco for the men who were lost, and for the direction that they followed on their paths of life.

In ceremonial garb, Bucko Teeple prepares to complete the prayer observance begun near the wreck of the *Edmund Fitzgerald* in July, 1995. The on-shore commemoration took place on Whitefish Point, with Lake Superior in the background. (Photo: Alan R. Kamuda)

A representation of our striving toward higher things?

Oh yes, even toward the Afterlife.

You completed the ceremony on the same day?

I was able to get to the shore at Whitefish Point later that day and complete it there. That part was a little different. I actually smoked the ceremonial pipe. That ceremony takes probably 10 minutes. The pipe is lit in a traditional way--not with a match but with what we call a *skittogin*, which is a kind of punkwood. You use a flint and steel, and strike a spark, and the punkwood starts to smoulder. Then a little piece placed in the pipe ignites the tobacco. The dried punkwood has a soft, velvety feel to it.

You met some of the families of the victims?

I did talk with several members of the families of the *Fitzgerald's* crew. That was both prior to the dive and later. All the family members that I had met before the bell recovery were there when it was brought up out of the water. That was July Fourth. They were also there on July 7 in Sault Ste. Marie, when the bell was transferred from Canada to the United States.

I believe I met some members of the families before I made the dive on the *Fitzgerald.* They were all at the Ojibway Hotel in Sault Ste. Marie.

The understanding was that the whole recovery project was made possible because the families wanted the bell brought up?

That was critical. As Indian people, we understand that there's desecration and robbery from graves. We've experienced that. And we know that that still happens today. We have our gravesites torn up, or bothered, by all sorts of things and people--you name it, it happens.

The families had made their request to the Great Lakes Shipwreck Historical Society, for assistance in recovering the bell. Had it not been for that, we wouldn't have been able to join the project.

Can you tell us a little about your work in Sault Ste. Marie?

Well, I'm a member of the Bay Mills Indian community, and work for the Sault Ste. Marie Tribe of Chippewa Indians. The community here in Sault Ste. Marie has about 3,000 to 4,000 members. The overall membership in the tribe itself is in the neighborhood of 23,000. They live throughout the United States, but the largest group is in the eastern Upper Peninsula--about 8,000 persons.

You work as spiritual leader?

I get that title, but I don't really work full-time at that. My work here is in research and planning. Folks do call me a spiritual leader because I take part in religious ceremonies pretty frequently. My regular work is in economic development.

Is the pipe ceremony used on other occasions?

Yes, many others. For example, it's used in naming ceremonies,

228 Asleep in the Deep

the fall feast, spirit ceremonies, births and deaths. It goes far back in our history.

V

Craft Masters

Not enjoyment, and not sorrow,
Is our destined end or way;
But to act, that each tomorrow
Find us farther than today.

-- From "A Psalm of Life,"
Henry Wadworth Longfellow

RAY BOESSEL JR.

(1992)

His pictures make him look like a modern-day voyageur. In his workshop on the Bigfork River in Minnesota, some 125 miles from Lake Superior, he pursues a trade that a voyageur would appreciate.

He builds birch-bark canoes the Indian way, culling the materials from the forests around his home and assembling them in the 70- x -40-foot "factory" called the Hafeman Boat Works. In the 16 years ending in late 1996 he had built 201 canoes that, to his knowledge, still ply the waters of the Great Lakes, their fantastic networks of rivers and smaller lakes--and other waterways in Canada and distant parts of the United States. The longest he's built measured 26 feet, the shortest two feet, a scale model. As a craftsman, he's deeply into the history of the birch-bark canoe...

* * *

Let me fill in some background... The boat, as everyone knows, has been an integral part of the transportation picture on the North American continent for centuries. As not everyone knows, the canoe has been one of the most versatile boats ever built for use in North America.

Jacques Cartier probably saw it first. The King of France, Francis I, sent Cartier out in 1534 and again in 1535. The purpose was to find precious metals and, if Cartier had time, maybe a Northwest Passage across the upper part of the continent. What Cartier actually found was Indians, Native Americans, using birch-bark canoes. About 70 years later the fur trade began. The traders used bark canoes whose LOA (length overall) was as much as 37 feet. This "maitre canot" or *Montreal canoe* could carry cargo weighing three and a half tons or more.

There were also smaller canoes that the fur traders could use on

Ray Boessel, Jr., dressed for Rendezvous Days.

hazardous interior waterways like the Ottawa and French rivers. These were called North canoes. The Algonquin Indians probably taught Europeans to make canoes on their own. If you lived like the voyageurs lived, you'd appreciate the high bows on these craft. On the Great Lakes the bows could cut through all but the biggest waves. Also, the canoe could be hauled out of the water and turned over. Voila! You had a very serviceable raised canopy to sleep under. You might call it a "canoe-py."

Canoes lasted as fur freighters for some 250 years, to about 1850. Through much of this time they were built at the trading posts of big companies. The Hudson Bay Company was one. Others were the North West Company, the XY Company, and the American Fur Company.

What's the building technique--theirs and yours?

First you've got to find the right materials. It's a little challenging because nature doesn't create two identical trees. So you've got to find straight, good-sized birch trees. The tree supplies the canoe's outer shell. Then you need some roots from the black spruce. You use that to sew the sheets of bark together. Cedar trees provide wood for the ribs and planking; you can use spruce resin for pitch to seal cracks.

Say you've found a straight tree of the right size. You've got to examine the bark to make sure the creases or lines that encircle the tree are just right. If they're too deep the bark may crack and start leaking. If the creases are too shallow, the bark could separate and cause blisters.

The bark also has to be the right thickness. Too thin and it won't be strong enough. Too thick and it isn't flexible enough. By the way, heavier bark means a heavier canoe. Light is lovely when you're portaging or putting the canoe on the rack of your car. The average weight of a 16 foot canoe is 50 to 60 pounds, depending on the materials used.

The woods serve as your materials warehouse.

Once upon a time there was plenty of material available for building canoes. You could build a canoe using one sheet of bark. Today, with some depletion setting in, it's more common to use several pieces sewn together.

The cedar for the inside framework needs to have a straight grain. Also, the tops of the trees should be healthy. That way, you know the tree has enough sap in the trunk to make the wood split easier. You use a wooden wedge, a metal froe, or a heavy knife to split the cedar for the ribs and lining of the boat. You can split down to about 1/4 inch from the heartwood of the tree. The heartwood then makes stiffer ribs that hold the shape of the canoe.

The roots are critical. There are no nails or glue in a traditional bark canoe. So you're looking for spruce roots from five to 30 feet long, the longer the better. Finding really good, long roots is like discovering the pot of gold at the end of the rainbow.

I work alone, but my wife Christie may help as time permits. So do the boys.

How do you assemble the materials?

The bark canoe is built on a frame, from the outside in. That's the opposite of the method used to make the modern strip canoe that substitutes canvas for birch-bark. You set the frame and then put on the skin or outer shell in making the strip canoe. With the bark canoe, once the bark skin is ready, you bend it up by putting a frame on the bark to hold it down. The frame shapes the bottom of the canoe and stakes or forms hold the canoe sides in place.

Once the gunwales are attached to the bark and the center frame is removed, you put in the planking and then the ribs. The planking goes into the canoe lengthwise in approximately four-foot sections. That simplifies the future repairs if they become necessary.

All this sounds simple. But it's much more demanding, and scientific, than it sounds. It's quite a trick to put in the permanent ribs, sew in the thwarts or cross braces, and then, with the canoe off the stakes or forms and upside down, to seal any seams or cracks in the bark. At one time canoe makers used tree resin, charcoal, and animal fat or grease as a sealant. The grease tempered the pitch for colder weather. But on hot days that sealant got soft and ran. It became hard to keep the canoe from leaking. Now we use modern caulk--our only concession to modern technology.

How do you learn to make a birch bark canoe?

Mainly from my wife Christine, who has built scale models since she was 13 years old. She learned from her German grandfather and I also apprenticed with him for about three years.

Christie's grandfather, Bill Hafeman, taught himself to build bark canoes as early as 1921. He built canoes until he was 85 years old, at which time my wife and I began carrying on the business here on the Bigfork.

We make canoes in three basic sizes and styles--and also custom models. The three basic sizes are the 13-foot and 16-foot Chippewa and the 17-foot Voyageur. We no longer take orders for the 20-foot and 26-foot Voyageur freight models because of the availability of materials. We also build and sell five- to 10-foot scale models. We can build to specifications without a problem. A lot of people love the models. They display them. They're conversation pieces.

People seem to romanticize them--has that been your experience?

Yes. But there are lots of misconceptions about bark canoes. Most people think the white side of the bark, the outside of the tree, should be on the outside of the canoe. It isn't. The bark naturally curls toward the white side. So the white is put on the inside of the canoe. Also, with the yellow side out, you have less drag on the water. That side is smoother.

Probably the most important reason for having the yellow side out is because it is the side that absorbs the water. That makes the bark flexible. It gives when it hits a rock in a rapids--without cracking the bark. The white side of the bark doesn't allow water through, and if properly sealed on the seams the canoe will be water-tight.

There's another myth--that bark canoes are fragile. Canoes are really quite strong once the bark soaks in the water for about 15 minutes. I've hit rocks in rapids, and have even been stuck on the rocks. The bark didn't crack or tear. If the canoes were fragile, the trading companies couldn't have used them for over 250 years without going bankrupt. If canoes full of freight, weighing sometimes as much as 4,000 pounds, had been lost, even occasionally, the companies would have changed their methods of transporting hides.

Can you keep busy building canoes?

Sure. I work now and then as a canoe builder for the White Oak Society of Deer River, a town not far from here. I've done a number

The Bigfork River serves as proving ground, highway, and excursion retreat for Ray Boessel and his sons, with a birch-bark canoe as the means of transportation.

of fur trade presentations for groups and schools, and also for the White Oak Society. It has a reconstructed fur trading post in Deer River. The White Oak Society sponsors Rendezvous Days in late July, early August. The fur trading post is complete with a voyageur village that comes alive during the rendezvous. We all dress up for that occasion. The Boessel family turns into a family of voyageurs. I usually do a canoe building workshop during the rendezvous. Birch-bark canoes.

Occasionally I go to other places to put on canoe building workshops. These are mostly sports shows. I've done them in southern Minnesota. I've gone to sports shows as far east as Pittsburgh, as far south as Kansas City. I think I've done one in Cleveland, Cincinnati. Two in Indianapolis. One in Lincoln, Nebraska. When I finish the canoes at the shows, they go into museums or whatever. The show sponsors own them, but they may just give them away. They usually go into museums, but not always. These are full size canoes, 16 and 17 feet long.

So basically I build canoes. In the summer we work in the shop. I hunt up my own materials. I may spend 60 hours in the woods, just searching and hauling. Then when I have everything I need it may take

24 hours to finish a canoe. I do one a week in the summer, start to finish.

In winter we turn our house into a shop and build scale models on the kitchen table. I build about 10 to 15 full-size canoes every summer, about 20 scale models a year, five and six feet long mostly.

You have visitors there on the Bigfork?

In summer we have people coming here from all over. Groups come from around the country, and even from foreign countries. We've had visitors and buyers from Texas, Nebraska, Georgia, New York, Florida, California. Also the Great Lakes states and Canada. We've sold scale models to people from Germany, Norway, Japan.

We always give visitors free tours of our shop. The welcome mat is always out. A lot of people know we're on a historic fur trade route. They're interested. If I have a canoe ready, I'll let people take a ride. They may want to try a ride to see if they want to buy. Or they may want to be able to say they were in a real birch-bark canoe.

Do you ever see or hear from the owners of your canoes?

Sure. They send letters saying their canoe works great. There are some that I see occasionally. There's one man from Kansas, he brings his canoe back almost every year. We do some bindings and check for leaks, and make sure it's ready for the summer. We'll see him then at rendezvous.

I got a picture not long ago from one of our owners. He's got a 17-footer. The picture showed the canoe loaded with two moose--I think a bull and a calf. He figured the total weight was about 2,000 pounds. It looked in the picture like he had a freeboard of about three inches.

One guy has three of my canoes. He's a mail carrier, a real nice guy. First he bought a 16-footer, then a 17-footer. Then he bought a 26-footer. He does rendezvous also.

My wife's cousin is married to a fellow from England. They live here now, in Minnesota, but when they lived in England they would bring a group over to visit us. These people were in the RAF--the Royal Air Force. This has gone on several years now. The groups might be four people or 15 people. They usually take a canoe out and paddle it around on the river in front of the shop. They come over here

236   Craft Masters

and rent canoes and travel through the Boundary Waters.

From what you've said, you're living with history--the fur trade, the rivers, the lakes...

We are. The Bigfork flows north to the Rainy River, and that goes out to the Chain o' Lakes. That would be part of the fur trade route. The Rainy River goes into Rainy Lake. I think the Bigfork part of the fur trade route must be 200, 220 miles. It's 220 miles from the head of the Bigfork to the Rainy River. That's according to the river map that I have. Chasing after beaver hides, the voyageurs would probably have traveled that whole distance. Somewhere up north there's even a portage so that you could get over to the Mississippi River system. I'm not sure what all the contacts are between those systems.

There are several lakes there where the Bigfork starts. There's Bowstring, and Dora, and Sand. Dora Lake is actually where the Bigfork starts. This river was written up in a book put out by *National Geographic, The Wild Rivers of North America*. That must have been in 1983 or '84. Bill Hafeman, my wife's grandfather, was still working in the shop yet, that's when they were there. The book said the Bigfork was one of the top 10 rivers in the United States, as far as canoeing.

I never did get a copy of the book. It was a hardback. They had a picture of my wife's grandfather working outside the shop. He was 92 when he died in 1990. His wife, Christine's grandmother, is 92 (in 1992).

It's really been a great pleasure working here on canoes with people who appreciate them.

TERRY L. SEARFOSS

(1997)

By his own account, Terry Searfoss began his "lackluster sailing career" at the ripe age of 9. In the eight-foot sailing dinghy hade by his father, he patrolled the Lake Huron main near Caseville, Michigan, where the family had a summer home. One boat led to another, and another, which is when Terry realized that there were few McDonald's franchises in the North Channel. A talent for putting elements of meals into edible formats surfaced.

Terry set aside his training in fine arts and a budding career in advertising. The rest is succulent, nutritious history. So many people came to him asking for copies of his recipes that he decided to stop running a copy machine into the ground. He put together his book, The Two Burner Gourmet. *The book came out in 1991, went into a second printing in 1992, and into a third in 1994. Terry became the guy you see preparing Portugese Poached Eggs before crowds at boat shows from here to Seattle.*

The culinary system that Searfoss developed, the one he espouses in his book, grew out of the author's aversion to work, especially the kind that consigns one to a "hot tiny little galley while everyone else is having fun." You can, he maintains, make it easy on yourself and eat like an oriental potentate, even as a seaborne cook...

* * *

Your book combines off-trail humor and practical advice with mouth-watering recipes--by design, I presume?

It's really just telling the truth with a little twist added. Those meals were actually what we ate while cruising, and I've been cruising since about 1970--on the Great Lakes, off the east and west coasts, and in the Gulf of Mexico.

My theory is that you don't have to eat peanut butter-and-jelly sandwiches from one end of a cruise to the other. Why not a plump chicken breast in an elegant lemon and wine sauce? Or a thick, juicy sirloin steak stuffed with oysters and Roquefort Cheese?

You're suggesting that any clown can do it? In any kind of galley?

Of course. The main thing is that about 80 or 90 percent of cooking on board a boat is the planning. You need to have that can of beans and franks on board if it's your favorite meal. You need to have the steak. You don't just run into a grocery store the day before you're

238   Craft Masters

leaving on the Big Cruise and buy whatever strikes your fancy. Why buy something hoping that some day you may use it?

People ask me how I provision a boat for the summer. I say, Well, I don't. I only provision for when we're going on a trip. That really freaks them out. They've read these articles about what you need. "You've got to have so much flour and so many pounds of beans, so much of this and plenty of that." I say, Well, that's for live-aboards, or for people who are making passage. For a week-long cruise, or two weeks, you just plan your meals. If you want to have eggs and bacon one morning, and cereal the next morning, and coffee cake the third morning, you've got to have that stuff on your shopping list.

Sounds like what a thrifty housewife would do...

Sure. What I also point out at my seminars is that if you're going to have sandwiches, you want to know what kinds of sandwiches you're going to have. You can have bologna sandwiches--they're cheap and the bologna lasts longer. But you've got to write down that on your trip you're going to have bologna sandwiches. Will you have them on Monday, Tuesday, and Wednesday? That gets pretty boring. Why not vary it with turkey one day, salami another day? All it takes is writing it down.

You start planning far in advance of a cruise?

I used to. Now I wait until about a week beforehand. It's gotten a little different. We've got Mr. Computer to help us out. A lot of my stuff is in computers now.

When I'm at a boat show, say a 10-day show, and will be doing maybe 42 different demonstrations, I can make up my daily shopping list for that 10-day period in less than 20 minutes. That's kind of handy.

Finding space to store dry goods and canned foods should be a snap. All you have to do is a little boat exploring... The real problem will be keeping track of where you've put all the goodies. Some experts suggest that you draw a diagram of the boat and make a list of exactly where the cans of tomatoes, the pitted black olives, the tuna fish, the potato chips, etc., etc., etc. are hidden.

It's a great idea..., but I found it a pain...
Since I plan and schedule all our meals for the entire cruise well before we leave port, I've got a pretty good idea of what I'll be serving and when I'll be serving it... So instead of storing the ingredients all over the boat..., I simply put them and any '*pre-packaged*' ingredients required in a single brown paper bag. Tape the bag shut... Then, with a broad tipped marking pen, label it "2nd & 3rd day... Week II" for identification.

-- The Two Burner Gourmet, p. 8

Seminars are your main activity now, year-round?

Yes, but not quite year-round. I'm doing maybe a dozen boat shows a year. A lot depends on the length of a given show. Some of the shows are nine days, 10 days, so you can only get a couple in during some seasons. When they're four days long, as most of them are in the summer and fall, you can take in more of them. At each show I'm doing seminars anywhere from three to six times a day.

You're doing them repetitively at each show?

Well, my seminars are broken down into different categories. I'm not constantly doing the same thing. When I'm preparing meals like that before groups, I can switch the meal plans to suit my hunger tastes. I can do a Drunken Chicken, or Portuguese Poached Eggs, or a Chinese Chicken Salad--just about anything I choose.

Is there a progression in your presentations?

Yes, there's a basic approach and a main topic. The basics are the equipment you have available, the actual provisioning, and then the storage. Form there you go on to how to look for recipes and how to plan meals. My book helps there because I've got a chapter on meal plans, with nine different plans for two-day to five-day menus.

The main concern that I have to overcome is that you need lots of equipment, or that you need special equipment, to produce world-class meals. Thinking it's too difficult to cook on board their boats, people start figuring that you just make reservations at the next harbor of refuge. They give up.

The other part is that too many people get caught up in the idea that they have to go and buy a special pressure-cooker, or a special stove. I try to reel them in a little bit. I just try to show them that if you think of what you're doing, and how, you don't need a lot. If you plan, you could have a 14-year-old kid do the cooking for you. It's Hungersville if you wait until mealtime comes around and say, "What are we going to have?"

At a show, do you use the minimum of equipment or have you a full boat of pots and pans, gadgets, utensils?

I have just what I use on my boat, or on any boat. There's one pot, one skillet. My three can-openers. One knife. One bowl. I really pretend that I'm on board a boat. I even use a little cooler for fresh foods.

Your book says you have a little bag when you give one of these seminars. Is all your equipment in that bag?

That's it. My pots and pans, all the other things. It's just an old thing like a duffelbag. If I want to I can throw in my foul-weather gear, my boots, my bathing suit. I can carry everything I need for cruising.

Are there items in there that you couldn't do without while giving a seminar--some absolutely essential items?

Terry Searfoss prepares one of his specialties in a typically cramped galley.

Yes, my knife and my dutch oven. I've got one good knife, and it'll do just about everything I want it to do. A multiple-purpose instrument. It's not as efficient for boning as a boning knife, and not as good for other things as a filet knife or a French knife. But I don't need four knives. The one I have gets the job done.

Don't get me wrong. It's wonderful to have all those fancy gadgets. If you have them, don't throw them overboard. But they aren't essential.

When cooking, or giving seminars, do you favor some main ingredient--fish, fowl, meat?

No. Really, I try to point out to people that they should keep it simple and go for variety. That's true especially when you're dealing with storage on board. You remember that chicken doesn't last as long as beef, and you've got pork that's somewhere in between, so if you use your chicken and then your pork and your beef, you can usually get through the first couple or three days.

I run into people who want to barbecue all the time. I say, That's fine, but how do you make pancakes in the morning on the grill? You can do the hotdogs while you're underway, do them on a grill, but what happens when it's raining?

There are people who fish and then cook them up and eat them. More power to them. It may be worth it to break your routine, or plan. But I don't plan on eating what I catch because I don't catch anything. I could fish with a magnet; it wouldn't work.

Caked on, baked on, burnt-on food, cemented to the bottom of the pan? It's not supposed to happen, but it does... You don't have to use a hammer and chisel to get it out. Just add a little water, bring it to a boil, and take your wooden or plastic spatula and gently scrape it off. If it needs a little more friendly persuasion, add some dish detergent. Still stubborn? Try adding some bleach. If that doesn't work, throw the pan out and send the recipe to NASA.

-- The Two Burner Gourmet, p. 19

242   Craft Masters

It's obvious from your book that cooking on board is a lot more than just cooking. It's garbage disposal, dish-washing, water conservation, sanitation, what else?

All of the above. You have to plan those things too. People should be aware of these other aspects. They're important even when you're at home.

Look at water conservation. If you're at home, you can take a shower for half an hour. On a boat, if you do that the water tank is going to go dry on you. So you have to know how to take a shower. You can shave with a half-cup of water. How much water do you need to brush your teeth?

Do you find that a lot of people are afraid of cooking on board a boat?

You betcha. One thing is, they're scared of the stove units. They think of all the accidents they've heard about, the ones that made the papers. But those accidents are all the results of stupid mistakes. The answer is to understand, or be familiar with your cooking source. I mention in the book, without going into too much detail, that many smaller stoves in boats can be taken out and put back in. They're not molded into the hull. You could take the stove out and put it in your back yard. That way, you could get used to the controls. After that it's a matter of following some basic safety procedures.

There was one story about a stove that blew up and sank the boat. But the cook in that case was pouring fuel into the reservoir while the stove was hot. It wasn't the fault of the stove.

Have you a favorite recipe, or recipes?

That's kind of like asking, "Who's your favorite kid?" When we make up our menus for our cruises, we tend toward the exotic, the bizarre, the stuff we don't normally get at home. Everyone has special family meals that they schedule for family occasions. We do those on the boat.

That doesn't mean putting more time into the cooking?

No. With that recipe for Carpetbagger Steak, as one example, it's just grilling the steak. The difference is, we're stuffing it with bleu cheese, mushrooms, oysters, a little parsley, and bread crumbs to bind it all together. That makes it a little different, but not harder.

When you're provisioning for a cruise, do you think economy?

Always. I collect newspaper cents-off coupons for weeks ahead. I'm loaded with hints for saving money. Do you think you'll need a gallon of milk? Buy four quarts. It'll cost a little more, but if one quart container goes bad, you haven't blown the whole supply.

Whenever possible, I like to re-supply along the way. You've got limited stowage anyway. Why not buy fresh lettuce if it's there in a dockside grocery store? You can serve your Hearty Macaroni Salad on unwilted lettuce.

How about leftovers?

I have one favorite that I use in seminars. I show people how to make gazpacho with a day's leftover vegetables. You can let it grow day by day if you're careful. Got a half-tomato left from lunch? Toss it into a plastic zip-lock bag. Too much celery from the Bloody Mary swizzles? Into the bag. As you go along, you can marinate it all in a red wine vinegar and lemon juice mix. Add some hot sauce, Worcestershire, and canned tomato juice. Add whatever's left from the dinner veggies. At the end, in goes a can of minced clams, juice and all. Don't throw in the can.

You know what's one of the great features of that gazpacho? You serve it right out of the plastic bag and then there's no bowl to clean.

Have you ever noticed how friendly and sociable boaters are? It seems that every time you turn around, they've got a drink in their hand. And they're never shy about asking others to come aboard and join in. Well, contrary to popular beliefs, they're not a bunch of lushes, social drunkards, or misfits. Nope! They're just a dedicated group of individuals, preserving an ancient seafaring tradition of camaraderie and bonding. A way of celebrating a job well done.

It seems that a long long time ago, after surviving a treacherous storm or after an excellent display of teamwork and seamanship, to reward them for their

244   Craft Masters

performance, the skipper would order up an extra ration of drink for his crew. So the way I see it, cocktail time is just another way of keeping in touch with our heritage.

-- The Two Burner Gourmet, p. 46

The zip-lock bag has come into its own with the on-board cook?

For me it's a critical component. I use those little tiny zip-locks when a recipe requires dry spices and seasonings. I just pre-measure the ingredients and stash them with the appropriate menu. It's also handy to transfer rice, pasta, and other boxed foods into zip-locking bags. They're far more compact, easier to stuff into tight storage spaces.

Does giving seminars, presenting cooking shows on cable TV, and helping to crew racing boats cut into your own personal summer cruising time?

I can't always count on the three weeks on the Great Lakes that I'd like. Last year (1996) I was lucky to get away for about nine days. This year I'm planning on doing better. I've got a 19-foot Lightning that hasn't been in the water for a while, but I'll get there some day. Most summers I'm cruising on SE's anyway. There's an SE 29, an SE 31, some others.

What's an SE?

Somebody Else's. A boat owned by a friend.

Any hankering to get back into painting and drawing, into advertising?

No, well, maybe yes about painting. It'd be wonderful to sit on a dock and set up an easel and go to work. But advertising? Not any more. That's a ratrace. I've given that up along with 3,000-mile cruises. If you want to make passage, I'll fly to the Fiji Islands and meet you there.

That's because you're traveling so much nowadays?

Maybe. I've been up in Portland, then Seattle in recent weeks. And I just got back from the east coast. I'm going down to Charleston, South Carolina this weekend. You can say I box the country. But whether you're in a civic center or an amphitheater, the tents and the job are the same.

In the early '80's I owned a sailboat with friends. A Tanzer 28. It was an ugly looking boat, but a six-foot-one guy could stand up in the galley. On other boats, when I'd stand up in the galley I could rest my elbows on the deck. So the Tanzer was really kind of nice. We cruised a lot on it. Then we sold it, and it's still around on the Lakes. It's a 1974 model, and some of these older boats are better than a lot of new ones. They have more storage room. Today they make these big salons down in the cabin area, and the salon goes from hull to hull basically. So you don't really have any storage area.

Your cooking philosophy--keep it simple and strive for variety--would work for RV travel, camping, all kinds of outdoor living, it seems.

You've discovered my secret. I spent a lot of time looking for recipes, but they taste as good on land as on water.

PAUL D. BRUGGER

(1997)

Sixteenth-century goldsmith Benvenuto Cellini didn't invent the "lost wax" method of making metal castings, but he practiced it well ahead of Paul D. Brugger of Erie, Pennsylvania. The fact is that cire perdue, *or lost wax, goes back as a craft to about 6,000 B.C. Artisans of ancient Greece, Rome, Egypt, and the Far East used the method to make the bronze masterpieces that now dazzle museum visitors*

246   Craft Masters

throughout the world. As for Cellini, historians say his only surviving work in gold is the richly ornamented "Saltcellar of Francis I," created for King Francis I of France.

In nearly a quarter of a century of practicing the arcane craft of lost wax casting, Brugger has achieved a rare level of mastery. The expertise didn't come easily. Brugger "apprenticed" to himself for some 10 years before he felt comfortable with the process. Before he completed his 1,600-square-foot basement workshop, he worked partly in the family kitchen--with the encouragement of his wife Mary Ann. He researched the history of lost wax casting, unearthing among other things a treatise on the subject written during the Chou dynasty in China in 1122 B.C. Brugger also talked with experts in various fields, and found that his long-ago studies in organic and inorganic chemistry at the University of Pittsburgh came in handy.

Among the bronze castings Brugger has produced are a historic bell, a figurehead representing the famed Lake Erie Monster, and assorted other works in the shapes of birds and other animals, yacht racing and other trophies, and a historic bronze cannon...

* * *

Is it possible to describe in layman's terms what lost wax casting involves?

The process starts with a drawing, a picture, or sometimes an existing model. Then you create an armature or frame or other material and build a rubber mold around it. After making a wax image, complete in all details, from the rubber mold, you wrap the wax in a special ceramic mold that encases the artwork.

In the next step you subject the ceramic mold to heat at about 1,800 degrees Fahrenheit. The wax melts and is lost. The resulting void in the mold retains the memory of the art and you can pour molten bronze or other metal or ceramic material into the mold. In the last stage the mold material is broken off the bronze casting. The casting is polished and treated with an acid to produce the desired sheen and color.

The creative part comes early on, when you're shaping the wax image?

Yes. At that stage you're producing the three-dimensional model of the final casting. What you have in wax you get back in metal.

The Niagara *bell was obviously a major project—can you tell us about it?*

I think in doing that one we actually utilized both an ancient process, the lost wax method, and some space shuttle technology. The new age technology came into play at the stage where the wax becomes encased in the ceramic fused silica. This is the same material that the National Aeronautics and Space Administration uses for the tiles on the space shuttles. The silica can withstand temperatures ranging from 3,000 to 5,000 degrees Fahrenheit. Once we melted the wax out of the ceramic mold, we could pour the molten bronze.

The Niagara League of Erie asked me to make that replica. The original bell and the one I made for the *Niagara* both weigh about 150 pounds. That presents a problem in weight management. To obtain the needed extra manpower I enlisted the help of Dave Stadler and some of his employees at Stadler's Superior Bronze Corporation on Poplar Street (in Erie, PA). They spent more than half a day pouring the liquid bronze, allowing it to set, and then knocking the mold material off the casting. That was the final stage; the whole project took about 12 months from start to finish.

You were able to duplicate the original bell perfectly?

Down, or up, to the year 1799 that identifies the year in which the bell was first cast. We also duplicated the six configurations on the bell's crown. These represent a sort of royal crown. I believe the tonal quality of the new bell is identical to that of the original bell.

That reminds me that we did deviate from the model in one way. That original bell has a crack in it. We filled in the crack to make the replicas.

Replicas--plural?

Yes. I made the first one for delivery in 1990, to coincide with the restoration of the *Niagara*, Admiral Perry's flagship at the Battle of Lake Erie. That bell is on view for visitors to the *Niagara* during the tourist season. Erie, of course, is the *Niagara's* home port. Then last year (1996) the City of Erie commissioned me to make a second

248   Craft Masters

Posing with the small naval cannon that he made from an original found in Lake Erie, Paul Brugger acts out a mock attack on the brig *Niagara* in the harbor at Erie, Pennsylvania. (Photos courtesy Paul Brugger)

Mary Ann Brugger joins her husband, Paul, in a toast to the bell that Brugger made for the brig *Niagara* by the lost wax method. The bell remains on exhibit on the *Niagara* during the summer tourist season.

A bit of American history goes to China: Paul Brugger's second replica of the historic *Niagara* ship's bell hangs in a park in the Chinese city of Zibo. The city of Erie sent the replica to sister city Zibo as an expression of friendship.

duplicate for Erie's sister city, Zibo, China. That bell is now in China.

What's the history of the original bell?

It's generally believed that the original was the ship's bell from the British warship *Queen Charlotte*, one of the ships engaged in the Battle of Put-In Bay in September, 1813. The *Queen Charlotte* was the first British ship to surrender to Commodore Perry. After the battle Perry supposedly took the bell as a war prize, then placed it aboard the *Niagara*. In another version the bell was on board the British warship *Detroit*, the British flagship at the Battle of Lake Erie.

There's some mystery and confusion about the rest of the bell's history. It was apparently used as the courthouse bell here in Erie for years, starting in the 1820's. It disappeared in 1856 and surfaced again a few years later. But at that time it had developed a crack and couldn't be rung. It went on public display at City Hall and stayed there for years. Then it sort of got lost. It was in the basement of a local tavern, Dickson's tavern, crack and all, for about 30 years. That's when I used it as my model. The original bell is now in the Erie Historical Museum.

Can you tell us about the Lake Erie Monster and your casting of it?

It's a curious story. I was a kid, maybe 13. We had this boat out at my aunt's cottage, about seven miles east of Erie. Someone had to take the boat back. I volunteered. It turned really dark.

That seven-mile trip turned out to be I don't know how long. Then, close to Erie, off Presque Isle, I saw this monster.* It had fiery eyes and flared nostrils, a swirly tongue, armor-like skin. It had curled lips, and fangs.

---

* Sightings of the Lake Erie Monster have been reported through much of the twentieth century. A cluster of such reports surfaced in the mid-1980s, some of them coming from groups rather than individuals. In *Tales of the Western Reserve*, author Shelley Pearsall describes what may have been a prehistoric cousin of the monster: "He had a body that stretched 20 feet in length, and he was covered with gray armor, as impenetrable as steel." The Great Lakes Historical Society in Vermilion, Ohio has been assembling research on the "monster" for several years, and notes that fossilized remains of the "cousin" mentioned by Pearsall are on exhibit in the Cleveland Museum of Natural History, Cleveland, Ohio. The fossil is identified as *Dunkleasteus*.

You made the casting from memory?

Of the head only. The casting is a figurehead, 105 pounds in weight, and 44 inches long. I can't forget what that thing in the water looked like, so it was easy to recreate it. I made the figurehead for a neighbor, Dr. Doug Nagle, and the casting is now on the bow of his motor yacht *Westerly*. The yacht docks in Erie harbor in summer.

In the case of this monster casting, I first made a plaster of Paris mold of the bow. Then I made the casting so it would fit exactly onto the bow.

You're not the only one who's seen the monster.

I know. I've read about some of the others. The monster even has a name now--South Bay Besse, like the Loch Ness Nessie. People who have seen it describe it as a sea monster, a serpent, a black snake-like thing about as thick as a bowling ball. Most of the sightings have taken place along the south shore of Lake Erie. They've been coming in since about 1960. But there was one, I believe 60 or 70 years ago, from the eastern shore of Lake Huron, on the Canadian side.

The people who report these sightings are very hard to discount. One was the president of a two-million-dollar corporation in Cincinnati. He was a high school senior in about 1960. While fishing from a pier in Sandusky Bay, he heard a noise behind him. He turned to see some rats on the pier. He had decided to throw some stones at them, but when he turned back and looked into the water he saw *it*. It came out of the water a foot to a foot and a half, and was as long as a car, according to this witness. That sighting took place on a clear, calm night, one pretty much like the one I was enjoying as a kid. The others who have seen the monster were a schoolteacher, a counselor at the University of Toledo, a housewife, an auto salesman.

My mental picture of the monster or serpent, or whatever, is still very clear. The first step in making the casting was to draw a very detailed picture of it. I was even able to sculpt facial detail. The whole project took nearly two years. I made a film of the highlights as I went along.

You've made other figureheads?

A number of them. One of my favorites was the head of the bald eagle that I had mounted on the sailboat I once owned. That was the *Victoria*, a 65-foot yacht that was all block and tackle. I wasn't using the boat that much and it's sold now. But it still has the American Eagle figurehead.

Erie Harbor must be crowded with your work...

Besides the Monster, the American Eagle figurehead, and the *Niagara* bell, the Erie Yacht Club is practically a one-man show of my castings. The International Arrow Ice Boat Trophy is one that I'm very proud of. It's another bronze, and shows an ice boat in action. The Yacht Club keeps it in a trophy case. Two other trophies in the trophy case are a second International Ice Boat Trophy and the Governor's Cup Trophy.

There must be seven or so of my castings in the Yacht Club trophy case. They were done in different media.

For the Yacht Club's 100th anniversary in 1995 I made a one-third-size casting in bronze of the *Niagara* bell. It's buried now in a time capsule in the Yacht Club grounds.

Have you done other historic pieces?

A number of them. Remember when the *Providence*, the Revolutionary War sloop, visited the Great Lakes? That was in 1995. The captain had asked me to cast a bronze bell for the ship. For me it was quite an honor. They wanted a 1700's style bell, To make it look authentic I put a line drawing of the sloop on the front surface of the bell. The finished bell was eight and one-half inches in height and across the base. It's about half the size of the original and weighs about 25 pounds.

One other commission came from the Erie Museum, and there's a little story behind it. Some years ago someone found a cast iron cannon about 16 miles west of Erie--in the lake in about six feet of water. It had been there, apparently, since the early 1800's. The theory is that it was lost off the tow rail of a British vessel that patrolled Lake Erie and other Great Lakes prior to the War of 1812. The museum wanted a bronze casting and I was able to use the cannon itself as my model in making the mold. The cannon had a carriage, so I built that out of solid rough-sawed lumber.

You've covered the waterfront, it seems, with different types of castings.

Each one is a challenge. I've done miniatures like the Cooley Trophy, a clay casting with a solid gold overlay. It shows four card players with cards in their hands and each player on a separate chair at a round table. The casting is a tribute to Byron Cooley, one of the founders of the Erie Yacht Club's Pinochle Club.

I've also done birds, for example two bronze cranes that fall in what I call the "fine arts" category. That category also includes the historic replicas. The cranes were done for a private client's front yard. There have been other birds, including a swan that now stands in a private home in South Carolina. Another bronze in the Erie Yacht Club is a replica of *The Little Mermaid*, the statue that stands in the harbor of Copenhagen, Denmark.

I've really been concentrating mostly on maritime and nautical works. That's what I'm primarily interested in.

Visiting the Erie Yacht Club, former Gov. and Mrs. Dick Thornburg of Pennsylvania get a closeup view of trophies made by Paul Brugger (second from left). (Photo: Ron Norman Studio, Erie, PA)

What decided you to go into this second career?

When I retired from the A. Brugger and Sons Funeral Homes in 1991, I wanted to stay busy. That business has been in the family for three--now four--generations. I had already read about this 6,000-year-old craft and even experimented with casting. I decided to explore it full-time. They call it *investment casting* when it's done industrially, but of course I wanted to do more artistic, more historic things. It's been a great way to stay busy. I tell people that now that I'm retired I can work as hard as I want. (Laughs.)

Some things I didn't foresee. I didn't think I'd have to spend more than a year on a single casting, as I did with the *Niagara* bell. Some others have taken 18 months and more. Much of that time goes into preparing the model. The harder the model, the longer it may take. The Lake Erie Monster took about a year to complete.

You can do everything in your basement workshop?

I can do all the operations up to the finished shell mold. Then I have to go outside for help in pouring the metal or other medium. In my basement workshop I have hammers and nails, air and electric grinding tools, compressors, scales, saws, jeweler's glasses, and gas burners to melt wax. I may have left something out. Supplies that I keep on hand include drawing papers, metal screening, ceramic and rubber materials, and so on. The "studio," as I call it, has temperature and humidity controls.

At one time I used sand to make molds. Now I use the fused silica that I mentioned. That involves checking the specific gravity of the ceramic slurry.

You must feel like a modern inheritor of an ancient craft.

I do. I've made maybe 300 castings and have as many more to go.

WINSTON SMITH

(1993)

_____

_____

The Bilge Buoy Boat Bailer is his invention but not necessarily the monument by which he will be remembered. True, the bailer represents an achievement--ingenuity applied to a basic problem: keeping a small, open boat dry. But Winston Smith has also written two small books of poetry, "Long as the Rivers Flow" and "Peninsula Poems." He's a licensed commercial aircraft pilot who, as a World War II flyer, flew over the Himalayan "hump" and back to base 128 times. He's an A&P--an airframe and powerplant mechanic. He's taught aviation and power mechanics and flown gliders in competitions. He lives out there on the Lost Peninsula that juts into Lake Erie and belongs partly to Michigan and partly to Ohio. In the case of the boat bailer, exasperation was the mother of invention...

* * *

Year in and year out it was the same story. I'd go down to the dock in the spring and there was my boat, half full of water. I decided to do something about it. I was wearing out the coffee can, doing the bailing.

My background in power mechanics led me to the solution. I knew that many small boat owners don't have electric bilge pumps. A lot of them don't want to put on heavy canvas covers or do the hand bailing that you have to do if rain or snow collect in the bottom of the boat. Or if there's a small leak.

I was thinking weight and mass. I thought I'd try to use waves and the rocking motion they give to a boat to power a small pump. Waves make the boat rock, obviously. The mass is supplied by the boat. The resulting energy drives the pump, which has a rocking arm and a submerged horizontal plate.

You did some experimenting?

Yes, quite a bit. We spent three years working up a saleable product. Some people thought it was a Rube Goldberg, but we tested the first model on others. They thought it was great. Goodbye coffee can. At one point we had a trailer-mounted demonstrator unit that we built. We could use it to show the bilge pump in action and for testing purposes. A small electric motor provided the rocking action on the demo. That simulated the rocking action that a boat would experience in the water.

We found that that early model would pump five gallons of water, or more, per hour. That's with even a slight boat movement. With increased movement, such as would be the case in windy weather, the pump would get rid of up to 20 gallons an hour.

Is the pump installed permanently?

No. It's for use only when a boat is docked, anchored, or moored. When you're getting under way, you remove it. With a wrench you can take it off entirely. You can remove part of it without tools. That's because the pump is attached to the boat with a bolt that passes through the carlock socket. Boats that don't have carlocks and sockets can use the pump by installing it with a mounting bracket.

I should mention also that the Bilge Buoy is designed for use on boats with 24 inches or less of freeboard at the point where you're mounting the pump. We can adapt it for larger boats if we have their specs in advance.

You've obviously got moving parts on the pump. How many of them?

In the first version we had four moving parts. But that became our prototype. This year (1993) we put the finishing touches on a new model that has one moving part. Just like the first one, the new model is for use on small boats that don't have electric bilge pumps. The later version works if the boat moves through an arc of one inch. But it weighs only about three pounds, half the weight of the earlier model.

Both of these pumps, the prototype and the later model, are for use when the boat is docked, moored, or anchored. Both models can be attached to the boat by tightening a nut. It can be installed in a minute or less.

One difference between the two pumps is that the new model bails at a somewhat slower rate. But it would still be adequate unless you're

256 Craft Masters

Between the Ottawa River (foreground) and Lake Erie and Maumee Bay on the horizon, the Lost Peninsula has its own water world. Winston Smith (inset) developed his Bilge Buoy Boat Bailer in a workshop not far from the Peninsula's tip.

in a monsoon. We've manufactured both models in my one-car garage. We're on the Ottawa River here, and I've got a 22-foot sloop, the "*Halcyon,*" and a 12-foot outboard.

You've patented the Bilge Buoy?

Yes, but I had to do the library research first. That was hours of work, mostly in the Toledo-Lucas County Public Library. I studied patent law and patenting procedures. We finally got Patent No. 4,953,490, dated September 4, 1990. I had to prepare the application papers.

The language of the application had to be technical--power mechanics-ese. Listen to this: The pump is a--and I'm quoting here--"a wave-operated boat pump...whereby said upper pumping tube is connected to the bottom side diaphragm pump and descends in an essentially vertical direction to a connection with a top opening of said bilge water discharge assembly, and said standpipe tube is connected to an upper opening and rises in an essentially vertical direction to, above, and over the gunwale of said boat and then down-ward, giving the said standpipe tube an overall U-shape for increased flow."

I wish I knew that language. What kinds of reports on the pump have you gotten from people who have used it?

They were all very positive. One friend put pumps on two rowboats that he keeps on the St. Marys River in northern Michigan. The craft have remained dry since he started using them. There was no power available where he docked the boats, so the wave-operated boat pump was a godsend.

Another friend used it for a year, giving it a real road test. Then he came back and said the pump worked perfectly. Before that, his boat always sank at the dock in strong winds and heavy rains.

Do you work alone?

My son Gary has helped me. We work in the garage. We do all the work ourselves except for one thing: parts go out to be plated.

I should mention that the pumps are self-priming. In the first model we had two check-valves and a hose. The single moving part on my second version was the pump apparatus that moves up and down on a baseplate. Our materials are mostly plastic or brass.

Can you tell us about your aviation experience?

I've been flying for 60 years. In the Far East I was with the U.S. Air Transport Command. I received the Distinguished Flying Cross after 128 flights over the Hump and back. We were carrying supplies over the mountains to China, Chiang Kai-shek's people.

I guess once a pilot, always a pilot. I was with the Toledo Board of Education as an instructor and director of the Aviation Center. I started as a mechanics teacher in the Macomber Vocational High School in 1949 and retired in 1981--33 years in all. The Aviation Center was FAA (Federal Aeronautics Administration) approved for aviation and powerplant mechanics. With the FAA for some years I was also a pilot examiner--testing pilots on what they knew and their flying skills.

I even built my own sailplane. That was a favorite hobby for years. I once took a sailplane up 28,000 feet. That was in Colorado. I belong to the Adrian Soaring Club--have for years. Adrian's about 40 miles from here.

I have to confess to a love of boats also. I've been interested in boating since I was a kid. I've lived here on the Ottawa River for 40 years, and we're surrounded by boats. The Lost Peninsula Marina is

258   Craft Masters

right behind us and Ohio is a couple of blocks away. We can be in Lake Erie in minutes. We're on this point of land between Maumee Bay and the Ottawa. A great place.

Tell us about your books.

Writing them has been one of the great pleasures of my life. They're sort of local history in poetry. I draw on Native American themes and the history of the region back to the early days before there were settlers. I publish the books myself--another home industry of mine. They're really hand-crafted.

It seems to me especially poignant that the Indians and the whites couldn't live together. It ought to be possible. It's a big country.

You were all over the map in World War II. Do you still travel?

Yes, now and then. My wife Freda, and I have been to England twice, once to Hawaii. This past summer we went to Nantucket. We stopped at Mystic, Connecticut on the way back to visit the maritime museum there.

"REV. EDWARD DOWLING, U-D PROFESSOR, AUTHORITY ON GREAT LAKES SHIPPING"

The Rev. Edward Dowling's interest in Great Lakes shipping began as a child in Chicago on the shores of Lake Michigan and led him to become a top expert on the subject.

Fr. Dowling, 89, a retired priest and engineering instructor at the University of Detroit, died from kidney failure Saturday, May 18, 1996, in the Colombiere Center in Clarkston.

"He was one of the foremost historians on Great Lakes shipping," said the Rev. Arthur McGovern, his last superior at the University of Detroit Mercy. "The dinner room at U. of D. is decorated with his paintings of Great Lakes ships."

Fr. Dowling had one of the largest personal collections of Great Lakes shipping memorabilia including 35 to 50 rare research books, 120 albums filled with 8 by 10 photos, charts, navigation routes and record sheets for up to 3,000 models.

He also was an accomplished artist, painting about 1,000 ships, many pre-1900 models.

"He was cordial, shy and always very respectful... He would go up north during the summers to research and paint," Fr. McGovern said.

He also has written numerous articles on travel and commercial shipping. He also wrote the 1967 book, *Lakers of World War I.*

He was one of the original organizers, and president, of the Maritime History Society of Detroit; president of the Great Lakes Maritime Institute of Detroit; and vice-president of Steamship Historical Society of America.

In 1992 he donated his personal collection of Great Lakes memorabilia to the University of Detroit Mercy and in 1993 he received the American Merchant Marine Museum's Nathaniel Bowditch Maritime Scholar Award.

Fr. Dowling, who received his master's degree from Xavier University in Cincinnati in 1933, was ordained in 1940 into the Jesuits.

He taught engineering graphics at U-D from 1942 to 1973. He then became an archivist professor for the school. He moved to Colombiere in 1993.

--Obituary, *Detroit News,*
May 22, 1996

MATTHEW L. DALEY

(1996)

Matthew L. Daley is engaged in a slow-motion race against time. As a library assistant at the university of Detroit Mercy Library, he has the primary responsibility for organizing and preserving the library's

Marine Historical Collection. The project, already three years old in 1996, calls for seemingly endless identifying, re-filing, and indexing/cataloguing of the collection's tens of thousands of photographs--most of them of Great Lakes ships--and assorted other records, books, paintings, models, and memorabilia. Unless Daley does his work well, the acids that infest many storage formats will take their toll of prints, negatives, and other valuable records.

The collection emerged from the life-long hobby of a single man, Edward J. Dowling, S. J. (Society of Jesus). Over some 60-plus years Father Dowling wielded his cameras, applied brush to canvas, stocked books, clipped articles, copied documents, and just plain collected. Known officially as the Marine Historical Collection, Edward J. Dowling Photographic Collection, the archive today occupies an 18-by-24-foot room on the third floor of the UDM Library. A small anteroom serves as the Research Room. Matt Daley has come to know the collection perhaps better than Father Dowling ever did. He's delighted to know that one man's legacy has become a library's treasurehouse of Great Lakes history...

* * *

Father Dowling started having an interest in ships when he was 5, when he saw his first Great Lakes ship in Chicago. He was captivated by it, and it became a lifelong pursuit. We have some of his original books, which have a child's handwriting inside of them, which we think is pretty cool. Yes, they are part of the collection. He has several of that era. He began to collect items--books, photographs--starting at a very early age. He began to paint about 1918 or so, when he was about 12; his father was an architect in Chicago. He learned architectural drafting, which is what he taught here.

He studied classical languages, but he taught drafting. He started to network with people. His family took annual cruises on--I think it was the Northern Transportation Lines. His favorite ship was the *Manitou*, which you can see there on the side.

A cruise ship?

A cruise ship. His family would go on a cruise on that ship every year. One of his fondest memories was to ride on that boat, come back; they always went to the Manitou Island shoal in northern Lake

Michigan. That was a fun thing. When he joined the priesthood in the 1930s, he began to work at Sugar Island. At that time he got into photography, and more into painting; that's when the most productive period of his life started, up until around the 1980s.

He made many connections with pilots and sea people in the Sault Ste. Marie area. He worked--began to publish, around 1945, when he first began to write for *Inland Seas* (journal of the Great Lakes Historical Society).

That's the Great Lakes Historical Society--Vermilion, Ohio.

Yes, it is. In the '30s he began to collect photographs, sometimes from the islanders, or people who would go up there on vacation. He got to know Albert Young, and got a number of pictures from him--and from the company that he had up there. He established a real broad base, and he just kept working out and out. When he was assigned here in 1940, to teach engineering graphics, he was instrumental in founding the Detroit Marine Historical Society. He was one of the founding members of the society. They put out the publication, *The Detroit Marine Historian.* He edited that publication off and on, and even as late as 1978 he was its editor. He used photos from his collection, and he would write up all the information. He got to know just everybody. He was shy, and yet when he got past that he was very charming. That's how he made lots of contacts.

The collection has been growing since the early '30s?

Yes. He started out with his own personal works, his own photographs, and books. Books that we get now--some of them are donated to us as gifts from people whom he knew, or from people who had asked him questions and gotten help from him.

One of his main interests was the "Lakers" of the First World War. We have an extensive collection of those photographs. He wrote and published a book on that. We have about two dozen copies of the book. The title is *The Lakers of World War I,* University of Detroit Press, and it was published in 1967. The book has 107 pages. It's illustrated throughout--all his photographs. He took some of them personally, others were from people he had talked to. He would contact them and they would send duplicates. Many of our photographs are duplications of other photographs, but we've found

Matthew L. Daley

Father Dowling

that our duplicates are the originals because the originals are gone. Many of the photos in this collection say, "From the Collection of So-and-So." But when we would write to the people responsible for these collections, they would write back and say they had no interest in getting the photographs back. They were gifts.

He left a vast collection of photographs. We're counting--we estimate that we have about 35,000 photos. We also have nearly as many negatives, probably 30,000. We are working on preserving those. And we'd like some day to have the negatives all turned into pictures--prints.

Are the negatives sorted--are they accessible to researchers, archivists, others who may want to refer to them?

Yes, they are. They are very accessible. We have them all broken down by ship's name. We have mylar sheets, and we'll have them in small plastic packages so that the acid doesn't eat into the negatives. It's a fairly simple procedure, but it's time-consuming.

So the collection has been growing since he came here. He made many contacts through the Detroit Historical Society, then he branched out into the national arena--through the Marine Historical Society of America. Their publication is "Steamboat Bill." He acted as an advisor on that.

Would you have some other statistics?

We have about 40-45,000 negatives. We have probably around 2,500 books, around 3,200 issues of various publications. Some of them are *U.S. Naval Proceedings, Inland Seas*, others. We also have a few artifacts and around 40 paintings of his. We also have a record of other paintings and where they went; we want to get a student assistant to come in and help us track down those paintings. If they-- the recipients--don't want them, we want them back.

He gave paintings away to just about anybody. He was very generous about that. We have a small binder of his paintings, and there are notes--"Where did such and such a painting go?" But we've found some. One turned up at the Henry Ford Museum. We're pleased to have them out. We don't have any problem with their being out, but a lot are gone. There may be a thousand or more like that.

This is the last work he did. The *Zenith City*. (Points.) We also have a partially finished work that he was painting. There are here a number of his very early paintings that we're really glad to have, plus some sketches. That one, the *Zenith City*, was done in 1994. He painted right up to the date of his death. But he was very frustrated because not only was his vision bad, but his hands would shake. He was very precise, and strove for absolute accuracy.

The collection has always been in this room?

No, it was transferred down here recently, in 1993. When I first got here, I was involved in moving it from Father Dowling's old quarters over to this room in the library. He went to the retirement center up at Clarkston--the Jesuit center, Colombiere. He left everything that he had. That was in August, 1993. I'm not sure what he moved--he was moving in stages.

We've created the research room, which used to be an old supply room. It's right out there. It's got all of our boxes right now. They just came in yesterday. We are very strict about how we set up our procedures for researchers--how they utilize this collection. We work with the Dossin Great Lakes Museum on Belle Isle and also with the Reuther Archives down at Wayne State University. Much of the technical advice we get is from them. We also work with the Institute for Great Lakes Research in Perrysburg, Ohio. Whatever researchers can't find here we refer to them, and whatever others can't find there, they refer to us. So we have a nice reciprocal relationship.

We're coming along very well. We haven't had any real big setbacks. Father Dowling had all this arranged for his understanding; he apologized when he gave it to us. He was like, "I don't think you

264   Craft Masters

guys are going to find everything." We've had to go back and search. We've created a list of all our research journals. The registries. Shipping manuals. We want to put those on-line so we can find them on the computer. We're creating a Web page for all of this so that World Wide Web users can track us down. As soon as we get the photographs into acid free folders, we'll catalogue them properly.

We started doing this back in September, 1993. He's got so many photographs--and each one he would scotch tape into the books. The acid has started to decay the pictures. So we had to cut each corner out, label it, get the folders, track it down. Some of the names are blurred, and we can't tell what the subject is. We've had to spend days trying to compare pictures and complete identifications. It's a slow process. But as we've gone along, we've gotten real good at it and are moving along well. We're probably more than half-way through.

How long do you think it will take to finish?

Another year or two. Once we have it done, we are going to apply for a grant. Right now we can't do that--we haven't gotten the photographs ready yet. We do have this distant vision of a unified database system, with Bowling Green, Kingston, Canal Park in Duluth, and so on.

As for official written materials on the collection, we don't yet have much. Like I said, up to now it's been, "Oh my goodness, we've got a disaster on our hands. We've got to try to straighten it out." The index right behind you indexes all the photographs we have. Father Dowling created that just before he left for Colombiere. Those highlighted in yellow means we have found the photographs.

Is the Edmund Fitzgerald *listed here?*

Yes, it is. He photographed it and painted it. He also had things from a large number of publications. Newspaper clippings, documentson the ship, that kind of thing. He kept meticulous track of the *Fitzgerald*. These other photos were organized by fleet--or at least by name. It seems to me that it was a special interest of his--or that he mentioned it as a special interest. That would be a year ago now.

The top ship, the model (on a cabinet), that was his very favorite ship. The *Duluth*. We want to use that on our brochure. It will be a kind of trademark. It's a package freighter. The model was given to

Surrounded by portions of the Dowling Collection, Matthew Daley and Christine Yancy, university archivist, work on files. The model (upper right), built by Father Dowling, is the *Lake Grampus*, a laker constructed in 1919.

From the Dowling Collection: The SS *Lake Larga* went into service in 1918. Only 10 years later, in 1928, the Ford Motor Company, owner, scrapped the Laker for unknown reasons. The ship wears the "dazzle camouflage" common among many ships of the World War I era.

him by friends. We've also made contacts with other friends of his. Mr. Al Jackman has been working here on a book on the vanishing canalers, which we're helping him complete.

Mr. Jackman runs a book distribution agency, named Great Lakes Memories, which deals in nothing but Great Lakes ships and memorabilia, models, videos, and so on. He's been very helpful when we needed to find books, or back copies of journals that Father Dowling had. Mr. Jackman and Father were friends for years, since the late 1940s.

You'll have archival materials from other sources--books, photos, whatever?

Yes. We usually try to work reciprocally with our researchers. If they find anything new to us, we say, Please let us know. Then we can go and find it. We usually get the same researchers back two or three times in a year.

I myself do research for my own studies. Others are here doing hobby work. They have a favorite ship and want more on it. We also have people here who are doing genealogy. Maybe looking for a particular ship on which one of that person's relatives worked. This is a very nice arrangement for tracking that kind of thing. We even have companies writing to us, looking for vessels that they no longer own, but did have at one time. We get some pretty strange requests.

These look official--U.S. Treasury Department.

Again--he got those from the Coast Guard. He knew people and he just kept picking things up. These over here are real neat and we have lot of fun going through them because they help us find the exact sizes. We've found various mistakes in them... In here are many of the small pamphlets and newspaper articles on anything and everything. Some from the 1930s. A lot on fleets. Some of his original manuscripts. He's even got a couple of steamboat tickets in those files that we're going to pull out. And we're very glad of that because some of those are very rare.

There are about 4,000 glass negatives here. We're going to take those out and put them in a special location. He didn't take these pictures. He found them in curiosity ships, in antique stores. Some of them were given to him as gifts.

He was a natural-born archivist.

He was. Here are a few more models. Father Dowling built that model of the *Titanic*. We're going to get some glue and fix it. A piece is broken off. That drawing is the *Crescent City*. I asked him if that was a pastel, and he said, No, it's crayon. The year there is 1924. The *Crescent City* was an automobile carrier. He would go out on breakwaters many times and draw and photograph.

Over here he's got his research guides--the *Blue Book of American Shipping, Beeson's Marine Directory, The Ship Master's Association Directory*. The directory goes from 1897 all the way to 1967. The Ship Master's Association became the I.S.M.A., or International Ship Master's Association, later. Then there are these small books, like pocket guides, that tell who commands what ship. They're the *Great Lakes Red Books*.

Here, in these folders, the ones with E.J.D. on them, we've got all his publications. Here also is what is probably the meat of our collection--all his fleet listings. A lot of these things were published in the *Detroit Marine Historian*. Most of them are hand written on the backs of other paper. He was very frugal, and didn't want to waste paper. The only problem with that paper is that it disintegrates; so does the handwriting. So we've started to make photocopies of all these. They're so light even the photocopier doesn't pick them up.

How many of these fleet listings are there?

About 60. There are also lists of the publications. *Marine News*, others. A lot of smaller notations from various years. He published magazine, newspaper, and journal articles. There are about 30 in all.

You're immersed in this sea of records and photos--if I can use that phrase. Have you ever been on a Laker?

I've never sailed on one, no. One of my goals is to find out how to take a trip on one or to win a trip on one. I will say I've visited all the museum ships on the Great Lakes, from the *William A. Irvin* in Duluth to the *William G. Mather* in Cleveland. I couldn't rate one higher than the others--they're all delightful.

Remember the first Laker you ever saw?

268   Craft Masters

Very well. It was the *Philip R. Clarke* of the U.S. Steel fleet. I was about 5 or 6 and was visiting the Soo Locks with my parents. We were just south of MacArthur Park. The *Clarke* coasted out going downbound. Just as my parents and I reached the fence the *Clarke* sounded its horn. At a distance of about 200 feet, it was very loud. I jumped a foot in the air. My parents roared with laughter.

You're aware that some of the ships represented in these archives pass in the Detroit River?

I know. The river is about six miles from here as the crow flies.

Is there a chance you could become another Father Dowling?   A collector?

No, I don't think so. The whole thing fascinates me, and I'm soon going to have a bachelor of arts degree in technology and cultural history, with emphasis on the Great Lakes. But I've got plans to go on to a master's degree. I expect to be busy. Maybe I'm just not the collector type.

VI

Movers and Shakers

Build thee more stately mansions, O my soul,
As the swift seasons roll!
Leave thy low-vaulted past!
Let each new temple, nobler than the last,
Shut thee from heaven with a dome more vast,
Till thou at length art free,
Leaving thine outgrown shell by life's unresting sea!

-- From "The Chambered Nautilus,"
Oliver Wendell Holmes

DAVID P. KENSLER

(1992)

He's a warbird collector/restorer, a wartime-vintage airplane hobbyist. His company is Warbird Aircraft Restoration and Salvage, Inc. of Waterford, Michigan. He owns the F4F-3 Grumman Wildcat that was fished out of Lake Michigan in late 1991. After nearly four years of restoration the Wildcat flew again on June 20, 1995--almost 52 years since its last flight. It went on exhibit in the Kalamazoo Aviation History Museum in the fall of 1995 and in August, 1996 it returned home to the Oakland/Pontiac Airport. Dave Kensler's story is that of the discovery and restoration of the Wildcat--and of locating the pilot who survived the June 21, 1943 crash into 220 feet of Lake

Michigan water.

* * *

It all started with an innocent telephone call from a military aircraft broker in December of 1991. He said he had an airplane, an F4F-3 Grumman Wildcat, for sale that just came out of Lake Michigan where it had spent the last 49 years! He said that I just had to come over and see it. "Sure, just what I need--a money pit!"

Give us some background?

In 1978 my brother-in-law, George Everett, invited me to go to the Oshkosh Airshow. Until that time I had never even been in small airplanes and knew virtually nothing about them. During that visit I walked through the "Warbird" area and saw up close these military airplanes of all descriptions that were privately owned. To say the least the experience opened my eyes to a very exciting though

Before it was converted for use as a World War II aircraft carrier (USS *Wolverine*), the *Seeandbee* ranked as the largest sidewheel steamer in the world. Built in 1912, it could carry 2,300 passengers. It saw 28 years of luxury service on Lake Erie before its conversion. The painting of the *Seeandbee* hangs in the Inland Seas Maritime Museum in Vermilion, Ohio, a repository operated by the Great Lakes Historical Society.

financially remote possibility--that "someday" I could actually own one of these magnificent airplanes.

Over the next several years I was able to scrape the necessary funds together to start and complete my private pilot training in rented Cessna 172's. To date (1992) I have accumulated 1,200 hours and an instrument rating in a very mixed bag of airplanes.

In 1988, with the support and understanding of my wife, Brenda, coupled with some luck in the business world, I was able to purchase a 1952 Harvard MKIV. It had taken me 10 years to go from dreamer to owner/pilot.

This set the stage for the F4F-3?

It did. The first sight of the Wildcat was a very poor fax that showed that it was an airplane but little else. I showed the picture to my full-time A&P (airframe and powerplant mechanic) and restoration chief--Mike Dodman--and asked him what he thought. His basic response was that I was crazy. I called Mark Clark of Courtesy Aircraft, Rockford, Illinois back and said we felt the project was more than we could handle financially and that the Wildcat would probably be better off in the hands of a more substantial restoration shop. Mark disagreed and said that the plane was in exceptional condition and warranted a personal inspection. After kicking around the possibilities we made the trip over to Chicago to do a "quick" inspection of the Wildcat with the basic intention to just see it and no more.

Legend had it that there were over 100 military airplanes of all types in Lake Michigan. The problem was to get them out and have clear title from the Navy. Due to the U.S. retaining ownership of everything forever coupled with the great cost and complexity of location and recovery, most people have long given up on even trying to secure one of these planes.

This situation was unique in a number of areas. It seems that the Navy had authorized a salvage company to do a survey of the airplanes in Lake Michigan and to bring up those worthy of recovery due to the great demand from various museums and manufacturer retiree groups that wanted to secure these planes for their use. In lieu of payment, the Navy allowed the salvage company to retain and sell two airframes in order to recoup their expenses. The two airframes were the ones that we were the first to see. Mud and water were both still dripping from the airplanes on our arrival. The paint was in such a good condition that we originally considered leaving it alone.

After about 45 minutes Mike came over and stated with a very startled expression that he "couldn't find anything wrong with one of the aircraft." He had looked very carefully in all the usual places for corrosion and structural damage but found nothing significantly wrong.

That's after 49-plus years in Lake Michigan--a collector's dream.

We had to decide right there and then. The firm asking price was $250,000 cash. Whenever I have found myself in similar circumstances I have always done the same thing--call my wife and get her opinion. After a short conversation, she agreed that it might be a rare opportunity that probably wouldn't ever come around again and that if it looked that good--go for it! So, after some quick negotiations I said yes.

The airplane we purchased--with clear title--is a Grumman built F4F-3 Wildcat and is extremely rare. This was the first of the famed "Grumman Cats": Wildcat, Hellcat, Bearcat, Tigercat, and Tomcat. There hasn't been an actual Grumman Wildcat flying for many years. It is the fixed-wing variant and only 285 were ever built.

This four-machinegun fighter was the same model airplane that John Thatch and Butch O'Hare flew in the battle of the Coral Sea in 1942. A lot of the bad press heaped on the Wildcat was not aimed at the F4F-3 but the F4F-4 variant due to the extra weight of the folding wings and the addition of two more 50 caliber machineguns without a corresponding increase in horsepower. These changes had a dramatic impact on the performance of the airplane.

Currently there are only 19 Wildcats registered in the U.S. Of those, only nine are currently airworthy. Most of these are in private collections or museums. There are no flying Grumman Wildcats. This point has spurred our efforts to do a world-class restoration.

A historical sidelight is that the F4F-3 under the British name Martlet was the first American airplane to shoot down a German airplane. On Christmas Day 1940, almost one year before Pearl Harbor, a Junkers 88 tried to sneak in and bomb the Royal Navy shore base at Scapa Flow in the Orkney Islands; two Wildcats intercepted it.

After transporting the plane back to Pontiac, Michigan's Oakland/Pontiac Airport via Worldwide Aircraft Recovery, we started

A trainer careens off the deck of the USS *Wolverine*, one of the two converted sidewheel steamers that served as aircraft carriers in Lake Michigan during World War II. The plane crashed in the lake, but the pilot was unhurt. (Photo: Chicago Maritime Society)

in on the rehab work.

The nitty-gritty taking place under Dodman's direction?

Yes, and there were some specific discoveries during the first inspection:

1. There was 1943 air in the tires.
2. There was oil in the oil tank, oil coolers, and lines.
3. There was gas in the gas tank.
4. There were 2,000 pounds of oxygen in the air bottle.
5. The struts were up and properly inflated.

The first questions were how and why was this airplane in such good condition. These questions led to my search for the history of our Wildcat. We started with a very poor copy of the Navy's accident report that was our only original source of information on the plane.

In this report we found some very important information that spurred the quest for more details. We had the bureau number--12296; the pilot's name--George Anthony Hahn; the accident date--June 21, 1943; and the cause of the accident--prop control failure. This information gave us something to go on. We started our search, which led to the Grumman History Center in Bethpage, Long Island, New York, and the Grumman historian, Peter Kirkup.

It turns out that our airplane was built on February 13, 1943 as part of a batch of 100 airplanes of the grand total of 285 F4F-3's built by Grumman that were originally going to be F4F-7 Reconnaissance float planes, or Grumman "Wildcatfish." Ultimately they were finished as fixed wing F4F-3's and turned over to the training command at Glenview Naval Air Station north of Chicago. Our airplane was only 68 days old when it went into the water.

A little known fact is that over 12,000 pilots carrier-qualified on Lake Michigan during WW II. Training on two converted sidewheel passenger steamers--the *Wolverine* and the *Sable*, the cadets flying from the various fields surrounding Glenview would proceed out to the two training carriers to complete their required number of landings, usually in the same type aircraft they would be flying in combat.

Our airplane went into the lake after a takeoff from the *Sable*. An interesting note is that President George Bush carrier-qualified on the *Sable* approximately one month after George Hahn's incident with our Wildcat. We also answered the question as to how this airplane was in such good condition. Grumman had built the airplane to government specifications that required the plane to operate in a saltwater environment for its projected 250 hour operational life.

You had answered the <u>where</u> question--<u>where</u> the plane was found--and what that had to do with its preservation.

The airplane was down about 220 feet, some 30 miles northeast of Glenview. The constant temperature, lack of sunlight (no ultraviolet light), lack of vegetation, and low oxygen content of the water at that depth all joined in preserving the airplane. It also helped that the plane was upside-down, nose-down, buried in mud. As we disassembled the plane we encountered one discovery after another.

Here are just a few of the highlights:

1. After charging electrolyte several times, the battery held a full charge
2. Several position lightbulbs worked
3. Most of the gear assemblies were still filled with grease and totally unaffected by 49 years under water
4. Trim wheels and various other control systems were fully functional
5. All rubber gaskets, etc., were still soft and pliable
6. The manual hand landing gear retract system worked on the first try
7. Most of the bearings were functional and greased
8. The spirit level in the gunsight worked perfectly
9. Of the 3,000 plus screws in the plane, only 10 had to be drilled out.

Since our restoration efforts one of the most asked questions was "What happened to the pilot?" So we started to see if we could find the pilot who did such an excellent job of putting the plane in the water with no structural damage. All we had to go on was his name--George Anthony Hahn.

After several months of dead ends, we wrote the FAA to see if George ever received any civilian pilot certificates. About three weeks went by and we received a letter stating that a George Anthony Hahn had indeed received several civilian certificates and that his last listed address was dated 1973.

You can imagine how excited we were in calling information and getting a phone number. After several anxious moments, I dialed the number and a man answered. I asked if he was George Anthony Hahn and he said yes. And then I asked if he put a Wildcat into Lake Michigan in 1943 and after a pause, he said yes. After that statement and a huge sigh of relief, we started a very long conversation during which George went through the training accident caused by the faulty prop governor control on the Curtis Electric propeller.

276   Movers and Shakers

After carrier qualification, George went on to fly F6F Hellcats in the Pacific to the end of the war. After the war, he became a CPA under the GI bill. He was 21 years old on that June day and stated that we were lucky we didn't find him in the plane because his parachute straps had become tangled and he truly felt he was going to drown. Now, at 71, George has agreed to come and be present when the Wildcat takes to the air on our scheduled completion date of June 21, 1993--50 years to the day after it went into Lake Michigan.

(Note: There were some "gotcha's." The restoration took nearly four years.)

ROBERT A. "BOB" MANGLITZ

(1996)

On November 16, 1990, the S.S. Badger made its last voyage across Lake Michigan as a railroad car ferry. Operating between Ludington, Michigan and Kewaunee, Wisconsin, the 410-foot, 4,300-ton ship had carried railroad cars, passengers, and automobiles on a twice-daily, year-round schedule. Its passing seemed to sound the death knell for the cross-lake ferry service between Michigan and Wisconsin that could trace its beginnings to 1875, when the westward-creeping tracks of the Flint & Pere Marquette Railroad had reached historic Ludington.

Fortunately, the Badger story didn't end there. In 1991, the late Charles Conrad, Ludington native, magnate, and visionary, "put his money where his mouth was." While the entire Ludington region breathed a sigh of relief, the Badger underwent a face-lift. Workmen paved over the railroad tracks that had accommodated up to 32 railroad cars in a single cargo. The ship by degrees became a comfortable, well appointed passenger-motor vehicle ferry, with railroad cars no longer part of its future and with a mandate to run only between May and October over the 60-mile route between Ludington and Manitowoc. The ship returned to service on May 18, 1992.

Charles Conrad died in 1995, having lived long enough to see his dream of a revived cross-lake ferry come to life. Robert A. Manglitz, chief executive officer of Lake Michigan Carferry Service, Inc., took over the task of further implementing--and possibly expanding--the historic tradition. Bob Manglitz paints in the details only weeks after the Badger *completed its fifth season as the Great Lakes' only passenger-oriented cross-lake ferry...*

* * *

How do you see the Badger *and the ferry service as they relate to the communities involved?*

For both communities, Manitowoc and Ludington, the car ferry service has importance far beyond the mere fact that there's an easy way to cross the lake at its waist. You can look at this in terms of both employees and passengers. We employ some 220 people at both ends of the ferry route across the lake and on the *Badger*. Not only is that a boon as far as employment is concerned; the communities believe-- they *know*--that the service enhances their images. When we inaugurated the new summer service for passengers and motor vehicles in 1992, we had press coverage that you wouldn't believe.

Just to give you an idea... The story was covered in more than 400 newspapers in major markets throughout the United States and Canada. We received radio coverage in 15 major markets and TV coverage in 25 major markets. The whole thing put Lake Michigan Carferries on the map along with the two communities and the Great Lakes themselves. It was almost as if the country welcomed the renewal of ferry service on the lake.

All that's over and above the economic impact on the two communities.

Absolutely. That's hard to figure because both Ludington and

Manitowoc draw thousands more visitors each year because of the ferry. One estimate puts the economic advantage to the two cities at $15,000,000 to $20,000,000. That's for each city. West Shore Community College, outside Ludington, has done some extensive research on this.

I don't think anyone can measure the psychological impact of the restored car-ferry service. A lot of people, employees and others, tell us that it's exciting to be part of this process of growth, and to see the *Badger* take on new life as a passenger vessel. We also have many passengers writing to us to pass on thanks and compliments. They appreciate the fact that the historic tradition has been revived--they feel it's something that *should* live on.

The prospects look positive?

Very. The passenger counts have increased by 150 percent over the last year of the railroad operation. The counts have, in fact, gone up every year since we carried 110,000 in 1992.

Do you foresee any expansion of the cross-lake ferry service?

It's always in the backs of our minds. We wouldn't go back into ferrying railroad cars across the lake. That takes year-round operation, and really isn't economically viable in today's context. You get into a curious bind with that kind of service. You have to commit to the year-round service, but doing that makes it impossible to develop fully the potential of the car ferry as a passenger-oriented operation. That's why we've concentrated on the passenger service as a primary focus.

We did make a major commitment of financial resources to renovate the *Badger* to meet the needs of passengers. We decided first how we wanted the ship to look as a refurbished passenger-auto ferry. Paving over the tracks was one major initial step. Then we expanded the passenger areas and applied new paint. We did a lot of mechanical work to ready the *Badger* to sail again. When we were done--right now--we had a ship that will carry up to 620 passengers and 180 autos, tour busses, recreational vehicles, semi-trucks, and even bicycles and motorcycles.

You've added some passenger amenities?

A lot of them. We have the "Upper Deck Cafe" serving buffet-style breakfast, lunch, and dinner. The "Badger Galley" on the main deck offers a variety of sandwiches, salads, snacks, and beverages. On a typical four-hour crossing no one needs to go hungry.

There are attractions for all ages. The "Badger Boatique" offers a selection of souvenirs, clothing, and reading materials. There's a small museum chronicling the important highlights of car-ferry history. Next year (1997) by the way, we'll be celebrating the 100th anniversary of Lake Michigan car-ferry service. Every day, on every trip, we have a story-time for our families and younger passengers. The stories deal with the Great Lakes as a fresh-water resource and the ways in which young people can help protect the Lakes. There's also a video arcade and movie lounge with lots of comfortable seating.

About seating--we put in some additional aircraft seating in the upper aft areas. That was part of a project that also involved replacement of canvas curtains with sliding glass windows. There's also plenty of outdoor seating for those who want to take it easy and watch the glorious lake go by, nap, or read a book.

You have staterooms also, I believe.

Yes, we do. There are 42 staterooms for people who want to rest or even spend the night in an authentic car-ferry stateroom. The staterooms have 84 berths.

Robert Manglitz, president and chief executive officer, Lake Michigan Carferry Service, Inc.

All this is the result of the dedication of one man--Mr. Conrad?

He was the prime mover. He was an individual who throughout his career always placed challenges and opportunities for his employees above the profit line. He owned a number of corporations in his lifetime, but I doubt that he was as passionate about anything as he was about re-starting the ferry service. Lake Michigan Carferry Service is really his creation. If he hadn't invested in the company and the project, it wouldn't have come into being. I'm convinced of that.

There's one thing--I don't believe his dream has been realized completely. He hoped to have all three of our vessels operating on the Great Lakes--not only the *Badger* but also the *City of Midland* and the *Spartan*. That may be possible some day. Sometime in the near future we'll be researching the possibility of utilizing another of our car ferries for a run between Ludington and another location on the Lakes.

The next likely candidate for activation would be the *City of Midland*. In many ways this ship is more passenger-compatible than the *Spartan* or the *Badger*. It would start with more accommodations and passenger space available.

Are there stats on the current operations of the Badger*?*

Sure. The ship travels approximately 22,200 miles per season, or about 110,000 since we went back into operation in 1992. Before that, the *Badger* had traveled somewhere in the neighborhood of 3,295,000 miles, most of them between Ludington and Milwaukee, Wisconsin. The *Badger* now makes 430 one-way trips each season.

Would you have some details on the history of the Badger*?*

Yes. She was built in 1952 by the Christy Corporation of Sturgeon Bay, Wisconsin. The cost of construction was $5,000,000.

The *Badger* was launched on September 6, 1952, and began daily service on March 21, 1953. Car-ferry service between Michigan and Wisconsin has really been in existence for 100 years next year (1997). After the *Badger* ended its cross-lake voyages in 1990, it lay idle for a year and a half. It has a beam, or width, of 59½ feet and is the equivalent of four stories in height.

The *Badger*, outside and inside. A view inside the car decks (top) suggests how the ship can transport about 180 vehicles of various sizes. Docked in Ludington (bottom), the ship readies for another trip across Lake Michigan to Manitowoc.

You might be interested in our propellers. Each one is 14 feet in diameter. The two of them are solid four-blade cast steel with a weight of 15,400 pounds. The anchors weigh 7,000 pounds each. The *Badger's* average sea speed is 18 miles an hour. Her max speed is 24 miles per hour.

You've carried some famous personages?

We have, yes. The list of entertainers is a long one, and dates back to the *Badger's* start in 1953. The entertainers include Jack Benny and Mary Livingston, Cary Grant, Tyrone Power, and Agnes Moorehead. There were also Artie Shaw, the band leader, Tammy Wynette, Little Jimmy Dickens, The Who, and Weird Al Yankovich.

A number of baseball players have also crossed the Lake with us. There were George Kell, Harry Heilmann, Larry McPhail, and Eddie Matthews. The Angolan Olympic basketball team crossed with the

282   Movers and Shakers

Badger and so did the tennis stars, Pancho Gonzales and Vic Seixias. There are probably some that I've overlooked.

The history of car-ferry service goes back to 1897. But weren't there attempts before that to establish such a service?

Several of them. In 1875 the Flint & Pere Marquette Railroad chartered the 175-foot side-wheeler the *John Sherman* to provide service between Ludington and Sheboygan, Wisconsin. After one season the *Sherman* was found to be too small for the volume of freight generated on the route.

In 1882, two wooden bulk freighters were built to run between Ludington and Milwaukee shuttling grain, passengers, and package freight. The steamers were 145 feet long with hulls that were strengthened to withstand heavy ice. By 1890, the fleet was expanded to give bulk steamers with expanded service to Manistee, Michigan and Manitowoc, Wisconsin. Although successful, the railroad management was keenly observant of a new innovation developed by the rival Ann Arbor Railroad. This innovation threatened the future of the Ludington steamer fleet.

James M. Ashley, former governor of Montana and then president of the Ann Arbor Railroad, had a long-standing dream that became a reality in November 1892. The 260-foot wooden hulled *Ann Arbor I* carried its first cargo of loaded railroad cars across the open waters of Lake Michigan between Frankfort, Michigan and Kewaunee, Wisconsin.

Was that the end of the F&PM?

No. Within a few years the Ann Arbor ferry fleet was expanded to three vessels serving several Michigan and Wisconsin ports. This marked a revolution in cross-lake shipping. But during this period the F&PM went ahead with plans to develop a similar fleet of car ferries. Capitalizing on Ann Arbor's lessons, the F&PM in 1896 placed an order with naval architect Robert Logan to design the first steel-hulled cross-lake ferry. The construction contract was awarded to the F.W. Wheeler Company of West Bay City, Michigan. The new ferry was 350 feet long, 56 feet wide, and capable of carrying 30 train cars.

Launched in December, 1896, and ready for service by February,

1897, the ship was named *Pere Marquette*. She developed 2,500 horsepower generated by two fore-and-aft compound engines and traveled at about 12½ miles an hour between Ludington and Manitowoc. This was the real start of long-term ferry service.

The *Pere Marquette* was an immediate success and proved to be a fine icebreaker. The Robert Logan design was so good that it set the standard for many railroad ferries built in the twentieth century on the Great Lakes and abroad.

By 1900, the F&PM was merged with the Chicago & West Michigan and the Detroit, Grand Rapids & Western Railroads. The combined railroad was called the Pere Marquette Railway. The PMR acquired a wooden car ferry named *Muskegon*, later called *Pere Marquette 16*.

You recently hosted a meeting of the Historical Society of Michigan...

Yes. They had more than 160 people at the meeting. Most of them visited the ship on September 21, the first day of their meeting. Then about 85 members of the Historical Society went across the lake with us the next day--across and back. While in Manitowoc, they visited the Wisconsin Maritime Museum. They had the bad luck to visit there while the submarine exhibit, the U.S.S. *Cobia*, was out for refurbishing. But the other exhibits are just as marvelous.

The captain who took the *Badger* to Manitowoc was Bruce Masse. We have two licensed, experienced captains, Captain Masse and Capt. Dean Hobbs. They trade off every two days in the summer running season.

Have you formulated plans for a 100th anniversary celebration?

Not totally. We know we'll have an extra-special "Carferry Days" celebration when the *Badger* goes back into service in May of 1997. These days are held every year--a whole weekend of festivities near our docks in Ludington. The city takes part, and they have rides, games, tours of the *Badger*, refreshments, just about everything you'd have in a carnival.

Now that I think about it, that's not as far off as it sounds.

284   Movers and Shakers

POST OFFICE TO THE GREAT LAKES

"Maintaining a 116-year tradition, sailors passing through the Detroit River have come to look forward to a special kind of mail call. In the bend of the river just west of the Ambassador Bridge, they may receive a letter from home.   A wedding invitation.   A birth announcement.   A gossipy, newsy missive with pictures of former classmates. A document that needs to be signed.

"In the early days, when the tradition was young, John Ward Westcott used his rowboat to greet the sailing crews with welcome letters and packages. Today (1989), the tradition continues from a 45-foot mailboat, the *J. W. Westcott II...* The *Westcott* and the family business that operates it have their own zip code--48222. They run their friendly communication system under contract with the U.S. Postal Service--and have been doing so continuously since 1948."

;-- Magazine report, August, 1989

JAMES HOGAN

(1989)

In 1996 the tradition has flourished for 123 years. James Hogan, great-grandson of the founder, is vice president and general manager of the J. W. Westcott Company. The year 1995 saw the company using its two radar-equipped boats, the 45-foot J. W. Westcott II *and the 40-foot* Joseph J. Hogan, *to deliver slightly under 400,000 pieces of mail and freight to lakers passing up or down on the Detroit River. At river's edge the company works out of the single-story building, almost in the shadow of the Ambassador Bridge, that it first occupied in 1955.*

The 10-person fulltime staff not only delivers mail and packages to the ships that pass in the day or night; they bring mail and freight off the ships for dispatch through the postal system or other channels. The Westcott company is also "a nautical bookstore, with well over 175 different titles and with written aids to navigation, both U.S. and Canadian; a chart agent; and the 7-11 of the Great Lakes, providing various kinds of snack foods, pop, pizza, and assorted edibles and potables. All we need is an hour's advance notice from the ship as it approaches our headquarters."

But let Jim Hogan tell it as he did in 1989...

* * *

A trip to deliver the mail can be a real experience. After receiving a call from a ship, a call that often includes orders for newspapers and other supplies, our "postmaster" and a crew of one race to load the appropriate mail and other goods onto the *Westcott II*. Since the big ships can't stop, the *Westcott II* simply ties up alongside them. The ship's crew lowers a pail from their deck to the *Westcott II*.

The mail goes into the container and is hoisted up by the sailors on board. Larger packages may, literally, be thrown up to the deck. All this time the ship and our boat are yawing and rolling in the hefty currents and swells of the Detroit River. With the loading done, and with incoming mail secured on board our boat, the freighter gives a toot on the ship's horn. That's a salute to our people. The whole operation averages about seven minutes.

All this started in 1874?

Yes. My great-grandfather, John Ward Westcott, began the service that year. He did use a rowboat at first. For the pickup and delivery service he provided he charged a fee on each piece of mail. The fee ranged up to 25 cents per item, a substantial overwrite on the basic charge for postage.

No one minded the extra cost. The service became critically important, I think largely because it brought ships and crews up to date on personal, shipping trade, and national-international news--and of course made it unnecessary for through traffic to dock to pick up mail and supplies. At one time, before hiring halls and union cards, my great-grandfather even hired sailors for ships that were shorthanded.

Tied up to a Great Lakes freighter, the *J. W. Westcott II* seems to be engulfed in Detroit River spray. During the shipping season, delivering "mail by the pail" or bag is a nonstop task. (Photo courtesy J. W. Westcott Co.)

The story goes that Captain Westcott would make sure that the sailors got on board as the ships passed.

My great-grandfather died in 1913. He had proved the need for the kind of service he was offering. By the time of his death the firm was using several rowboats. But it was no longer carrying mail. Starting in 1895, the federal Postal Service used a series of boats of its own to make mail deliveries and pickups.

The firm obviously survived.

It survived that and other competition. It was providing a range of ancillary services, like delivering supplies, packages that the postal service couldn't handle, and other things like food and personal items. Over time the company used a diverse collection of boats that changed with the times. There was one constructed in 1920.

The *J. W. Westcott II* was built in 1949. By 1948 the postal service people had decided that they'd be well advised to contract out the water-borne mail service. The contract went to our firm. We've been doing this job as part of the postal service ever since. But none of us is *in* the postal service.

It's always been a family business, always adapting to conditions and needs?

We have to . I represent the fourth Westcott generation that has run or helped run the business. My father, Joseph Hogan, ran the business for some years and my mother, June Westcott Hogan, was also active in it. I've been working here since 1974 and have been general manager since 1983. We operated without a backup vessel for 25 years, and finally got a former Corps of Engineers survey boat, the *Joseph W. Hogan*, re-named after my Dad. Our people work shifts, seven days a week, 24 hours a day. We work some 252 days a year, during the shipping season. That season begins in April and runs until December. Sometimes, depending on the weather, it runs into the first or second week of January.

In winter we go over the boats, overhauling them. We work over every inch. They're dependable, solid boats. We used to depend on other boats to pinch-hit for the *Westcott* when she went out. Now we don't have to.

You had other locations before moving here?

Several--all on the river. This building is about right for us, medium-sized, about 70 by 80 feet in extent. It's a good location, foot of 24th Street, and what I call a conservative building, with basic necessities. You have to remember that we use the building only eight to eight and one-half months a year. We have a couple of offices here, some workrooms and a warehouse area.

You ferry people to or from the ships?

Yes. A crew member on one of the freighters may have to go ashore for personal reasons. A freighter may change officers, literally in mid-river. Some of the people heading out to the lakers are pilots. The pilots are needed on the Great Lakes from Montreal westward through the lakes and rivers. We don't supply the pilots. We only provide transportation to and from the ships.

We get calls, usually, an hour or more in advance of the ship's arrival opposite our headquarters. They call us on the marine band. Then we have to rush around getting together everything that's going to them. We tell the ship what we're going to be delivering. Our deck hand and captain on duty do this work. They may have to prepare 30 to 50 different items from oil to dish soap. Freight forwarding is our ticket. We consider anything that comes through our door a piece of freight. We are compensated accordingly.

We're a Mobil Oil consignee. That means we handle the Port of Detroit shipments of Mobil lubricants.

How does mail get to you on its way to the ships?

Mail is processed through the general mail facility in downtown Detroit. It's divided by zip code so that everything marked 48222 finds its way to us here at the Detroit River Station. It arrives by postal truck each day and we subdivide every shipment into pigeonholes and No. 3 sacks, making everything ready for delivery.

The boat crews send mail through us, as you know. They provide their correspondents with full forwarding addresses. That means the name of a sailor or officer, the name of the ship, and "Detroit, Michigan," with the 48222 zip code.

As a licensed chart agent we stock a lot of charts--all those needed for travel in the Great Lakes, the east coast, and the southeastern coastal waters. We can get any charts that anyone would need within hours or a day or two. The charts can be for waters anywhere in the

Relaying passengers to or from passing "lakers" is also part of the service performed by the J. W. Westcott boats and personnel. A ladder simplifies the transfer from the *J. W. Westcott II* to the deck of the laker. (Photo courtesy J. W. Westcott Co.)

world. We've been rated among the top 4 percent of the licensed chart agents in the United States.

Do you receive calls from boats docked on the Detroit River?

Yes. To deliver these items, we use a truck. We can go dock to dock. A ship may need to have a parcel picked up. They may want replacement or repair parts. They sometimes call for cleaning equipment, electronic parts or gear, soap, light bulbs, rags, almost anything. We have wholesale outfits where we can get just about everything we need. That's true for boats docked or passing through. But the bulk of our work is with the moving traffic on the Detroit River. Ninety-nine times out of a hundred we can approach the ships visually. We sit on the high side of this bend in the river and can see three and a half miles in both directions.

Of all the stuff we move, maybe 40 or 45 percent is mail, Federal Express parcels, or packages shipped in other ways. We do get some mail that has been mis-addressed; it has the 48222 zip code. That number was designated specifically for the J. W. Westcott Company.

With a history as long as yours, there must have been some incidents that made news.

There were a lot of them. One was in a history of our company written in 1979. That item was about the famous *Erie-Tashmoo* race in 1901. In October, 1900, the story runs, President Parker of the White Star Line boasted to a reporter that his steamer, the *Tashmoo*, could beat any other steamer on the Great Lakes, including the *City of Erie* and the *City of Buffalo*. These two were passenger steamers operated by the rival Cleveland and Buffalo Transit Company. Parker said he would back up his claim with $1,000. The manager of the C&B Line wrote to my great-grandfather asking if it were true that Parker had made such a statement and was serious.

Grandfather, as a neutral observer, held the stakes--$1,000 from each competitor. The race took place June 4, 1901. The *City of Erie* beat the *Tashmoo* by a mere 45 seconds. The course stretched between Cleveland and Erie, Pennsylvania. The two vessels ran the course in just over four hours and 20 minutes. Besides holding the stakes, my great-grandfather had helped make some of the incidental arrangements

290   Movers and Shakers

for the race.

Your great-grandfather was famous after that?

Probably before and after. It was a rather unique service that he provided, and still is. We believe we're the only water-borne post office in the world.

OSWEGO: TRADITION REVISITED

"The Great Lakes comprise the largest fresh water system in the world and directly or indirectly serve the needs of over one hundred million people for industry, transportation, drinking and cooling water, and recreations each day. However, all is not as it should be with the Great Lakes, as you are well aware...

"It is imperative that we develop a program to promote a positive interest in the Great Lakes resulting in a stimulated and concerned public through which lasting solutions can arise. The alternatives before us are clear: If we choose inaction as our course, then we must accept the inevitable consequences. If we choose to face the issues confronting the Great Lakes now and resolve to apply our combined effort to restore this part of our heritage, our history, and our future to the place where it belongs, there is hope."

-- Dr. Henry A. Spang, talk before the Oswego (N.Y.) Maritime Foundation, reported in "Mari/Times" newsletter, Spring, 1983

HENRY A. SPANG

(1997)

He proposed the Education Through Involvement (ETI) program way back in 1983. The occasion was a meeting of the Oswego Maritime Foundation, "a nonprofit organization dedicated to public service through maritime recreation, research, and education." Suiting action to the word in subsequent years, Dr. Spang became project director and was a prime mover when the keel for the good ship OMF Ontario *went down in 1988. Summer in and summer out he exhorted, supported, and organized as volunteer shipwrights, welders, carpenters, and others hammered and fitted, eventually producing the completed hull that stretched 85 feet along Oswego's waterfront.*

One hundred and fifteen years to the day after the last locally built schooner had slid down the ways, Henry A. Spang watched and cheered as the new incarnation of an honored tradition splashed into Oswego Harbor. The Ontario, *he could properly figure, was his baby as much as anyone's. More important, she was the sea-going embodiment of the program he had advocated: an educational effort geared to all ages and fired by the four basic concepts of history, heritage, resources, and ecology. The floating classroom that the* Ontario *would become had, in brief, those concepts as her guiding beacons.*

In early 1997 Henry Spang details how the schooner project came alive, recalls the thrill of the 1994 launching ceremonies, and describes what will happen when she takes to the water as a schoolship...

* * *

It's been a long, hard road.

In a way. But we've had a lot of help. It's been a community project since the beginning. I doubt that it would have gotten this far if that hadn't been the case.

292   Movers and Shakers

Before we started construction in 1988 we were able to test our on-board ETI Program. We did that in 1985 when the brigantine *St. Lawrence* came to Oswego from Kingston, Ontario for a visit. The *St. Lawrence* docked at the OMF (Oswego Maritime Foundation) Education Center down at the docks. More than 1,000 visitors flocked to the *St. Lawrence* during an open house and tour of the ship one evening.

Then the next day we brought two groups of 25 young people on board the *St. Lawrence*. All of them were in the OMF sailing scholarship classes. The two groups sailed into Lake Ontario on the brigantine while learning about Great Lakes history and the Lakes' heritage. They were able to collect and sample the water to learn about the balance of aquatic life. Mike DuGuay, a local guitar troubadour, kept the groups in the sailing spirit with sing-a-long sea chanties.

A smash success?

It was. The simulation, or dry run, with our program taught us that we were on the right track. The materials we were teaching would do their jobs once we had our own schooner.

It was a lucky chance that the *St. Lawrence* was 85 feet long-- exactly the length that we were envisioning for our schooner. So the simulation was perfect in every way. We were planning to have groups of up to 25 or so take classes once we had a ship of our own.

The principles behind the instruction had already been laid out?

Yes. They're very straightforward. The ETI Program was created, first, to foster an appreciation of our maritime history. Second, it was designed to increase understanding of the Great Lakes heritage. Third, it had the purpose of enhancing knowledge of Great Lakes resources. Finally, it would, we hoped, develop an awareness of how fragile the Lakes' ecosystem is. So we had four guiding principles that we could summarize as history, heritage, resources, and ecology.

We were hoping, and are still planning, to involve not only school children but seniors, community and civic groups, business organizations, and professional associations. That means just about everybody with an interest in the Lakes.

Was Education Through Involvement a working, viable program from the time the St. Lawrence *visited Oswego?*

Definitely. We went into schools with the program during the 1980s and later, after construction of our schooner started. The *St. Lawrence* gave us a great boost and got the community behind the whole thing. Suddenly we could see just how it would work.

We laid the keel for the schooner in 1988. The excitement started to build at that point. When weather permitted, and work was proceeding, we almost never failed to have 10 to 20 people working on the ship. She's 85 feet long and has all the necessary facilities, so it's been a massive task. All the workers have been volunteers. They've been skilled and unskilled, men and women. Most of the materials came to us through private contributions. We even had people donating special technical services and equipment.

You were "clerk of the works?"

Yes. That meant I had to coordinate all the schooner-related activities, from public programs on ETI to design changes, special displays, and onshore promotion. But starting in 1988 the ship was taking shape in front of the entire community, or the entire region, and we had a constant stream of visitors.

You had to handle work assignments?

Among officials and guests attending the ceremonies marking the launch of the *OMF Ontario* in July, 1994 were (left to right) Nelson Puccia and Elliott Wood of Gear Motions, Syracuse, New York; Bill Gallagher of Industrial Precision, Inc. of Oswego, and Dr. Spang.

294   Movers and Shakers

I did. I scheduled project volunteers, ordered materials when it was necessary, and did a lot of "gofer" tasks. When I had time, I helped with cleaning, grinding, painting, that kind of thing. I never had such a great time in my life.

All this time, while the ship was under construction, the ETI Program was going into schools?

Yes, and the schools took it from there in some cases. The Minetto School, for example, integrated regular school subjects with the ETI materials. Fourth-grade students researched and wrote papers on the history of schooners in the Great Lakes as part of the history curriculum. We found as we went along that fourth graders were at about the perfect age and stage of schooling for the materials we were offering. It's ideal because in New York State a classroom theme in fourth grade is New York history. And of course part of that is Oswego's own history as a ship-building center.

Other schools did similar things, or they had their students visit the construction site on field trips. The kids started to treasure the pictures that were taken of them with the ship in the background. About 1990 Joe Lackey, another well known local singer, wrote an original song, "The Schooner Song." It starts out, "There's a tall ship being built, down along the shore..." The song became part of all the public things we've done. Lackey was a schooner volunteer, and sang the song at the launch ceremonies.

Can you tell us about that? It was a day of triumph?

No question. Eleven years had passed since I first broached the idea. We had the site decorated, of course. There had to be at least 1,000 people there. The president of our Foundation, Dr. J. Richard Pfund, acted as emcee and delivered the opening remarks. We had a talk on the Traditions of Shipbuilding by a student of that subject, Col. Edgar Denton, who is retired from the U.S. Army. Chaplain Larry T West of the U.S. Coast Guard gave the Blessing of the Ship. We had had a ship-naming contest throughout the county before the ceremonies, and were able to honor a fourth-grade student, Amanda Malone, for her winning submission: the *OMF Ontario*.

A schoolship in the making. Volunteers hammer and pound (top) as the *OMF Ontario* takes shape. Using scaffolds, workers (center) put final touches to the bow. The launch (bottom) on July 2, 1994 drew a fascinated crowd.

296   Movers and Shakers

We launched the schooner on July 2, 1994 with Oswego's history in mind. Exactly 115 years earlier, in 1879, the schooner *Leadville* had been launched at the same spot where we launched the *Ontario*. One of the dozens of ships built in the eighteenth and nineteenth centuries, the *Leadville* is gone now--we don't know where. But the tradition lives on.

You broke a bottle of champagne?

That was the high point. To launch our floating classroom we had help from members of the Goble family. A direct descendent of that family, which owned the shipyard where the *Leadville* was built in 1879, did the honors with the champagne bottle. That was William Quirk. He's something like three or four generations down the line from the 1879 owners. Mr. Quirk's great-aunts, now in their 80s, were also there. We felt it was a genuine honor to have them take part--and historically meaningful.

Any glitches in the launching and christening?

Just one, and luckily we solved it. The firm that was going to supply a crane, to lift the ship and move it toward the harbor, found that the crane was on assignment in the Midwest. The ship weighs about 30 tons because she's got a steel hull--and will weigh 42 tons when she's finally outfitted and serving as a schoolship.

Well, we had a mad scramble to find a replacement crane. We did find one and everything went off smoothly. We had dignitaries there, of course, including our Oswego mayor, Terrence Hammill, and Dr. Rosemary Nesbitt, director of the H. Lee White Marine Museum in Oswego.

The volunteers who had worked on the Ontario *were there?*

All of them, about 500 people in all. Their names will be inscribed on a plaque on board the *Ontario*. The list includes everyone who has worked on the project from 1988 on. It includes the late Wilbert Pullen, one of our older volunteers. He wanted to help out even though he was in his 80s. He passed away about a year ago.

The Ontario *is now in the water. Can you rest easy?*

Not really. We wish everything else were finished, but I don't think that will happen for another two years--until about 1999. We'd be happy if it were done a week ago, in fact.

This winter (1996-97) we're building skylights off-site--away from the schooner and the ice and snow. We're also preparing the wooden hatch covers and the main companionway hatch. We've gotten the materials for the spars and have been working on those.

We made great progress last summer. Our volunteers did all the cutting, fitting, and welding on the above-deck structures. That includes the hatch coamings for the chain and line lockers. We finished the crew cabin and the cabins for the classroom, the aft cabin, and the deckhouse. The last-named will serve as a navigation station.

Last summer we also did a lot of welding. We completed the bulkhead that separates the engine compartment from the galley. There's some other welding to be done on the fuel, water, and waste storage tanks.

She'll be a two-masted schooner?

Yes. Two 70-foot tall masts. She's about 16 feet at the beam.

What will students of any age find once they step aboard?

There's a classroom, but we believe classes, or sessions, will be held out on deck in fair weather. The students will be offered three-hour programs. As much as possible it'll be a hands-on learning experience. There will be segments on marine terminology and on our nautical heritage. Other areas we'll talk about will be life at sea as it once was lived, the ways in which the Great Lakes served as highways for the movement of people and goods.

On the more scientific side, we'll have a number of projects. A key one, for example, will be taking water samples and testing them. We'll add that information to the shipboard database--our shipboard computer--while also teaching about the ecology of the Lakes. We'll get into pollution and ways of preventing it. Part of our equipment will be water-testing facilities.

The classroom work will be informal. We'll have singing--sea

298   Movers and Shakers

chanties for the most part, but other things too.   We'll stress
coordination and teamwork in a variety of ways, including the singing.

The crew will help?

Yes. They'll be both teaching and learning--learning to run the
ship, for example. We'll have a six-person crew, and they'll be able to
live aboard. The six will include a captain, who will be a hired
professional, and a first mate. We haven't chosen any crew members
yet, but except for the captain they'll all be volunteers.

The Ontario *will sail the lakes?*

She'll have two basic missions. One will be to serve as a
schoolship here in Oswego harbor. The other will be to tour Lake
Ontario. She'll also probably visit the Finger Lakes and Lake Erie.
Her ports of call will include cities and towns in Canada. We plan to
sail her down to New York City for the Statue of Liberty Fest.

How far she'll travel we don't know yet. But wherever we stop
we'll offer the same Great Lakes program. The whole purpose is to let
people know about the Great Lakes, to help people understand what a
treasure the lakes are, and to indicate ways in which everyone can
preserve them.

Sounds unique...

We think it is.* We've been told that the *Ontario* will be the only
American ship of its type on Lake Ontario that is dedicated entirely to
public service. We haven't found or heard of any other program of its
type in the region. And of course no one will pay for the shipboard
classes. We want to welcome anyone who's really interested.

Will you be part of the teaching corps?

---

*Actually, a "schooner classroom" scheduled for a 1998 launch was under
construction in Milwaukee, Wisconsin in mid-1997. A 97-foot three-masted
schooner, the "vessel of learning and tourism" was a project of the Wisconsin
Lake Schooner Education Association. The launch was planned to coincide
with the 150th anniversary of Wisconsin's achievement of statehood.

299

I think we all will--all of us in the Foundation--sooner or later. I'm still teaching high school biology, botany, and zoology, but I really expect to take part in the ETI program on board ship.

Your background must have prepared you for this...

I think it did. I was born and reared in Lorain, Ohio, on Lake Erie, and have owned boats since 1960. We still have an 18-foot Lyman Islander and a couple of small sailboats. I served as mayor of Fair Haven, where I live, from 1976 to '78.

As a kid in Lorain I had a neighbor who was a carpenter and boatbuilder. I was allowed to watch and help. In 1954, with the neighbor's help, I made a pair of water skis. I was never so proud of anything in my life.

Still use them?

Yes, I do. (Laughs.)

DAN McGEE

(1996)

For some people, the life would be a one-way ticket to the cuckoo's nest. The nearest neighbor lives about a quarter of a mile away. The supermarket where The Wife does her weekly supershopping is in Alpena, Michigan, 25 miles distant by two-lane highway. Deer, coyote, and foxes roam the cedar, pine, and birch forest that covers much of the 100-acre "estate." On clear days you can see islands off the shore of Canada, some 30 miles across Lake

Huron. But you can't get there without a boat. The nearest bridges are in Port Huron--the Blue Water Bridge--and at Sault Ste. Marie--the International Bridge.

For Dan McGee and his wife Marianne it's the life of Riley. The couple are as happy as if they had just won the lottery. They find it exciting and, in nearly 16 years as "keepers" of the Presque Isle Light, they've built a tourist attraction that brings more than 100,000 people a year to their remote corner of the Wolverine State. Dan remembers how they got there and how they did it...

* * *

We moved to the lighthouse about 1981. I'd say this is our 16th year. I saw an article in a newspaper. We were traveling up to Mackinac Island, and we stopped in a motel in Rogers City. There was a small article in the paper. They wanted someone to take care of a lighthouse. I said, That's the job for me. I drove back to the lighthouse. I talked to the lady who was movin' out--she had been there a couple of years--and she told me who I should talk to. So I went over there and talked to them.

I was just in a position where I was sellin' my farm downstate. I was going to move somewhere, and so we decided the lighthouse was the thing to do. We had been in Armada, Michigan. We did get a tour of the lighthouse, and went through the buildings. You know at that time they had no idea there would be a museum there or anything--the job was just for a caretaker. But it required that somebody live there.

So you put in the museum?

Yeah, after we moved in there, and found out about the Coast Guard, and all that, I started asking--What's the house there, next to the lighthouse? It's just abandoned. If it gets deteriorated we'll tear it down. By then I had met some of the locals up there, and we formed an organization that we called the Presque Isle Historical Society. We all threw $5.00 in as a membership fee.

Then we had an annual picnic. There's always been an annual picnic at the lighthouse. The Lions Club came in and cooked chicken and they took the money. That was the tradition. And the funds went to charity. So I said, I think we should turn this thing around--we need

Taking the role of a lighthouse keeper of the late 1800s, Dan McGee wears an authentic keeper's uniform of the period.

the funds here. So we took over the chicken dinners, the Society did, and the money started pouring in for the lighthouse. Then we had people who wanted to climb to the top of the lighthouse. They'd donate money to be able to climb. That money started goin' to the Society. We thought that was more important than the national charity that we were supporting at the time.

So once we had that started we started on the house. We spent about six or seven years working on it. We stripped the paint, and then we started getting grants. We got a grant for $30,000 and then another one, I think, for $10,000. Then I got the Coast Guard to rebrick the tower in 1988. They bricked all the way up to the railing. It was one of these snafus--the contract called for bricking up to 90 feet, and when they got to 90 feet they quit. Then they had to come back some years later and finish the top portion.

The women did the work--Elsie Marcellus has passed away now, but she was the president of our Society at that time. She knew that the bricks were falling--we had to rope it around, about 100 feet around the lighthouse. We couldn't allow anybody near there because of falling bricks.

So Elsie and my wife and some other women went up to Alpena. The commander of the Coast Guard happened to be appearing in

Alpena, you know, for something, maybe to give a speech. He gave his speech and afterward--we had a petition drawn up, a couple of hundred signatures.

And it worked?

We had pictures, before and after. They showed fallen bricks. The ladies said, Sir, we need to talk to you. Okay, he said, after I'm done here. Then he finished and they got this Coast Guard commander and the ladies gave him what-for. (Chuckles.)

The next thing we knew a letter came down and they said, We will brick the tower. That was in '88, so they must've gone down in '86 or '87. Without them, the ladies, it would never have been done because the Coast Guard isn't much into repairing lighthouses. I think we have the only lighthouse that's been re-bricked in the country--I don't know of any other one. They just peeled off the old bricks and put on the new ones--white ones.

So it's completely safe now?

Yes, absolutely, it should last for generations now. Then the museum opened about the same time. We were doing all this inside work, and one day we said, Let's open it to the people. The public was askin' to come and see it, you know? So we said, Come on in, see what we're doin'. And that worked kind of good because everybody could see us while we were still working. One guy came in there and said, Here's a hundred dollars, I like what you're doin'. That kind of thing boosts your spirits up, you know?

I was talkin' about those grants. They started comin' in. I got a federal grant to re-roof the house. We put original roofs on both houses. We had to have new restrooms with the public comin' in there--we built the restrooms with a grant. Then we got new lighting, new wiring, new furnaces--it just progressed to where it's at today. I think one grant covered both roofs. Another covered the restrooms. And a third took care of a lot of other things there.

Did you have a formal opening day?

No, not exactly. Because as I say we opened it up a little, then we finally just left the doors open. Then we just straightened everything up--I guess it just happened. Now we have a lot of stuff. A lot of it's been donated. Antique stoves, and furniture, and period stuff and photographs and shipwreck stuff--whatever we feel is appropriate for lighthouses.

The lighthouse used to be open three days a year--big days. That's open to climb to the top. Now, under a new policy I started this past year it's been open every weekend. If it goes through as it has this year, I think next year (1997) it'll be open every day.

You worked on the museum building as a carpenter?

Oh yeah, I did, well, I was there, you know. I kind of took charge of it. I did the sanding of the floors, using a big commercial sander. People helped me, and we also tore out rotten wood. I got a lot of help from a guy named Ben from Ohio. He came up there and he took a likin' to it, and he did a lot of the real fine work. With one of the grants we put in new windows. A window company came and did that. I had to fight with them because they wanted to put plastic track in the windows, to move them up and down. I said they've got to be wood so we have wood to wood. "They'll swell up," he said. That's okay, I told him.

How big are the two houses?

The museum has four rooms downstairs and three upstairs. Our home is four up and four down. All the rooms are equally divided. It's like a square house and the stairway went right up through the center. All the rooms are 12 x 12 (feet). That's the way they built them in 1905. Now one of the upstairs rooms has been made into a bathroom, so we have a huge bathroom upstairs.

The lighthouse is 113 feet tall?

Yeah, that's the measurement we have. Some places you'll read that it's 109 feet. But I think 113 is right. We're the tallest structure on the Great Lakes. There are 144 steps to the top. That's from the sidewalk outside to the top, the ventilator.

We do have about 100 acres, and it's on a peninsula that juts out into Lake Huron. So it's basically limestone. That's the base, and all that grows on limestone is cedar trees and white birch and pine. It's a long, narrow piece of property--it's 100 acres, but there's quite a lot of lake frontage, you know?

We've cut trails through the woods. But the first project we did, there was a foghorn down at the end. What we call the end, to the north. All that was left there was the footings, so we built a pavilion over the top of that, a roof. It's about 24 x 40 (feet), something like that. And then we have picnic tables under there, and it's floored. There are places for fireplaces there--you know, you can cook outside. We maintain about 20 picnic tables on the grounds. So people like to come down there by the lake. If it's raining you can get under the pavilion. We've had picnics out there, and weddings--we must have had a dozen weddings. There's something romantic about getting married at a lighthouse. Most of the weddings are just on the grounds because of the configuration of the tower--there's not that much room at the top. But you can go down to the water, with the lighthouse in the background, or else stand right at the foot of the lighthouse.

Where is the gift shop?

There's like a lean-to that's not included in the house. The gift shop is in there--it's about 12 by 30 (feet). There's a full basement in that house, so we use that for storage. The gift shop is just crammed with lighthouse stuff, we can't get another thing in there. Then there are four or five steps, and people can go up into the museum. We don't have an admission fee for that, but there is a donation box there and a sign-in book. And then they can walk around there, the two floors, all of it restored. The gift shop has t-shirts, sweat-shirts, key chains, all kinds of lighthouse models--I think we have models of every one that's made on the Great Lakes. We have light-up lighthouses, lighthouse jewelry, souvenirs of other kinds. You name it, we got it.

Does Marianne handle all that?

She does it all. She does the ordering and the buying. She has a girl who works for her. It's a real project, but it supports our whole operation. We turn enough money there to cover expenses. In fact, Marianne and I are paid a salary now.

We just dedicate the whole summer to keeping the place going. We're open seven days a week. And the grounds are open all the time until dusk, you know. Then the museum is open from 9:00 to 6:00 every day. And the gift shop--either Marianne's in there, or I'm in there, or somebody else is in there--it's open all the time. People come from all over the country, and I've always felt that it must be heartbreaking to drive a long way and then hear, Well, we're closed on Wednesday of something like that. Lighthouse people come from all over. Some from long ways. We try to accommodate them. They're lighthouse buffs, a lot of them.

Next year we hope to have the lighthouse tower open all the time, as I said. There's been a major change in the lighthouse. It was owned by the Coast Guard. And now the Coast Guard this fall gave it to the township. So the Historical Society has to negotiate a new lease with the township. And if things go the way I would like it, then we'll be open all the time.

You open up there on May first--is that the custom?

Yeah, usually. But I've had a foot of snow on May first. I used to put May first, but because of that I usually put "May through October." If the weather's nice, and the sun is shinin', then we open it up. But I can't open up the restrooms until it can't freeze any more, so...

You have plenty of parking for visitors?

Lots of parking. That's one thing I've fought for over the years. We had a road there. It's been widened out and there's all parking all around there. We've got room for motor homes--for the biggest rigs there is, at the end of every cul-de-sac on the grounds.

Getting acclimatized in a place like that must be a little bit of a challenge.

It wasn't really hard. For groceries there's a party store down the street. Everything closes in the wintertime. But Alpena's 25 miles away, the major town. So you go there and instead of buying two rolls of toilet paper you buy two dozen, you know? Marianne can shop for an entire week. We've got a freezer in the basement.

The interior of the "new" Presque Isle Lighthouse, built in 1870, boasts exhibits of Great lakes ship artifacts as well as displays of Lake Huron lighthouses and shipwrecks.

Restored with white glazed brick, the Presque Isle Lighthouse measures more than 100 feet from its base to the ventilator ball at the top. Its Third Order Fresnel lens produces a light visible 21 statute miles out in Lake Huron.

It's hard to schedule your day. We've got people coming there at all hours. I've had people come there and sleep overnight in their cars or vans to photograph the lighthouse at sunrise. Or they want to be there when the light goes on at dark. There's somebody there--I have to be careful when I walk outside, I have to be presentable, you know? (Laughter.) It's not like livin' in town--I don't have any close neighbors, and I'm never surprised to see two or three cars parked. There'll be people setting up their tripods and cameras, and trying to photograph the lighthouse. They may be trying to get the clouds in the picture.

The light operates on a 15-second cycle. That means it's on for five seconds and off for ten. The ships can tell by that what light it is. They just time it. There's a NOAA (National Oceanic and Atmospheric Administration) apparatus up on the tower too. A weather-observation gadget. I don't really have much to do with the light. If it's out, of course, I'd call the Coast Guard. This is the new lighthouse, you know; it was built in 1870, with the building that's now the museum. Our house was built in 1905.

You have sort of feast-days, holidays, special events...

Yeah, we used to have an annual picnic. Now we have one even earlier than that--we have an annual wooden boat show up there. That takes place the third weekend in June, which is the third weekend before Father's Day. That will be down at the harbor, and then the lighthouse is always open in conjunction with that. We're about a mile from the harbor. It's a brand-new harbor put in by the State of Michigan. People can go up on the lighthouse and then go see the antique wooden boats--and that's turned out to be quite an event. Then we also have an arts and crafts show that day.

That's our first big weekend, then we have the annual picnic, which falls on the Saturday nearest the Fourth of July. That's when we used to have the tower open, but that's probably going to change now. Then we've always had a Labor Day pig-corn roast, on the Saturday of Labor Day weekend. Those are the main events that push us through the summer--fund-raisers, you know? The July Fourth picnic features barbecued chicken. Over the years we've acquired two big barbecuers that we got in North Carolina. They've got big tires on 'em. We can do about a hundred chickens an hour. We crank 'em out and people buy 'em as fast as we cook 'em. And all the volunteers pitch in the night before, and do all that has to be done, and we have a beer tent there and I have a band with live music. We draw over a thousand people for that. There are pony rides for kids and different things, you know.

Our attendance on the Labor Day Saturday can be as good as the Fourth of July. It depends on the weather. People come from long distances for that--they call us up and want to know what's going on. A lot of 'em plan their vacation around it. We have quite a few kids-- we're not overrun, but the families do come. Also, there's a lot of retirees who live up in that area.

Now, your brochure says you have a collection of horns and whistles. Ships' horns and whistles.

Yeah, I started by buying them at garage sales. I'm now up to about 35 of them. All the whistles can operate--I have an air compressor at the lighthouse. When I get school kids out there--let's say there are four grades from a certain school--I'll let them climb the lighthouse and then talk to them. Then I demonstrate all the different whistles. Everything--fishing boats, everything had a steam whistle way back when. I've got them in all sizes, from eight inches in diameter and four feet high all the way down to little ones, like popcorn wagon whistles. I can be heard for miles when I sound 'em off. (Laughs.)

I can even blow more than one at a time. I wear earmuffs when I sound them. When the kids are there, I have them stand back. Then I don't run 'em at full volume, I run them at reduced pressure, but it's enough sometimes to make your ears ring--it sounds just like a freighter, you know. I've got every tone imaginable. No two are alike. I could play a song if I had enough beer in me.

You've got a cannon on the grounds too.

Yeah, three of them. One was used as a line-throwing gun. Then I have another that I've acquired over the years. There's one that I like to fire. It was a warning gun. In a fog they had to use any kind of sound they could find. Bells, whistles, all the way up to a foghorn. That's part of the collection we have that's appropriate to the lighthouse. All three cannon can be fired. We do fire them now and then--but not with a big crowd. But you're dealing with gunpowder and that stuff, it could be hazardous.

We've also got a miniature tram on the grounds. A little railroad. Everything for the lighthouse came in by ship. There were no roads to Alpena in those days. So they had this little railroad car with four wheels on it, and they probably pulled it up using horses. They had two tracks leading up to the lighthouse--they probably used one or the other depending on where the storm was coming from--they'd come in on the lee side. They'd load coal, oil, everything on those little trams and pull them up the hill to the lighthouse. The lighthouse is 300, 400 yards from the water. I was able to acquire one of those one time and restore it. I don't have enough track to run it down to the water--if I had 500 feet of track I could.

We're not on a bluff, but we're above the water maybe 20, 30 feet up, so there's an incline down to the water.

Are you acquiring new things all the time?

If I can find them, and they're getting harder to find all the time. When I'm in Florida I go to Miami, Jacksonville, and look for things. They obviously had lighthouses all over Florida too. Then I'll go to steam whistle and tractor shows, any place that might have some of that old stuff, you know.

How big is your Historical Society membership?

It runs around 900, 1,000 Some of our members live all over the country, of course. Others are right there and work as volunteers. They pay a $5 membership fee and then sometimes a donation. And everything helps. We put out a newsletter once a year.

You're living with history out there--with the generations of keepers who tended the light in the old days...

We are. We even have a haunted tower legend. There was supposed to be a secret tunnel leading from the tower to a barn that used to sit a little ways off. The tunnel might have been dug so that keepers could get to the barn in a storm. The legend says loneliness got to one keeper's wife. She bugged him so bad that he put her in the tunnel and then bricked it up, sealing it. Well, we did find a tunnel under the tower, and it is bricked up. But we haven't heard the wailing that you're supposed to hear on stormy nights. Or if we did, it was the wind.

We had a couple of visitors there one day and I was showing them the trap-door that leads down to the bricked-up tunnel. The gentleman dropped his sunglasses into the hole. He was too big to go down after them, so his daughter went. She got the glasses, but then she came jumping up out of the hole. She said she had heard something down there. (Laughter.)

JOHN TANNER

(1996)

In late 1996 there are 82 of them, cadets in the process of learning what goes into the operation of a commercial ship on the Great Lakes. They harbor dreams, and many of their visions include scenes of life on the sweetwater seas. Some of them may end as masters of the large and small ships that ply the water routes from the great ocean in the east to Duluth and other points west. The dreams don't exclude voyages on the salt seas.

Between them and those challenges and those lifetime careers lies the work that the Great Lakes Maritime Academy requires of them: three years of study in the Great Lakes' only maritime academy under the tutelage of instructors who have been there and earned their credentials. The water ripples almost under their feet--Grand Traverse Bay. Their Academy enjoys the prestige and backup of Northwestern Michigan College, under whose aegis they attend classes. Because it takes familiarity with the absolute latest in technological advances to run modern "lakers", they attend labs that simulate what they will encounter when they go to sea. John Tanner, a seven-year veteran of lake-faring, was a faculty member for more than 20 years before becoming superintendent on July 1, 1995. He tells it as it is in this world of computers and monitors and schematics and simulated harbors and rivers...

* * *

Can you tell us about your student body--the 82?

Sure. They range in age from 18 to 48, proving that it's never too late to become a professional on the Great Lakes. Our minimum age is 17 or 18, with a high school diploma or the equivalent. The interesting thing is that we offer a three-year program and so, by the time they finish the training, they'll be 21, which is a requirement for holding a U.S. Coast Guard license to work on Great Lakes ships. Right now we have three women among our students. They're at different levels of instruction.

Besides having a high school diploma or its equivalent, prospective cadets take an asset test. It measures their math and English skill levels. This ensures that the future cadet should do well in his or her course work.

You've added things to your physical plant?

That's the exciting part. We've added quite a bit over the past couple of years. We have an entirely new radar lab. And it's updated-- it has more capability. We've added a ship-handling lab, or watch-standing lab, in which we have various harbors simulated, and we also have the St. Marys River simulated. The student will be on a bridge approximately 14 x 14 feet, with a wheel-stand and an engine telegraph--and you can look out a front window on the Great Lakes, with a 14-foot-wide, six-foot high screen. They'll see the St. Marys River. They'll also see the bow of their ship. They go through a certain stretch of the river, depending on their lesson of the day, and work with one another in the pilothouse, learning to pilot a ship safely. And that has proved to be just wonderful.

They can see themselves on a bridge.

Yes. They can do the things they would be called on to do on a real ship. The things they will be doing in the future. They also learn what to expect when they are in the river, making turns, and so on--how to act on the bridge of a ship.

We've also added an engineering lab that's computer based. Students will have two monitors, with a computer keyboard in front of them, and a mouse, and one of the monitors will have a schematic drawing of a piping system--an engine steam or diesel plant. They'll be able to use the mouse to open and close valves to bring this engine up from being totally cold to being a fully operational plant. They'll be able to go through diagnostic-type scenarios too. Ballast systems are part of this lab.

This has proven to be a fantastic training aid.

When were those installed?

The radar and ship-handling system was installed in November of

Unique among maritime training schools in the United States, the Great Lakes Maritime Academy trains officers specifically for the fleets of the Great Lakes shipping industry. (Photo courtesy Great Lakes Maritime Academy)

'93. The engine system was dedicated in October of '95.

Are there other physical changes?

Those are the key ones. You're talking about a million and a half dollars in equipment. We will be plugging more equipment into those systems. We're ready to purchase a simulation of the Detroit River, which should be ready in September of '97. And then later we'll add more rivers and options to the basic system.

The next big project is our harbor, which is in need of some repair. So we're going to be doing some work on it. We'll make it a little bit more sheltered. That's a big project.

Where do your students come from--have most of them grown up near the lakes or other water?

Right now approximately half of them are from Michigan. The others are from Minnesota, Wisconsin, Illinois, Indiana, Ohio and then they're spread from there all the way to Maryland, California, Florida.

They are mostly from states that are close to water. They get exposed to the water in childhood and are attracted to that kind of career. A great number of our students find the Great Lakes Maritime Academy--rather than we going out and finding them.

The courses would be of interest--you used to have two programs, or two tracks...

We still do. The one is for the deck--that's the person who does the maneuvering, the steering of the ship. He or she takes it out of harbor, across a lake, through a river system, through locks. He takes the ship into port. Loads the ship properly. And then takes the ship to an unloading port.

Now, down inside the ship, where the engines are, there's an engineering crew. These people make sure the engine's running properly, make sure we have water ballast when and where we need it. They make sure the ship has hotel service so that the people living on board the ship have the proper amounts of electricity, water, heat-- power for the meals they cook, refrigeration to keep the foods cold, all those types of things.

The engineer obviously has a multi-dimensional job. That person is actually running a little city. They have a sewage plant, they have

314   Movers and Shakers

water treatment, all of these things, plus the main engine has to be running to propel the ship.

When we're on board ship we can't call in anyone to help us--we have to fix everything ourselves. We can't go to Ace Hardware to get a bolt, we've got to have it aboard.

The students get on-board experience with both of these tracks--on your semester system.

Yes, they do. They start out in fall, they'll go two semesters on campus, then they're on board ship approximately 60 to 90 days, depending on the exact schedule. And then they'll come back for another academic year. They'll go back out for approximately 150 to 180 days, depending on the sea window. They'll get over 200 sea days--aboard the kind of ship that they'll actually work on, as licensed officers. So they really do get hands-on experience.

That's over 200 days during the three-year course. The school year has changed. We run on a semester system, with a 16-week study window. We start in late August and we run until approximately the middle of May, at which time the students go out to sea. They go aboard ships as cadet observers.

Have you added any courses in the past few years?

Now, a number of our courses deal specifically with our simulation equipment. That means they work with the simulation equipment to perform tasks. This underlines a student's ability to work in different ways, much more than a simple lecture would. We have an engineering class that deals with self-unloading systems. The self-unloading system on a Great Lakes ship is really the heart of the ship. When these ships unload themselves, the boom is swung out to a stockpile or a hopper. The cargo is moved along a belt system that's built into the bottom of the ship. It's moved by gravity as a series of gates are opened up, goes onto a belt below the hold, and goes from there onto an elevator system that takes it up onto the boom. And then it goes off the ship.

Our students have a course that deals specifically with that. It's critical. Just about all Great Lakes freighters are now self-unloading.

Haven't they scrapped some older freighters because they didn't have self-unloading systems?

That's correct. When you look back at that earlier time in our history, we probably should have saved some of those ships, because some might have been retrofitted. Right now a brand-new ship is very, very expensive.

Even though the boom apparatus must be extremely expensive itself?

Yes. It is expensive. They have to anchor that boom way down to an A-frame. They go right down to the keel of the ship. There's a lot of retrofitting, a lot of engineering that's involved in that. It's almost like reconstructing the ship.

How about your faculty? They've got the full responsibility for the academics...

We have four faculty members, and two support staff, to man the office. A part-time recruiter. And that's our staff. But in addition to that, NMC (Northwestern Michigan College) provides instructors for all academic classes--English, math, physics, chemistry, and so on. We are a division of the college. We have library services, dorms, and computer and other services that are also available in the college. They can link up with other research resources as needed.

When they're aboard ship our cadets send back a lengthy sea project. They have to describe what's happening aboard the ship, how they solved problems, that kind of thing.

All this stresses the hands-on aspect of the curriculum...

Yes, it does. We really stress that.

Are there women on the faculty?

Our recruiter is a graduate of the Academy, Margo Marks. We have three other graduates on the staff as faculty members.

What's the state of the merchant fleet nowadays?

The merchant fleet on the Great Lakes has stabilized in the past

Cadets in training at the Great Lakes Maritime Academy in Traverse City learn teamwork while rowing on Grand Traverse Bay. (Photo courtesy Great Lakes Maritime Academy)

few years, and they're working on the efficiency of the ship schedules. So more attention is paid to the scheduling of ships, and on ways to do that properly. That way, they get in more trips per year. That means more cargo and more efficiency for that particular year. They run year-round, just about, whenever they can. For instance, last year we had ships that ran into February. And they started out again in mid-March. That's because of the need for iron ore. Right now (mid-December, 1996) a good share of them are working, and they'll go on into January. In this particular year it's nice to have this weather break--it's quite mild.

The Lakes are really expected to close January 15. What they'll do with the remainder of the season is haul cargo on Lake Michigan, going as far north as Escanaba.

Is there a trend toward putting more 1,000-footers on the Lakes?

I think those things are certainly being looked at. It seems there's also going to be a need for a medium-sized self-unloader for river deliveries. Not every cargo can be hauled on a 1,000-foot carrier--you may have to go into a small port, or into a river.

That would apply, for example, in Cleveland--the Cuyahoga River. Ports like Toledo, where the thousand-footers go in, won't change. They'll continue to use those ports (as they have in the past).

Are there new ships under construction?

No, not now. The big ship-building centers are basically in Sturgeon Bay (Wisconsin), and the yard in Erie, Pennsylvania is still operational. Some new barges have been built.

Do you have an outstanding graduate annually?

Yes, we do. This year it was Chris Burkey. The award was given out at the graduation dinner, and that was held on May 18. We hold it at a Holiday Inn or a local restaurant--a place that can hold 100 or more people. That way families can attend, and we always do have family members there. We had 16 graduates this past May. Next year (1997) we should have 24 students in that class.

The graduating classes will be in the 20's in the future, as we see it now.

Do most of your grads go to unusual jobs, maybe land-based jobs, or do most of them go to freighters on the Lakes?

Most of them go to the freighters on the Great Lakes. That's why they come here. We do have some who go to other places for employment, but 90 percent, or as many as 95 percent, of them want to work on the Lakes. We have had graduates work on the *Lake Guardian*, the EPA (Environmental Protection Agency) ship, or on other ships of this type.

You have boats that are used in training?

Yes, we have the tug *Anchor Bay* and a newer vessel called the *Northwestern*, a wood-hulled vessel, and we intend to use it for training in ship handling and other things like navigation exercises on Grand Traverse Bay. We acquired the *Northwestern* in 1994. We're

318   Movers and Shakers

still going through Coast Guard inspection with the *Northwestern*, but we hope to have it in the curriculum by early next year. The tug is a 45-footer. The *Northwestern* is 80 feet long.

Do your students take rowing training?

Yes, they do. That's one of the first things they take when they come aboard. Starting in August of next year, the students will learn about safety and survival at sea. But one of the first things to learn is why a boat floats--a simple lifeboat--and how it's propelled. In this case it's propelled by people rowing.

The old adage that we use is, "If you all don't row, the boat won't go." So literally everybody has to put their oars in the water and row, which brings out teamwork, working together. It's really a basic lesson and a basic part of our curriculum.

Would a student's schedule on a freighter be pretty predictable?

It would be--it doesn't change that much. When they're on board ship the watch system is four hours on, eight off, under the direction of a mate or engineer. The schedule stays the same, but the activities change daily--loading, unloading, whatever.

They have a summer vacation?

The normal work schedule is 60 days work, 30 days off. For a person who wants a quantity of time off, it's possible to do some different types of things that would take time. For that it's an ideal occupation. For the normal worker in the United States these days, that's impossible. So it's a fantastic opportunity *if* you like the work and like to have time off like that.

Some of them will take special courses during their time off. They may work to upgrade their licenses or to get baccalaureate degrees. We have an agreement with Ferris State College--they can finish up a baccalaureate degree in a maritime specialty. Ferris State is about 80 miles south of here (Traverse City), at Big Rapids. They come out of our program with an associate degree.

Does the Academy offer any special student services?

The college offers those services. They can take advantage of counseling and other services. They can also request tutoring and it'll be supplied. We've really tried to cover all bases.

Do families visit?

Yes, they do. Each September we have an open house. Families come, and alumni come back. We have a picnic on the dock. We talk about the past and the future and get a chance to meet one another. Generally it's held on the second weekend in September. The families living in Michigan have the easiest time getting here, but sometimes we also have families from other states.

You've got a unique operation.

We think so. Unique in a lot of ways. Our John L. Horton Conference Room next to the main entrance overlooks the school's harbor and the west arm of Grand Traverse Bay. Also, we're the only maritime academy that trains students specifically for careers on the Great Lakes. We've had students who've come to acquire career skills after they've earned Ph.D.'s in other fields.

I think we're unique in the equipment area as well. I'm thinking of our sophisticated lab facilities. When our students graduate, they're qualified to take Coast Guard examinations--that's one criterion. They also have those associate degrees.

We think the ambience and living arrangements are unique. Students have dormitory residence available. Classes are small, usually with about 15 to 25 students a class.

There's also a tradition at the GLMA now.

Yes. If you took a tour of the Academy's facilities, you'd want to start in the reception area. A museum in miniature, the area houses a lighthouse beacon dating back to 1902, photos of Great Lakes boats, and other mementos. There's a beautiful old ship's wheel from the SS *Frontenac* of the Cleveland-Cliffs Iron Company fleet. The pilothouse from her sister ship, the SS *Pontiac,* was donated by the Cleveland Cliffs Company. One display case contains a variety of old navigation and timekeeping devices. One of the most striking displays

320   Movers and Shakers

memorializes Les Biederman, one of the people who founded the Academy in 1969. The display was dedicated to Mr. Biederman on his death in 1988.

We invite prospective students to come and visit--or anyone else. We're proud of what we have here.

"MAN OF THE SWIFT FLOWING RIVERS"

Man of the swift flowing rivers,
Paddler almighty, master of nature,
Long has he roamed the Vermilion,
The Des Plaines and the Embarras,
The North Branch and the Lower Fox.
And now, Spoon River surrenders
to his powered stroke.
Mr. Canoe of Chicagoland--
We salute you with paddles raised.
Terrible is his vengeance on those
Who would desecrate these sweet waters.
Oh Polluter, stand down in shame.

-- Anon.

RALPH C. FRESE

(1997)

Can one man touch off a renaissance? Popularize a form of water travel? Awaken a region to the drama and fascination of its own history? Hammer out a casting on a blacksmith's forge and go from there to a press conference with a big-city mayor? Inspire the cleanup of some garbage-filled rivers and streams? Design a canoe that earns universal acclaim among the paddling brotherhood?

Earn the nickname "Mr. Canoe?"

The answers: Yes. Ralph C Frese has done all the above. From his Chicagoland Canoe Base, "the most unusual canoe shop in the United States," he projects an aura of awe and excitement in the presence of American, maritime, and specifically Illinois and midwestern history while also spreading the gospel of Great Lakes region canoeing. The concepts dovetail, in his view. Some 200 stacked canoes fill the fenced yard outside his store. Only yards away is the workshop that houses his blacksmith's forge and canoe construction equipment. The store itself is a teeming crush of outdoorsman's clothing and equipment, books, canoes, paddles, and assorted other gear. The canoes include a number of New Town Canadiennes, the special model that Frese designed and whose manufacturing/marketing rights he has leased to the Old Town Canoe Company.

There may be a better way to introduce Ralph Frese. Look at the reverse side of his calling card, which reads, "Blacksmithing, Welding, Canoe Builder, Environmentalist, Historian, Lecturer..."

* * *

It must give you a sense of satisfaction to know that your name is on river trails, memorials, canoe extravaganzas, and various other events and things.

The satisfaction comes, I think, from knowing that we've made some progress. A lot of people are practicing environmentalists who might not have been, years ago. A lot of others are aware of the history of Illinois and the Midwest. Thousands of people realize that they can find wilderness escapes in their own back yards.

If you've seen the movie "Dennis the Menace," you saw an opening scene on the banks of a beautiful, scenic river. It's dawn, and there's a deer grazing at the foot of an oak tree. It could be summer in

322   Movers and Shakers

Canada. But that scene was filmed two blocks from my home, on the North Branch of the Chicago River.

There was a canoe in that movie.

I built it. A lot of my canoes have been movie stars. For the movie "Centennial," made from the James Michener novel, they wanted four birch-bark canoes. They wanted them right now. I got to talking with them and found out that the canoes were to be used by actors playing Pawnee Indians. The scene was on the Platte River.

I did a little quick research. It turned out that a German settler had written about the Pawnee and their canoes. But those canoes were dugouts made from cottonwood trees. The Pawnee never lived within 1,000 miles of good birch. So "Centennial" got authentic cottonwood dugout canoes.

You were already known as "Mr. Canoe?"

That started more than 40 years ago. I'm a blacksmith by trade, and still work at smithing. Back in the 1950s I was active with the Boy Scouts, and they were interested in canoes. It turned out that I was spending so much time describing canoes, and researching them, and telling people how to transport and use them that I decided to start building them. Then for me the canoes and the environmental work with the rivers came together. I started building canoes and canoeing more myself.

It seemed possible to dramatize how the canoe had opened up this part of the United States--in fact, pretty much of the northern part of North America. It was Samuel de Champlain who said, about 1610, that if you adopted the bark canoe of the Indian, you could travel almost anywhere within the continent. He had it right. The rivers are still there. They just need to be protected.

In 1957, thinking partly of the rivers, I started the Des Plaines River Canoe Marathon. That has become an annual event, with up to 2,000 canoes participating. I wanted to give our Scouts a place to paddle, but it's become a big thing. The Marathon attracted canoeists of all ages, and will celebrate its 40th anniversary this year. The canoes travel over a course that extends about 19 miles.

Ralph Frese displays photos showing canoes under construction in his workshop in Chicago. The symbol (right) decorates a brochure describing the services of Frese's Chicagoland Canoe Base, "Home of the Voyageur Canoe."

You had caught the canoe bug.

In the early '60s I decided to build a special canoe. I found some pictures of authentic birch-bark canoes and used them as my book of instructions. My first one was a 34-foot Montreal, the big fur trade canoe that could carry up to 7,000 pounds of trade goods and a crew of seven or eight. The first building project led to others.

We don't have much birch-bark around Chicago, so I decided to use the wood of the fiberglass tree. I made the skin from fiberglass that was the same thickness as birch-bark, then put hand-split cedar ribs and sheathing on the inside. Otherwise they're built just the way bark canoes are built.

Canoeing was catching on by this time?

People were forming brigades, holding canoe races and regattas, going on longer trips. We started holding an annual rendezvous on the Mississippi in southern Illinois. That took place at Prairie du Rocher. We called it the Fort de Chartres Rendezvous and we always held races as part of it.

I think John Harris visited that rendezvous in 1972. He was thinking of forming a brigade, and maybe heading it himself as director of the Tippecanoe County Historical Association, in Indiana. It took him a year and a half, but he got his own brigade started--*Le Brigade de Ouiatenon*-- and they're still holding their big canoe-fest in October every year. They call it the Feast of the Hunter's Moon. I've been there annually for years. I had one of my "Centennial" canoes there one year.

In the late '70s I figured up how many canoes I had made. There were more than 75 of them.

You were keeping your blacksmithing business going, promoting river cleanup, building canoes--what else?

Well, I was collecting canoes too. But that was pretty hit-or-miss. It started sometime around the late '50s. I was visiting my wife's relatives up at Eagle River, Wisconsin. One of the relatives owned a boat dealership up there. He had taken this thing in trade--a Rice Lake canoe, built of basswood in the late 1800s in Gore''s Landing, Ontario. It's so old they've forgotten how they were made.

I discovered years later that it was a Rice Lake product. But I picked it up. I couldn't bear to see it just sitting there, where no one placed any value on it.

Afterward I collected canoes where I could. They've come from all over the world. Some of them just sort of drifted toward my shop here. I turned the collection over to the Chicago Maritime Society a few years ago, more than 90 canoes. There's an Ecuadorian dugout among them along with a Wonacott stripper and a pretty rare Racine Lapstrake. There's a Moro Vinta, which is a double outrigger sailing canoe from Mindanao in the Philippines. It was found floating in New York's Greenwood Lake back in the '50s. Don't ask me how it got there.

I got a call a few years ago from a man who wanted to buy a boat trailer. He said he needed a way to carry a heavy canoe to the trout waters up in the Sierra Nevada Mountains. I asked him what kind of canoe he had. Would you believe it was a Philippine outrigger? For trout fishing? We talked about its suitability, or more accurately, its unsuitability. By the time we were finished he had a new Old Town Canadienne and I had an outrigger.

All this activity takes place while you're working as a blacksmith and welder?

Yes. For years I've worked at the forge at least three days a week. I make tools for carpenters, stonemasons, and other skilled workers. I make some castings. Years ago when they needed a cannot at Fort de Chartres, I made one. It's still there, part of the Fort's displays.

You know, building canoes and working as a blacksmith are both service businesses. They require that we be here six days a week. With one day a week off, you can't really travel very far. So, unlike people who could take whole weekends off, I made a lifelong hobby of exploring what I could reach in one day. Frankly, I haven't seen it all yet.

I got an idea. On Labor Day weekends, when canoe sales were kind of slow, I took advantage of the three-day weekend to go a little farther afield. And having a weird imagination, I thought of making it an adventure. A trip by voyageur canoe, and going places where people wouldn't ordinarily think of going. Then I hit on the idea of using a theme to twitch their curiosity a little bit. One year it was a visit to the Garden Peninsula, in Door County, Wisconsin, So we went cruising along the Garden Peninsula.

Another year it was the ghost of Lafayette. On the inside of the Garden Peninsular, in Door County, there's a ghost town, a former iron-smelting town. It's called Fayette, and is part of a state park now. There's old stone masonry and two iron furnaces that still sit there. So that was the trip that year. No one knew where Fayette was until we took that trip.

How many years did that go on?

Maybe 20. They called it "Frese's Follies." It got to be too much work for us, for my wife Rita and me. But the last trip was a beaut, what we called our Mississippi Heritage Trip. We started at Burlington, Iowa, visited Fort Madison, and that night slept outside the walls of the fort. From there we paddled down the river to Nauvoo, and got there in time for their Wine and Cheese Festival weekend.

You were into living history by then--reenactments of historic events?

Way into them. Our first big project in that department was the Montreal trip.

326   Movers and Shakers

How did you hit on the idea for that trip?

Well, Illinois was getting ready to celebrate its sesquicentennial in 1968. Of course I'm interested in the early explorers, the way we were discovered by the canoe, and so on. At one time we were part of French Canada. The trade goods traveled westward, down through the Illinois country and to the Mississippi. Anyway, in 1967 I was building these big Montreal canoes, up to 34, 35, 36 feet long. Thirty-four feet was an average size. Then I got to thinking, Wouldn't it be fun to take a Montreal canoe back to Montreal right at the time Canada is celebrating its centennial? All the supplies for the people in Illinois used to originate there, and now Illinois is a producer of farm goods, and a leading mining state, a manufacturing state. We could go back to Montreal and let people know Illinois was getting ready to celebrate its sesquicentennial in 1968.

I wanted to do the Montreal expedition in '67 so we could visit the Montreal Expo, the world's fair. I had been corresponding with Hugh McMillan, an archival detective and history buff who worked for the Canadian government. We decided to get two groups together, Canadian and American, and meet in the area of Sault Ste. Marie and travel the rest of the way to Montreal together. As it turned out, I had a party of 14 including some high school kids and grown men. One man was in his 60's.

You had the rendezvous without incident?

We were short of funds, so we drove from Chicago to the Straits of Mackinac. McMillan had two canoes and met us there. He had started in Grand Portage, canoeing and driving. We were all in costume, of course, and had a chance to be the honored guests at a reception in Sault Ste. Marie. We drove and paddled and portaged to Ottawa, having traveled on the Mattawa, French, and other rivers.

In Ottawa we attended a reception in the halls of Canada's Parliament. We got needled a lot by our Canadian friends. They took us into the back rooms, telling us that we were the first Americans who had ever been permitted in there. On of our people spoke Cajun French, and when the Canadians heard him talking in French, they rolled on the ground in hysterics. It's a completely different dialect.

Modern-day voyageurs approach the banks of the Wabash River near Lafayette, Indiana in the prelude to the annual Feast of the Hunter's Moon sponsored by the Tippecanoe County Historical Association. The Feast began under the inspiration of Ralph Frese and the Fort de Chartres Rendezvous that also takes place every year in southern Illinois. Frese has taken part in the Feast of the Hunter's Moon since it first drew canoe "brigades" in the middle 1970s. (Photo: ←*Paddler* Magazine)

Ralph Frese still works in his blacksmith shop, part of the comples that he runs as the Chicagoland Canoe Base. In the building housing the blacksmith shop he also builds canoes from the wood of the "fiberglass tree." (Photo: *Canoe* Magazine, now *Canoe and Kayak*) →

They gave you a sendoff to Montreal?

Yes, and we had a chance to stop at a lot of historic places along the way. We finally got to St. Helena's Island, near Montreal, and portaged up the leveed walls around the island. Then we paddled into the canals that they had built for Expo '67. At the Ontario Pavilion we were officially received by a representative of the Montreal government--mayor Jean Drapeau's people. We had brought along a pet raccoon, a piece of fur from Illinois, and in a formal scroll we announced that Illinois was hosting the International Coon Hunting Championships. The scroll also specified that we wanted Canada's coon-hungers to have every advantage--and to make it a fair contest we were bringing one southern Illinois coon so they could improve their breeding stock. (Laughs.)

The mayor's representative just split a gut. A member of the very exclusive Hudson Bay Beaver Club pretended to rant and rave--"What, all these years in the bush and all you've got to show for it is one lousy raccoon?" (Laughs.) Then we got a free tour of Expo and just had a ball.

You had made history of a new kind.

In a way. I think that trip to Montreal taught me what I needed to know about organizing reenactments. The experience certainly helped when we did the 1973 Jolliet-Marquette Tricentennial Expedition.

What's the story behind that?

A 300th anniversary was coming up in 1973. Father Jacques Marquette and Louis Jolliet had led an expedition down the Mississippi in 1673. On the way they really discovered the Illinois country, including the Chicago Portage, one of the seven keys to the North American continent. I knew from experience that the average person doesn't go to a history museum--and if a normal commemoration got any press coverage at all it would probably appear on the obit page of the *Chicago Tribune*. So I thought, Why not do a reenactment of the whole expedition and in effect bring history to the people?

This was what they call nowadays *living history*. One day I got a phone call from Dr. George Arnold, a professor at Southern Illinois

University who was the Illinois member of the Greater Mississippi River Road Commission. They were about to meet to talk about the anniversary and ways to celebrate it. Would I join them? Of course I would, and did.

They had read your mind, or heard of your reenactment plans.

Dr. Arnold had been at Fort de Chartres for our rendezvous, and had heard me spouting off. In no time after that phone call I was on the Illinois State Tricentennial Commission. They let me pick the seven members of the expedition, each one representing one member of the original Marquette-Jolliet party. My Jolliet was Reid Lewis, a high school French teacher, folk singer, and all-around fine leader. My Father Marquette was a real-life Jesuit priest, Father Joe McEnery, who had a Chicago parish.

They're in two canoes, in voyageur clothes, everything authentic?

Absolutely. These were 20-foot canoes that I had built. I couldn't go all the way with the expedition, but we got under way from the beach at St. Ignace, on Michigan's Upper Peninsula. The date was May 17, the date on which Marquette and Jolliet started down the west shore of Lake Michigan in 1673.

There were some hairy moments right at the start. We ran into six- to eight-foot waves under the Mackinac Bridge, the "Mighty Mac," and the water temperature was about 34 degrees.

Our crews lived off the land as they went, just the way the Marquette-Jolliet expedition did. Only our people were stopping at towns and villages along the way, and at every stop they put on a little pageant. Then the people on shore would provide a feast.

Did you make the Chicago Portage?

We did, what's left of it. We did the portage from a bend of the Des Plaines River, which wasn't the original route. That's been changed by the Sanitary District of Chicago in creating the Illinois Waterway. We got to St. Louis and at the museum under the Arch they had Father Marquette's original map on display. One of the members of the Illinois Tricentennial Commission had told them where to find the map.

We visited about 140 communities on Lake Michigan and the rivers. In each place we gave our program. Our itinerary didn't call for travel on the Mississippi below the mouth of the Arkansas River, but we did go up the Arkansas to Helena. On the 16th of July we attended a reception there. We had to give our program and meet everyone. Historically, it was on July 17th that Marquette and Jolliet turned back up the Mississippi from the mouth of the Arkansas. The problem was that our voyageurs were at Helena, Arkansas on the 15th of July and they had to be at the mouth of the Arkansas on the morning of the 17th. And Helena is 83 miles upstream. On the morning of July 16th they had severe thunderstorms, squalls, and what-have-you, and even so they paddled the 83 miles in one day.

Now you're heading back up the Mississippi?

Yes. A high point of the entire four-month expedition was our stay in Chicago. This was on Labor Day weekend. We set up a voyageur encampment on Michigan Boulevard. I got gymnasium mats, wrestling mats, for everyone to sleep on. Then the next day we had a beautiful mass and reception. The local Catholic parish had cut down every diseased white birch tree in every Catholic cemetery and built this huge platform out of birch logs. We had one of our canoes, overturned, to serve as an altar, with deerskin for an altar cloth.

I have one thing on audio tape. One of the speakers got up and asked the people in the front row of seats to please stand up and make room for the *voyeurs*. (Laughs.) Afterward we went to a press conference with Mayor Daley--Richard J. Daley.

The press must have eaten it up. The whole expedition must have given tens of thousands of people an inside view of history.

I keep a scrapbook, or I should say scrapbooks. I estimate that we got about 4,000,000 words in print that year. Local newspapers in the towns we visited did special editions on their local history. It was incredible, the fervor that spread up and down the Mississippi in particular. In each place my Father Marquette would give a brief talk about the brotherhood of the river. People came out by the hundreds to greet the voyageurs.

Each town must have been a different story.

Just as each river is unique, and has its own story. Put a canoe on a river and you're in heaven. Remember what (Henry David) Thoreau said in his book, *A Week on the Concord and Merrimack Rivers?* "With one thrust of the paddle we left all time, all history behind." That says it succinctly.

Everything you've done is practice for something else—that 1973 trip must have been preparation for the '76 Bicentennial Canoe Trip.

In a way, yes. I built the six canoes for that trip. There were 24 people taking part, most of them high school seniors. There were six or eight adults with them. They called it *La Salle: Expedition II* because it was a reenactment of the La Salle expedition down the Mississippi in 1681 and '82.

The story would make a book. The reenactors left Montreal in August of '76 and completed the 3,300 mile trip the next April in the Gulf of Mexico. They were sleeping on the ground in one of the worst winters on record. They did have one horrible accident over near Hebron, Indiana. They were portaging because the Kankakee River was frozen. They're trudging along this road, trying to make time because they have all these engagements in schools and with other groups, and a truck slows down to watch them in their voyageur outfits. Another truck hits that one from the rear and the first truck plows into the walkers.

It's a wonder no one was killed. I think that was the only night they didn't sleep out of doors. One had a broken arm, another had a broken leg. One had to have his spleen removed. And not one of them quit.

You had seen them off?

I was with them when they started in Montreal, and then I arranged a reception for them in Chicago. I completed the trip with them, from Kenner, Louisiana, to New Orleans, Venice, Pilottown, which was the last habitation, and then down to Mile Zero. That's at the mouth of the South Pass. I have pictures of La Salle--actually Reid Lewis--raising his sword once again to claim the entire Mississippi Valley region for

King Louis XIV and France.

The members of our La Salle expedition trained for nearly two years. They perfected canoeing and camping techniques. They learned French and memorized voyageur songs. They underwent very rigorous physical conditioning programs. But while traveling they had wind-chills down to minus-76 below zero. When the rivers were frozen, they portaged more than 500 miles.

They saw some of your favorite rivers.

I think all the rivers are my favorites. I've been working to protect them as long as I can remember. Three of my favorites are the Chicago, the Des Plaines, and the Fox. But there are 38 rivers in Illinois and I've seen and canoed on most of them.

My introduction to paddling came on the North Branch of the Chicago River. My father was a blacksmith, third-generation, and taught me that trade, but he thought my interest in the outdoors was silly. When I was about 14 I finally got a break. The kid next door to us had built a kayak at Lane Tech High School. He sold it to me for $15 when he went into the Marines. Now, $15 was a lot of dough in those days, but I had that boat for 25 years. I carried it on my bike to the North Branch.

People have maintained that you can probably explain the role of the canoe in the Creation.

There may be some truth in it. (Laughs.) The canoe certainly played a role in opening up the Great Lakes region. It wasn't the covered wagon that did that, nor the railroads.

Have you a big ambition--something you still want to accomplish in the way of conservation, historical research, reenactments, anything?

I'm living the life of Riley. I've got this shop (Chicagoland Canoe Base) and my workshop next door. The shop looks the way I wanted it to--with all that hand-crafted metal and special wood--and we've filled it with gear and canoes and books. People come in to talk, and thumb through the books, and pick up information on what to do and where to go with a canoe.

But I'm really just getting started. My main goal right now is to see my canoe collection housed in a museum, a display. I'd call it the Hall of Canoe. The Chicago Maritime Society is working on that and one of these days it'll come to pass. You know, the canoe is the oldest and most practical water-craft ever devised by man?

334 Movers and Shakers

APPENDIX A

VOICES FROM THE SWEETWATER SEAS

Our Interviewees...

Ray Boessel, Jr.
Hafeman Boat Works
R.R. 1, Box 187
Bigfork, MN 56628

Paul D. Brugger
5206 Wolf Rd.
Erie, PA 16505

Peter G. Code
51 George Henry Blvd.
Willowdale, ON M2J 1E4
Canada

Matthew L. Daley
University of Detroit Mercy
McNichols Library
4001 W. McNichols Rd.
P.O. Box 19900
Detroit, MI 48219-0900

Capt. Donald E. Erickson
7193 Huron St.
Taylor, MI 48180

Ralph C. Frese
Chicagoland Canoe Base, Inc.
4019 N. Narragansett Ave.
Chicago, IL 60634

Terry German
Extreme Explorer Productions
65 Lake Ridge Rd. South.
  Box 14
Whitby, ON L1P 1K6
Canada

Yvonne Hoag
3213 Fairlane
Midland, MI 48602

Capt. Jimmie H. Hobaugh
Le Sault de Ste. Marie
  Historic Sites, Inc.
501 E. Water St.
Sault Ste. Marie, MI 49783

James Hogan
J. W. Westcott Co.
Foot of 24th St.
Detroit, MI 48222

Ruth Hudson
5806 Burns Rd.
North Olmsted, OH 44070

Rev. Richard W. Ingalls, Rector
Mariners' Church of Detroit
170 E. Jefferson
Detroit, MI 48226-4391

David Irvine
Video-Craft, Inc.
37 Fawn Lake Dr.
Shelbyville, MI 49344

David P. Kensler
c/o Warbird Aircraft
  Restoration &Salvage, Inc.
1370 N. Oakland Blvd.
Waterford, MI 48327

Timothy J. and Doree Kent
Silver Fox Enterprises
P.O. Box 176
11504 U.S. 23 South
Ossineke, MI 49766

Verlen Kruger
2906 Meister Lane
Lansing, MI 48906

336   Appendix A

Capt. Fred D. Leete III
6321 N. Temple Ave.
Indianapolis, IN 46220

Robert A. Manglitz
Lake Michigan Carferry, Inc.
P.O. Box 708
Ludington, MI 49431

Dan McGee
Presque Isle Lighthouse
4500 E. Grand Lake Rd.
Presque Isle, MI 49777

Lee Murdock
Artists of Note
P.O. Box 11
Kaneville, IL 60144

Mark S. Nemschoff
Mark Nemschoff Sports Ltd.
Box 129
Sheboygan, WI 53082

Valerie Olson-van Heest
4848 Holton Duck Lake Rd.
Twin Lake, MI 49457

Peter Rindlisbacher
107 Brunner Ave.
Amherstburg, ON N9V 2B4
Canada

Camilla B. Ross
5502 S. Madison St., #3
Hinsdale, IL 60521-5149

Cheryl Rozman
102 Springfield Ave.
Gwinn, MI 49841

Terry L. Searfoss
The Two Burner Gourmet
1800 Wilson Ave.
Saginaw, MI 48603

Winston Smith
6550 Edgewater Dr.
Erie, MI 48133

Henry A. Spang
P.O. Box 257
Fair Haven, NY 13064

Deane H. Tank
340 W. Barry
Chicago, IL 60657

John Tanner
Great Lakes Maritime Academy
Northwestern Michigan College
1701 E. Front St.
Traverse City, MI 49086

Dwight "Bucko" Teeple
1099 E. Spruce
Sault Ste. Marie, MI 49783

David L. Trotter
7805 Royal Court N.
Canton, MI 48187

Charles Vickery
c/o The Clipper Ship Gallery
10 W. Harris Ave.
La Grange, IL 60525

APPENDIX B

In Memoriam

The Crew of the SS *Edmund Fitzgerald*

(Lost with their Ship November 10, 1975)

McSorley, Ernest Michael	Master, Toledo, Ohio
McCarthy, John Henkle	First Mate, Bay Village, Ohio
Pratt, James A.	Second Mate, Lakewood, Ohio
Armagost, Michael Eugene	Third Mate, Iron River, Wisconsin
Holl, George John	Chief Engineer, Cabot, Pennsylvania
Bindson, Edward Francis	First Assistant Engineer, Fairport Harbor, Ohio
Edwards, Thomas Edgar	Second Assistant Engineer, Oregon, Ohio
Haskell, Russell George	Second Assistant Engineer, Millbury, Ohio
Champeau, Oliver Joseph	Third Assistant Engineer, Milwaukee, Wisconsin
Beetcher, Frederick J.	Porter, Superior, Wisconsin
Bentsen, Thomas	Oiler, St. Joseph, Michigan
Borgeson, Thomas Dale	Able-Bodied Maintenance Man Duluth, Minnesota
Church, Nolan Frank	Porter, Silver Bay, Minnesota
Cundy, Ransom Edward	Watchman, Superior, Wisconsin
Hudson, Bruce Lee	Deckhand, North Olmsted, Ohio
Kalmon, Allen George	Second Cook, Washburn, Wisconsin
MacLellan, Gordon F.	Wiper, Clearwater, Florida
Mazes, Joseph William	Special Maintenance Man, Ashland, Wisconsin
O'Brien, Eugene William	Wheelsman, Perrysburg Township, Ohio
Peckol, Karl Anthony	Watchman, Ashtabula, Ohio
Poviach, John Joseph	Wheelsman, Bradentown, Florida
Rafferty, Robert Charles	Temporary Steward (First Cook), Toledo, Ohio
Riipa, Paul M.	Deckhand, Ashtabula, Ohio

338 Appendix B

Simmons, John David	Wheelsman, Ashland, Wisconsin
Spengler, William J.	Watchman, Toledo, Ohio
Thomas, Mark Andrew	Deckhand, Richmond Heights, Ohio
Walton, Ralph Grant	Oiler, Fremont, Ohio
Weiss, David Elliot	Cadet (deck), Canoga Park, California
Wilhelm, Blaine Howard	Oiler, Moquah, Wisconsin

Index

Abandoned Shipwreck Act, 103
Admiral Bayfield Award, 15f
Albany (schooner; shipwreck), 90
Alberta (Canada), 131
Alexandria's Locker (powerboat), 92
Algonac (Michigan), 142; home of Chris-
  Craft Corp., 144f; and Algonac Boat
  Show, 146
Algonquin Indians, 231
Alpena (Michigan), 299f
Ambassador Bridge, 284
American Eagle (yacht), 40; (*see also*
  Chicago-Mackinac Race)
Amherstburg (Ontario), 138
Anchor Bay (tug), 317
Anderson, Julia Ann, will establishing
  Mariners' Church, 189; vision, 197
Andrea Doria (passenger liner;
  shipwreck), 104f
Ann Arbor I (steamship), 282
Arabia (schooner; shipwreck), 106
Arctic (schooner; shipwreck), 81
Argonaut Rowing Club, 25, 26
Arkansas River, 330; and Helena, 330
Armada (Michigan), 300
Armagost, Janice, 202f
Armco (steamship), 127
Arnold, George, 329; (*see also* Jolliet-
  Marquette Tricentennial Expedition)
Arsenault, Rocky, 86
Arthur B. Homer (steamship), 168
Arthur M. Anderson (steamship), on Nov.
  10, 1975, 160f; Jesse B. Cooper,
  master, 160f
Ashland (steamship), 200
Ashley, James M., and Ann Arbor
  Railroad, 282
Ashtabula (Ohio), 203
Association for Great Lakes Maritime
  History, 140
Athabasca River, 8
Augusta (schooner), 101
Avafors (steamship), 169

Badger (steamship; auto-passenger ferry),

276f; improvements, 279; celebrity
  passengers, 281
Baez, Joan, 128
Bantu (yacht), 39; (*see also* Chicago-
  Mackinac Race)
Battle of Lake Erie, 130f; "Battle of Lake
  Erie," painting, 130f; 247f
Bay City (Michigan), 15
Bayview Yacht Club, 36*n*
Becker, Frank, 195
Beeson's Marine Director, 267
Belle River (tugboat), 176
Benfri (steamship), 163
Bennett, John, 93
Bennett Lake (Yukon Territory, Canada),
  71 (caption)
Bentley Historical Library, University of
  Michigan, 121
Bethpage (Long Island, New York), and
  Grumman History Center, 275
Biederman, Les, 320
Big Dipper (wooden runabout), 144
Bigfork River, 229f; and lakes
  (Bowstring, Dora, Sand), 236
"*Bigler's* Crew, The," 117-8; and juberju,
  117-8
Big Rapids (Michigan), 318
Big Sandy River, 69
Bilge Buoy Boat Bailer, 254f; as problem
  in power mechanics, 254f
Birch-Bark Canoes of the Fur Trade
  (book), 2; (*see also* fur trade)
Blanchard, Gov. James, 72
Blue Book of American Shipping, 267
Blue Water Bridge, 127
Boessel, Christine, 232f
Bowling Green (Ohio), 140
British Columbia, 4
Brown, Annie, 105
Brown, Brian, 105
Brugger, Mary Ann, 246; 248 (caption)
Buffalo (New York), 93
Burkey, Chris, 317
Bush, George, 275
Buzzi, Fabio, 51f

Cajun French, 328
Canada, 4, 5, 6, 18; *passim*
Canadian Broadcasting Company (CBC), 116
Canadian Coast Guard, 20
Canadian Maritimes, 131
Canadian Medal of Bravery, 113
Canadian National Rowing Team, 23
Canadian Pacific Railway, 107
Canal Park (Duluth), research facility, 264
canoe(s), birch-bark, 3, 230f; dugout, 4f; wood samples from, 5; construction methods, materials, 6f, 321f; *Cruiser, Loon, Monarch, Sea Wind* models, 64f; records, 74; "maitre canot" (Montreal) and North configurations, 230f; New Town Canadienne, 321; "Home of the voyageur canoe," 323 (caption); opened up region, 326f
Cape Vincent, New York, 17
carbon-dating, 4
Caribou Island, 165
Carl Bradley (steamship; shipwreck), 191
Cartiercliffe Hall (freighter), 129
Cartier, Jacques, and King Francis I, 230
Caseville (Michigan), 237
C-CURV (cable-controlled underwater recovery vehicle), in *Fitzgerald* reconnaissance, 173f
Cellini, Benvenuto, and lost wax casting, 245
Champlain, Samuel de, 322
Chicago, as *Lady Elgin* port, 97; and *Rouse Simmons*, 121, 149-50, 153 (caption); and excursion boats, 125
"Chicago Board of Trade" (schooner; shipwreck), song, 129
Chicago-Detroit run, 50f; assaults on speed record, 50f; Fabio Buzzi and, 51f; Tecno 40 chosen, 50f; route, 54f; and global positioning system, 54f; Hart Plaza finish line, 59; American Power Boat Association (APBA), 54, 58f
Chicago Historical Society, 99
Chicagoland Canoe Base, 321f
Chicago-Mackinac Race, 33f; weather conditions, 36f; route on Lake Michigan, 39; winners, 39; (*see also* Chicago Maritime Society; Jarymowycz, Boris)

Chicago Maritime Society, 33f; exhibits, 34; book projects, 34; and history of the Chicago-Mackinac Race, 34; holdings, 34f; work with UASC, 91; sketch, 101 (caption); and canoe collection, 324f
Chicago Portage, 328
Chicago River, 42f; tours on, 42f; North Pier, 42; for canoeing, 322f
Chicago's Era of Sailing Schooners (book) 34; (*see also* Chicago Maritime Society)
Chicago Tribune, and marine artists, 154; and reenactment, 328
Chilko Lake, British Columbia, 4
Chilkoot Pass (Alaska), 67; and Chilkoot Trail, 67n; part of "Gold Rush Trail," 67n
Chippewa County Historical Society, 177
Chippewa Indians, 210f; ceremony for the dead, 210f
Christian Radich (Norwegian tall ship), 153
"Christmas (Tree) Ship, The," song, 121; shipwreck, 149; (*see also Rouse Simmons*)
Christopher Columbus (whaleback ship), 35
chubasco (storm), 69; 70 (caption)
Churchill River, 8
cire perdue (*see* lost wax casting)
City of Midland (passenger steamer), 280
Clayton (New York), 17, 22, 146; and Boat Show, 146
Clearwater River, 13
Cleveland, 85, 128, 174, 200, 234, 317
Cleveland Museum of Natural History, 249n
Chipper Ship Galleries, 150
Clark, Mark, 271
Coast Guard, U.S. (*see* United States Coast Guard)
Collin, Robert "Broken Back," in Chicago, 122
Colorado River, Grand Canyon, 61f
Comet (ship), 35
Conrad, Charles, 276f
Continental Divide, portaging over, 69
Copenhagen (Denmark), and *The Little Mermaid*, statue, 252
Coplin, Larry, 81, 84n
Copper Harbor, 18, 164

Cormorant, HMCS (Canadian Navy diving vessel), 207f; and *Pisces II* (diving chamber), 210; and Newtsuit, 210f; and SDL-1, submersible, 222f
Cousteau, Jacques, 139
Creber, John, 210, 223 (caption)
Crosby, Sills, and Nash, 119
Cross Continent Canoe Safari, 64f
Cummings, Capt. Janet Provost, at Whitefish Point, 207f; escorts *Fitzgerald* bell, 209 (caption)
Cundy, Ransom "Ray", watchman, *Edmund Fitzgerald*, 179; in U.S. Marine Corps, 181; employed by Hanna, Oglebay-Norton, 181
Cussler, Clive, 109

Dailey, Pat, 128
Daley, Richard J., 330
Daniel J. Morrell, (steamship; shipwreck), 81, 127; and NTSB report, 168
Dave's Bay (Bruce Peninsula), 112
David Dows (schooner; shipwreck), 35, 96f
Dawson, Montague, 152
de Champlain, Samuel, 322
"Deep Blue Horizon," song, 124; (*see also* folk songs of the Great Lakes)
Deer River (Minnesota), and White Oak Society, 233f
Delphinus (powerboat), 15
Denton, Edgar, 294
Des Plaines River, and Canoe Marathon, 322; canoeing on, 329f
Detour (Michigan), 20
Detroit, (paddlewheel steamer; shipwreck), 82f; "walking beam engine," 84 (caption)
Detroit, City of, 6, 50f; Renaissance Center, 195
Detroit Historical Society, 262
Detroit, H.M.S. (warship), 130f; Project H.M.S. *Detroit*, 138
Detroit News, 194; Dowling obituary, 259
Detroit Public Library, 80
Detroit River, 15; and "post office to the Great Lakes," 284f; Port of Detroit, 288; simulation, 313
Devils Island (Apostle Islands), 174
Different Drummer (yacht), 39; (*see also* Chicago-Mackinac Race)
Dodman, Mike, 271f

Doherty, Don, quoted, 91
Donne, John, quoted, 188
Door County (Wisconsin), 325
Dossin Great Lakes Museum, 80, 83, 158, 263
Douglas, Stephen, 97
Douville, Henry, 106
Dow Chemical, 20
Dowling, Rev. Edward J., 258f; obituary, 258-9; and Colombiere Center, 258-9; and Detroit Marine Historical Society, co-founder, 261; and *Detroit Marine Historian*, 261f; and *Lakers of World War I*, book, 261; fleet listings, 267
Drapeau, Jean, 328
Drdla, Stan, 110
DuGuay, Mike, 292
Duluth, 10, 159f; home port, *Woodrush*, 171f
Duluth (package freighter), 264
Dylan, Bob, 119

Eagle (Coast Guard training ship), built in Hamburg, Germany, 217; original name *Segelschulschiff Horst Wessel*, 217
Eagle Harbor, 164
Eagle River (Wisconsin), 324
East Lansing (Michigan), 208; and Michigan State University, 208
Edmund Fitzgerald (steamship; shipwreck), painting, 138; and *William Clay Ford*, 157f; Ernest M. McSorley as master, 160f; and Coast Guard buoy tender *Woodrush*, 171f; scale model, 189 (caption); constructed River Rouge, 169, 195f; news of sinking, 179f, 195f; Memorial Dive '95, 207f; bell recovery a Canadian operation, 209f; Lloyd's of London, 211f; foreign press, 211; launch, reception, 213f; name *Seaway* proposed, 214; McSorley impersonated, 217; with namesake, 219 (caption); pipe ceremony for victims, 222f
Education Through Involvement (ETI), 291f; school interest, 294
Edward B. Green (steamship), 168f
Empress of Ireland, (passenger steamer; shipwreck), 104f
Environmental Protection Agency (EPA), 317

342 Index

Erickson, Joyce, 170
Ericsson, John, and Ericsson screws, 87f;
   and ironclad *Monitor* in Civil War, 88
Erie (Pennsylvania), 245; and Presque
   Isle, 249
Erie Historical Museum, 249f
Erie-Tashmoo Race, 289f; *City of Buffalo*
   (passenger steamer), 289
Erie Yacht Club, 251f; trophies, 251f;
   visit by Pennsylvania governor, 252
   (caption)
Escanaba (Michigan), 316
Evans, Don, 16
Evans, Doris, 16
Everett, George, and Oshkosh Air Show,
   270
Extreme Explorer Productions, 107f

Fader, Danny, 86
Fair Haven (New York), 299
Fayette (Wisconsin), ghost town, 325
Feast of the Hunter's Moon, 324, 327,
   (caption)
Federal Aeronautics Administration, 257;
   approved Aviation Center, Toledo
   Board of Education, 257
Ferris State College, 318
"Fertile Ground," folk song album, 121
Fitzgerald, Mrs. Edmund, and invitation to
   Fitzgerald launch, 206; in christening
   ceremony, 215 (caption)
Finger Lakes, 298
Pullen, Wilbert, 296
*Five Fitzgerald Brothers--Sea Captains
   All* (book), 214
Flaherty, Robert, documentary producer,
   145; and "Nanook of the North," 145
Flint & Pere Marquette Railroad, 282f;
   Pere Marquette Railway merger, 283
folk songs of the Great Lakes, 121f;
   albums, 121f; "The Christmas Ship"
   (*Rouse Simmons*), 121; "The Stomach
   Robber," 122; "Keeper of the Light,"
   123; "Deep Blue Horizon," 124; and
   Marblehead Light, 124f; "Lost on the
   Lady Elgin," 126; "Cold Winds"
   album, 128; "Safe in the Harbor"
   album, 128; "Freshwater Highway"
   album, 128; "The Great Lakes Song,"
   128f; "Requiem for the Mesquite," 129
Fons, Valerie, 68; (*see also* Kruger,
   Valerie)

Ford Motor Credit Company, 77
Fort Brady, 175
Fort Chipewyan (Alberta), 2, 13
Fort Dearborn (tour boat), 41
Fort de Chartres Rendezvous, 327
   (caption), 329; in Prairie du Rocher
   (Illinois), 323, 332
Fort Malden Volunteer Association, 138
Fox River, 332
Frankfort (Michigan), 282
Frazier, Phil, 222
French-Canadians, 10; in fur trade, 3f;
   lifeways, 10; (*see also* fur trade)
French River, 8, 231, 326
Frese, Rita, 325
Fresnel lens, Third Order, 306 (caption)
Frontenac (steamship), 319; and
   Cleveland-Cliffs Iron Co., 319
Frost, Esther, 21
Frost, John, 21
fur trade, 3, 6; canoes in, 2; culture, 3f;
   reenactments, 3f, 61f; rivers in, 8;
   trading companies (Hudson Bay, North
   West, XY, American Fur), 231; (*see
   also* voyageur)

Gambone, Guido, sculptor, 110
Gananoque (Ontario), on St. Lawrence
   River, 106
Garden Peninsula (Wisconsin), 325
George (yacht), 49
Georgian Bay, 17, 18; "sixth Great Lake,"
   104
Germania (luxury yacht; shipwreck), 100;
   Kaiser Wilhelm fleet, 100
Gibson, Bob, 128
Gifford, John, archeologist, 100
Glenview (Illinois), 274
Gloucester (Massachusetts), 154
Goderich (Ontario), 88
God figure, in painting, 152; in "Jesus
   Walking on the Sea," 153 (caption);
   (*see also* paintings, by Vickery)
Goliath (steamship; shipwreck), 87f
Goodman, Steve, 119
Gore's Landing (Ontario), 324
Goshawk (schooner; shipwreck), 95
Grand Canyon, 61f; (*see also* Colorado
   River)
Grand Portage, 71, 326
Grand Rapids, 93
Grand River, Grand River Expedition, 74f

Grand Traverse Bay, 310f
Gravenhurst (Ontario), 32
Gray's Reef, 208
Great Lakes, *passim;* great lakes of the
  Northland, 1; shipwrecks, 89; issues
  confronting, 290f; and education about,
  292f; only maritime academy, 310f;
  opened up by canoe, 326f
Great Lakes Cruising Club, 15, 21
Great Lakes Engineering Works, River
  Rouge, 168; ship construction pattern,
  168f; *Fitzgerald* launched, 215
  (photos)
Great Lakes Historical Society
  (Vermilion, Ohio), 249*n*, 270 (caption)
Great Lakes Lighthouse Stamp Series,
  123f; and National Anthem, 123; and
  Cheboygan (Michigan), 124
Great Lakes Maritime Academy, 204,
  310f
Great Lakes Maritime Institute, Detroit,
  157, 259
Great Lakes Shipwreck Historical Society,
  and *Edmund Fitzgerald*, 183f; and
  Shipwreck Museum, 185, 194; in
  Fitzgerald bell recovery, 227
Green, Johnny B., author, *Diving with and
  without Armor*, 88
Grierson, John, documentary producer,
  145
Grosse Point Light, 127
Grumman Wildcat (F4F-3), 269f; and
  other "cats," 272f; as Martlet, 272
Gulf of St. Lawrence, 107, 169
Gulinda (yacht; shipwreck), 183, 202
Gwalchmai, Robert, 223 (caption)

Hafeman, Bill, 233; in book, 236
Hafeman Boat Works, 229f; visitors, 235
Haggadone, David, 148
Hahn, George Anthony, pilot, 374f
Halcyon (sloop), 256
Hale, Dennis, 127; (*see also Daniel J.
  Morrell*)
Hall of Canoe, 333
Hamilton-Scourge Project, 130f; and
  waterfront park, 139; Society, 142
Hamilton Tiger Sharks, 105
Hamilton (warship; shipwreck), 130f; as
  Diana, 141; (*see also Hamilton-
  Scourge* Project)
Hammill, Terrence, 296

"Hang down Your Head, Tom Dooley,"
  song, 119
Harbor Beach, 55, 89
Harris, John, 323
Haskel Booster Systems, 115
"Head of the Charles, The," regatta, 26
Hercules Technical Ropes, 115
Hessel, Les Cheneaux Islands, 146
Highland Park (Illinois), 98
Hilda Marjanne (steamship), in *Edmund
  Fitzgerald* search, 161
Hires, Lamar, owner, DiveRite
  Manufacturing, 107
Hogan, Joseph W., 287
Hogan, June Westcott, 287
Holland (Michigan), 144f
Homer, Winslow, 154, 156
Houghton (Michigan), 170
Hubbell (Michigan), 181
Hudson Bay, 141
Hudson Bay Beaver Club, 328
Hudson Bay Co., 231; and major rivals,
  231; (*see also* fur trade)
Hudson, Bruce, 198, 201 (caption)
Hudson, Oddis, 198, 206
Hulsizer, Chuck, 222
Hunter Savidge, (schooner; shipwreck),
  85f

Illinois Historical Preservation Agency
  (IHSA), 96f
Illinois-Indiana Sea Grant, 96f
Illinois sesquicentennial, 326
Indiana Dunes National Lakeshore, song
  performance, 125; as painting venue,
  151
Indiana State Police, 220
Indianapolis (warship; torpedoed in
  World War II), 189f
Inland Seas, Journal of the Great Lakes
  Historical Society, 261
Innisfree (tour boat), 43f
Institute for Great Lakes Research, 263f
International Coon Hunting
  Championships, 328
International Ship Master's Association
  (ISMA), 161, 188; *Directory*, 267
Irvine, Joyce, 143
Irvine, Keith, 142
Iskra (yacht), 35f; (*see also* Jarymowycz,
  Boris, Chicago-Mackinac Race)
Island Goat Society, 41; (*see also*

344 Index

Chicago-Mackinac Race)
Isle Royale, 85, 165
isopod, possible new species, 114
Ives, Burl, 119

Jackman, Al, owner, Great Lakes
  Memories, 266
Jacobs, Bert, 151
Jarymowycz, Boris, 35; and *Iskra*
  ("Spark"), 35; and crew, 35
John A. McGean, (steamship; shipwreck),
  89
John Sherman (steamship), 282
Jolliet, Louis, 328f
Jolliet-Marquette Tricentennial Expedition
  (1973), 328; and Greater Mississippi
  River Road Commission, 329; and
  Illinois State Tricentennial
  Commission, 329f
Joseph J. Hogan (mailboat), 284f
J. W. Westcott II (mailboat), 284f;

Kalamazoo Aviation History Museum,
  269
Kamloops, (canaler; shipwreck), 85
Kamuda, Alan, photographer, *Detroit
  Free Press*, 208
"Keeper of the Light," song, 123
Kensler, Brenda, 271f
Kent, Ben, 3, 9, 11
Kent, Doree, 3, 9, 11
Kent, Kevin, 3, 9, 11
Kewaunee (Wisconsin), 282
Keweenaw Bay, 72; and Point, 163f
Key Biscayne (Florida), 100
Killarney (Ontario), 13, 18
Kingston (Ontario), 106, 141, 292
Kingston Trio, 119
Kirkup, Peter, 275
Kitchi-Manitou, Great Spirit, 225
Klein, Clayton, co-author, *One Incredible
  Journey*, 65
Kohler Power Systems, 50
Kruger, Valerie (Fons), 62

Lackey, Joe, author, "The Schooner
  Song," 294
Lady Elgin, 91f; subject of *The Lady
  Elgin: A Report on the 1992
  Reconnaissance Survey*, Underwater
  Archeological Society of Chicago
  (UASC), 91; and Edward Spencer, 91,

126; as historic wreck, 93f; "Lost on
  the *Lady Elgin*," song, 126
Lafayette, Marquis de, 325
La Grange (Illinois), studio in, 154
Lang, Peter, 119
Lake Athabasca, 3, 7
Lake City (Florida), 107
Lake Erie, 14; and painting subjects, 140;
  and monster, 248f; (caption); and
  schoolship *OMF Ontario*, 298f
Lake Erie Monster, 249f; sightings, 249n,
  250; (*see also* lost wax casting)
Lake Guardian (research vessel), 317
Lake Huron, 7, 13, 15, 78f; *Morrell*
  sinking, 127; freighter's route, 162; in
  picture, 306
Lake Larga (steamship), 265 (caption)
Lake Michigan, and Chicago-Mackinac
  Race, 33f; shipwrecks in, 78f; cruises
  on, 260f; aircraft recovered from, 270f;
  survey of aircraft in, 271; and only
  cross-lake ferry, 276f; and Jolliet-
  Marquette reenactment, 329f; *passim*
Lake Michigan Carferry Service, Inc.,
  277f; revived, 280
Lake Michigan historical tours, 43
Lake Ontario, 25, 30, 77; *Hamilton* and
  Scourge, 139f; and painting subjects,
  140; and schoolship, 299f
Lakers of World War I (book), 259f
Lake St. Clair, 56f, 131
Lake Superior, 7, 13, 18, 63 (caption); in
  winter, 72f; storms on, 162; and search
  for *Fitzgerald* survivors, 172f; ship
  missing, 179f
Lake Winnipeg, 7, 13
Landick, Steve, 62; in Ultimate Canoe
  Challenge, 62, 66f
Lansing (Michigan), 183
lapstrake boats, 24, 25
La Salle: Expedition II, 331f; cities, towns
  visited, 332
La Salle, Sieur de, 331f
Leadville (schooner), 296
LeBlanc, Romeo A., awards medal,
  certificates, 113
Lee, Robert E. "Bob", 192; (*see also*
  Dossin Great Lakes Museum)
Leopard Frog Cave system, 104f;
  appearance, age, 110f; "becoming the
  swimming dead," 112
Le Sault de Ste. Marie Historic Sites, 171f;

and Tower of History, 171f; and Walk of History, 175; and River of History Museum, 175

Leslie's Illustrated newspaper, 101 (caption)

Lewis, Reid, 329

Lightfoot, Gordon, and ballad, "Wreck of the *Edmund Fitzgerald*," 192; at *Fitzgerald* bell ceremonies, 201 (caption)

lighthouse keeper, life of, 300f; uniform, 301 (caption)

lighthouse(s), tallest, 303; (*see also* Presque Isle Light)

Lincoln, Abraham, 97

Link, Ed, 212

Little Current (Ontario), 22

Little Stream, cave, 113

Logan, Robert, naval architect, 282

Lomax, Alan, 126

London (England), 149

London (Ontario), 25

"Long as the Rivers Flow," poems, 254

Lorain (Ohio), and Producers Steamship Co., 176

LORAN (LOng RAnge Navigation), as necessary equipment, 95

Los Angeles, 67

Lost Peninsula, in Lake Erie, 254

Lost Peninsula Marina, 257

lost wax casting, 245f; ancient artisans and, 245f; *Niagara* bell, 247f, 248 (caption); history, 249; and Lake Erie Monster, 149; retirement hobby, 253

Louisbourg (Cape Breton Island, Nova Scotia), 142

Louis XIV, King, 332

Louisiana, 141

Lucy Smith (steam barge), in song, 122

Ludington (Michigan), 276f; and West Shore Community College, 278; (*see also Badger*, Lake Michigan)

Mackenzie River, 72

Mackinac Island (Michigan), 300; Mackinac Bridge, 329; (*see also* Chicago-Mackinac Race)

Mackinaw (Coast Guard cutter), 219

Mackinaw City (Michigan), 216

Malone, Amanda, 294

Mamainse (Ontario), 18

Manistee (Michigan), site of Century Boat

Show, 146; ferry terminal, 282

Manitou (cruise ship), National Transportation Lines, 260

Manitowoc (Wisconsin), 277f

Marcellus, Elsie, 301

Mares diving equipment, 114

Marine Historical Society of America, 262; publication, "Steamboat Bill," 262

Marine Museum of the Great Lakes, Kingston, (Ontario), 135

Marine Museum of Upper Canada (Toronto), 23, 31

Mariners' Church of Detroit, 170; rector, Rev. Richard W. Ingalls, 170, 180; site of memorial services, 188f; Brotherhood Bell, 188f; established by will, 1842, 189f; *Fitzgerald* memorial bell, 195f; and great Lakes Memorial Service, 195; and Frank Becker yacht, 195; honor guard at *Fitzgerald* services, 196 (photo)

Maritime History Society of Detroit, 259

Marks, Margo, 315

Marquette, Jacques, explorer, priest, 328f

Marquette (Michigan), 170

Marquette (tour boat), 41

Marquette Mining Journal, 186

Martin, Kim, 104f; in diving gear, 108 (captions)

Mattawa River, 8, 9, 326

Maumee Bay, 256 (caption); 258

McCarthy, Beth, 203

McCarthy, John, first mate, *Fitzgerald*, 200f

McCarthy, J. P., radio talk-show host, 146

McEnery, Joseph, 329

McGee, Marianne, 300f

McGovern, Rev. Arthur, 258-9

McGrath, Linda, 115

McGrath, Mike, 115

McGreevy, Robert "Bob," 86; *Morrell* painting, 84 (caption)

McMillan, Hugh, 326

McSorley, Ernest M., Captain, *Edmund Fitzgerald* (*see Edmund Fitzgerald*)

McVay, Kimo, 190

Menominee Indians, 14

Mentor-on-the-Bay, 17

Merchant Marine, 219

Merkle Camera and Video, 115

Michelangelo, 152

Michener, James, author, 322

346 Index

Michigan City (Indiana), 125
Michigan Habitant Heritage, journal, 11
Michigan Historical Museum (Lansing, Michigan), 119
Michigan Maritime Museum (South Haven, Michigan), 103
Michigan Public Television, 145, 148
Midland (Michigan), 17, 19
Midland (Ontario), 17, 106
Mid-Michigan International Television Association, 142f
"Mighty Mac," (Mackinac Bridge), 329
Miller, Candice, 223 (caption)
Milwaukee, as *Lady Elgin* port, 97; visited by *Fitzgerald*, 207; ferry stop, 280f; and "schooner classroom," 298n
Milwaukee Public Library, 80; Runge Collection in, 103
Minnedosa (schooner; shipwreck), 78f; largest ever built in Canada, 78; towed by steamer *Westmount*, 79; towing barge *Melrose*, 79
Mississippi Heritage Trip, 325; and river towns, 325
Mississippi River, 61, 70; record broken, 71; Chartres Rendezvous, 323; Heritage Trip, 325; mile zero, 332
"Mr. Canoe," (Ralph C. Frese), 321f
Montreal canoe, 230f, 323f
Montreal (Quebec), 4,6, 61, 287, 326; and Expo '67 visit, 326f; and LaSalle Expedition reenactment, 331f
Moore, Jeff, 86
Moore, Jim, 86
Moore, Sarah, 86
Moyer, John, 109
Musee de la Mer, 107; location, 107n
Muskoka Lakes, 25
Mystic Seaport (Connecticut), 258 M

Nagle, Douglas, and yacht *Westerly*, 250; (*see also* Lake Erie Monster)
Nanfri (steamship), 163
Nantucket (Massachusetts), 258
National Geographic, 195
National Oceanic and Atomospheric Administration (NOAA), 307
National Transportation Safety Board (NTSB), *Edmund Fitzgerald* hearings, 164f; in *Daniel J. Morrell* report, 168
Navy Pier, Chicago, 42, 53
Nelson, Fred, 121

Nelson, Horatio, painting, at Trafalgar, 154; *Victory* (flagship), 154
Nemschoff, K. C., 60
Nemschoff, Paul, 52f
Nemschoff Sports Ltd., team, 52 (photo, caption); 59
Nesbitt, Rosemary, and H. Lee White Marine Museum, 296
"New Bedford Whalers," song, 122
New Orleans, 70 (caption)
New York, 109
Niagara (brig; Perry flagship), replica, 247f; bell replicated, 247f; and *Niagara* League of Erie, 247 (*see also* lost wax casting)
Niagara Falls, 138
Niagara River, 141
"Night-Memory, A," 1
Norris, Chuck, 50
North Channel, 18
North Olmsted (Ohio), 200
Northuis, Steve, Grand Craft owner, 144
Northwestern Michigan College, 310f
Northwestern Mutual Life Insurance Co., 206f
Northwestern (training ship), 317f
Northwest Passage, 230
Northwest School of Wooden Boatbuilding, 23
Nucleus (bark; shipwreck), 82
Nuytten, Phil, inventor of Newtsuit, 212
Nye, Chauncey, 89

Oakland/Pontiac Airport (Pontiac, Michigan), 269f
Oakland University (Rochester, Michigan), 143
Obsession (powerboat), 89
Odyssey II (cruise boat), 44
Ohio State University (Wooster, Ohio), 199f
Ojibway Indian language (poem), 1
O'Hare, "Butch", 272
Old Town Canoe Co., and New Town Canadienne canoes, 321; (*see also* canoe)
OMF Ontario (schoolship), 291f; construction, launch scenes, 293 (caption)
Ontario Provincial Police, 113
Orinoco River, 73
Orr, Gov. Robert "Bob", and Sagamore of

the Wabash Award, 220
Ossineke (Michigan), 12
Oswego Maritime Foundation (OMF),
  291f
Oswego (New York), 141
Ottawa (Ontario), 326f; Parliament visit,
  326f
Ottawa River (Michigan/Ohio), 256
  (caption); 257f
Ottawa River (Ontario), 8, 231
Our Son (schooner; shipwreck), 121

Paddle to the Sea, 75
paintings, by Rindlisbacher, 130f;
  "*Naubinway* Ship in the Straits" (illus.),
  137; "Morning Salute: HMS *Ontario* at
  Carleton Island" (illus.), 137; by
  Vickery, 151f; "Farewell Chicago"
  (illus.), 153; "Jesus Walking on the
  Sea" (illus.), 153; "Song of the Sea"
  (illus.), 153; "Joy of Winter" (illus.),
  155
Pan American Games, 23
Pearsall, Shelley, author, *Tales of the
  Western Reserve*, 249n
"Peninsula Poems," book, 254
Pere Marquette (steamship), 283f; and
  successor *Pere Marquette 16*
  (originally *Muskegon*), 283
Perry, Oliver Hazard, Commodore, 247f;
  (*see also* Battle of Lake Erie; *Niagara*)
Perrysburg (Ohio), 93
Pfund, J. Richard, 294
Philadelphia, (steamship; shipwreck), 90
Philip R. Clarke (steamship), in Soo
  Locks, 268
Pickering Marine, 115
Pied Piper (yacht), 40, 41; (*see also*
  Chicago-Mackinac Race)
pipe ceremony, Chippewa, 222f; (*see also*
  Sault Ste. Marie Tribe of Chippewa
  Indians)
Pisces Underwater Club, 105
Point Pelee project, 82; Pelee Passage,
  138; shipwrecks, 138
Pointe aux Barques (Michigan), 82
Pointe-aux-Pere (Quebec), 107; location
  of Musee de la Mer, 104n
Pond, Peter, 65
Pontiac (steamship), 419, 319
Popo Agie River, 69; and longest portage,
  69

Portage River, 18
Port Hope, 89
Port Huron, 56, 81, 127, 191, 300
Port Huron-Mackinac Race, 36n
Portland (Maine), 245
PRAXAIR Specialty Gases, 115
Presque Isle Historical Society, 300f
Presque Isle Light, (New), 300f; museum
  opened, 302; haunted tower, 309-10
Providence (Revolutionary War sloop),
  251

Quebec City, 107
Queen Charlotte (British warship), 249
Queen's University (Kingston, Ontario),
  130
Quick, William, 296

Rainy Lake, 236
Rainy River, 8, 236
Reagan, Michael, 49f
reconnaissance surveys, shipwrecks, 92f
Reekie, John, 106f; owner, Alternative
  Dive Products, 106
Reid, Gary, 144f
Reinhart, Django, 119
remote operated vehicle (ROV), 99
Rendezvous Days, 230f
"Requiem for the Mesquite," song, 129;
  (*see also* folk songs of the Great Lakes)
Rimouski (Quebec), 107
Rindisbacher, Peter, 140f
Rindlisbacher, Eleanor, 130
Rindlisbacher, Ellen, 131
Rindlisbacher, Harold, 130
River Negro, 73
River Rouge (Michigan), port,
  construction site, 159, 197
Rocket (schooner; shipwreck), 81
Rockford (Illinois), 271
Rogers, Stan, 119
Rogers City (Michigan), 300
Rouse (Ontario), 21
Rouse Simmons (schooner; shipwreck),
  34; "The Christmas Ship," song, 121
Royal Canadian Yacht Club, 30

Sable (aircraft carrier), 275f
Sackets Harbor (New York), 140
Saginaw Bay, 20, 79
St. Clair River, 56, 81, 144, 145 (caption)
St. Ignace (Michigan), 329

348   Index

St. Joseph (Michigan), 203
St. Lawrence (brigantine), 292f
St. Lawrence River, 32, 146; Seaway, 169
St. Lawrence (skiff), 31
St. Marys (schooner; shipwreck), 92f
St. Marys River, 159f, 171; rapids named
   Bahwating, "The Gathering Place,"
   221; rowboats on, 257; navigating, 311
Sandor, Stephen, 30
Sandusky (schooner; shipwreck), 216f
Sanitary District of Chicago, 329; Illinois
   Waterway, 329
Saskatchewan River, 3, 8
Sault Ste. Marie, 13, 22, 171, 185, 203,
   207f; 220f; and Ojibway Hotel, 227;
   and International Bridge, 300;
   reenactment, 326
Sault Ste. Marie Tribe of Chippewa
   Indians, 221f; and Sugar Island group,
   221f; and *Anishnabek*, 221; origins in
   six bands, 222; Constitution and
   bylaws, 222; pipe ceremony, 222f; Bay
   Mills Indian community, 227
Sauvè, Moses, 32
Save Ontario Shipwrecks (SOS), 82; and
   Point Pelee project, 82; networking
   with, 100; member, 136
Schoolcraft, Henry Rowe, 177; original
   home, 177
Scourge (warship; shipwreck), 139; as
   Lord Nelson, 139
SCUBA or scuba (Self-Contained
   Underwater Breathing Apparatus)
   diving, 77f; conditions affecting, 80;
   nitrogen narcosis in, 87; training in,
   105f
sculls, 25; construction and
   characteristics, 25, 26; racing, 26f; and
   repachage, 26, 27; International
   Racing Association rules governing,
   27, 28; records, 28; Canadian National
   Rowing Team, 29 (photo); 1989 World
   Championships, 29
Sheboygan (Wisconsin), 4
Shelbyville (Michigan), 142
shipwrecks, 77f; in Great Lakes, 89;
   reconnaisance surveys of, 94f; (*see
   also* ships' names)
Silverstein, Shel, 128
Simon and Garfunkel, 119
Skagway, 67
Skiff Shop, The, 23, 24

Slate Islands, 18
Smith, Chris, Chris-Craft founder, 144;
   and Grand Craft, 144
Smith, Gary, 257
snorkeling, 105
Soja, Rob, 86
sonar, sidescan, 82f, 173
Soo Canada, 209
Soo Canal, Locks, 18, 20, 82, 162
Southwest Michigan Underwater Preserve
   Committee, (SWMUP), 92; part of
   Michigan Underwater Preserve Council
   (MUPC), 92; and Michigan's 11th
   underwater preserve, 102f
Spartan (passenger steamer), 280
Spencer, Edward, (*see Lady Elgin*)
Steamship Historical Society of America,
   259
Stockholm (passenger liner), 109
Storstad (steamship), 107; in collision
   with *Empress of Ireland*, 107
Sturgeon Bay (Wisconsin), 121; home of
   Christy Corp., 280
Sugar Island (Michigan) 261
Summers, John, 31
Superior (Wisconsin), 180
Suttons Bay (Michigan), 19

Tales of the Mackinac Race (book), 41;
   (*see also* Chicago-Mackinac Race)
Taney (Coast Guard Cutter), based in
   Portsmouth, Va., 177
Tanzer 28 (sailboat), 245
Taylor, Bill, 21
Taylor, Patricia, 21
Thatch, John, 272
"The Sea Hunt," movie, 105
"The Stomach Robber," folk song, 122
The Two Burner Gourmet (book), 234f;
   and planning on-board meals, 238f;
   and economizing, 243f
"The Undersea World of Jacques
   Cousteau," movie, 105
Thoreau, Henry David, author, *A Week on
   the Concord and Merrimack Rivers*,
   331
Tippecanoe County Historical
   Association, 324; and Le Brigade
   Ouiatenon, 324
Tobermory (Ontario), 104f; on Bruce
   Peninsula, 104
Toledo, 96, 317; and river ports, 317

Toledo-Lucas County Public Library, 256
Toronto (Ontario), 205
Traverse City (Michigan), 204
Treaty of Versailles, 99
Trent-Severn Waterway, 17
Trosvig, Thomas, 211
Troxell, Frank, 86
Two-Continent Canoe Expedition, 62, 72f; in *Sea Wind* canoes, 72; Ambassadors of Michigan, 72; and Gov. James Blanchard, 72; in South America, 73f

Undersea Research Associates, 77, 86f
Underwater Archeological Society of British Columbia, 100
Underwater Archeological Society of Chicago (UASC), 91f
Underwater Diving Technology, 216
U-97, World War I German submarine, 99
Union League Club, 149
U.S. Air Transport Command, 257
United States Coast Guard, at Sault Ste. Marie, 160f; in *Edmund Fitzgerald* loss, hearings, 160f; Career in, 171f; Readiness and Reserve Division, Cleveland, 177; in Desert Storm, 177; in memorial ceremonies, 188f; in bell recovery, 207f; Coast Guard Academy, 217; boot camp, Cape May, New Jersey, 218; represented at launch, 294; assisted, 300f
United States Naval Academy, 217
U.S. Naval Proceedings, 263
U.S. Navy, 271; and World War II battles, 272
U.S. Postal Service, 284f
University of Detroit Mercy, 258f; library, 259f; Marine Historical Collection, Edward J. Dowling Photographic Collection, 260f;
University of Pittsburgh, 246
Upper Peninsula (Michigan), 140; 146, 170, 199, 227, 329
USS *Massachusetts* (battleship), 46; and Underwater Archeological Department, State of Florida, 46; and *Massachusetts Two*, 46

Valley Camp (steamship; museum ship), 171f; original name (*Lewis W. Hill*), 176; bought by Wilson Marine Transit

Co., 176; and Republic Steel Co., 176; near historic homes, 176; photo, 177; *Edmund Fitzgerald* exhibit, 178
Vandalia, (steamship; shipwreck), 87
van Heest, Jack, 92
Varian, Howard, marine architect, 197
Verrazano, Giovanni di, 6
Victoria (British Columbia), 23
Victoria (yacht), 251
Victory (warship), Nelson flagship, 154
video production, 142f; start in, 143f; in Instructional Technology Center, 143; for Parke Davis Pharmaceutical, 143; Medical Center (Battle Creek, Michigan), 143; Video-Craft founded, 143; "Runabout Renaissance," 143f; "Runabout Renaissance II; Restoring Your Wooden Pleasure Craft," 147f; "The Role and Brush Method of Varnishing," 148
Voyageur News, 2
voyageur(s), and fur trade route, 3f; lifeways reenacted, 3f; in fur trade, 65f, 234f; voyageur village, 234; (*see also* fur trade, canoe)

Waddell, Clint, 61
Wahl, Werner, 86
Walter A. Sterling (steamship), 168f
Walton, Ivan, music collection, 121f; and "The Stomach Robber," folk song, 122
Warbird Aircraft Restoration and Salvage, Inc., 269f
warbirds, 270f
Ward, Eber, family, owners of *Detroit*, 83
War of 1812, 139f; *Hamilton* and *Scourge* and, 139; cannon found, 251; (*see also* Battle of Lake Erie, *Niagara*)
Waterford (Michigan), 269
Waterloo (Iowa), 152
Waugh, Frederick, 152
Waukegan (Illinois) 126
Wayne State University, Reuther Archives, 263
W. E. Fitzgerald (steamship), 214
Weiss, David, cadet, *Fitzgerald*, 203f
Welland Canal, 15f
Wells Burt (schooner, shipwreck), 95 (caption); 96f
West Bay City (Michigan), 282
West, Larry T., 294
Westcott, John Ward, 285f

350 Index

Westcott, J. W., Co., 284f; and zip code
48222, 284f
White, John, 6
Whitefish Point (Michigan), Coast Guard
station at, 158f; and Whitefish Bay,
158f; Hudson memorial at, 182
(caption), 187; visited by Cheryl
Rozman, 184f; near shipwreck, 198;
Fitzgerald memorial, 205; pipe
ceremony, 226
Whitworth, Rudy, 86
Who's Who in American Art, 150
Wild Rivers of North America, The (book),
236
William A. Irvin (museum ship, Duluth),
267
William Clay Ford (steamship), Ford
Motor Co. vessel, 158f; and *Edmund
Fitzgerald,* 158f; crew listed, 158;
capacity, 166 (caption): Donald E.
Erickson, captain, 191
William G. Mather (museum ship,
Cleveland), 267
Willis (schooner; shipwreck), 138
Wilson, Jack, 126 (*see also Lady Elgin*)
Wine and Cheese Festival, Nauvoo
(Illinois), 325
Winnipeg River, 8
Wisconsin Lake Schooner Education
Association, 298*n*
Wisconsin Marine Historical Society, 214
Wolverine (aircraft carrier; former
Seeandbee), 270, 275 (captions); and
Sable, 275f
Woodard, Cedric C. "Sid", pilot, 169
"woodies" (wooden boats), 142f; "Wild
about Woodies," article, 144; 1930
model reproduced, 144
Woodrush (Coast Guard buoy tender),
171f; in *Fitzterald* search, 171f; (*see
also* Edmund Fitzgerald)
Work, Henry C., composer, 126f

Zenith City (steamship), 263